Whitworth Porter

**Malta and its Knights**

Whitworth Porter

**Malta and its Knights**

ISBN/EAN: 9783742836878

Manufactured in Europe, USA, Canada, Australia, Japa

Cover: Foto ©Andreas Hilbeck / pixelio.de

Manufactured and distributed by brebook publishing software (www.brebook.com)

Whitworth Porter

**Malta and its Knights**

# MALTA AND ITS KNIGHTS.

BY

WHITWORTH PORTER,

LIEUT.-COL. ROYAL ENGINEERS.

# PREFACE.

In the year 1858 I published two works in connection with the subject of Malta and its Knights. One, a lengthy and elaborate treatise in two volumes, was a History of the Order of St. John of Jerusalem; and the other, a small work published locally, treated only of the fortress of Malta, and was, in fact, simply a history of its construction. Both of these books are now out of print, and even were this not the case, I have learnt from experience that they neither of them precisely fulfil the object I had intended. The first was too voluminous and detailed; and the latter, too bald and technical in its treatment to meet the views of the general reader. In the present volume I have endeavoured to obviate these objections. I have retained what seemed to me likely to prove of general interest in the larger work, and have suppressed all minor details. At the same time I have added very considerably to the narrative of the events which led to the transfer of the fortress into the hands of the English, a portion of the history, which, in my former works, had been somewhat too slightly sketched. In this latter branch of the subject, I have received considerable assistance from Captain William Gatt, of the Royal Malta Fencible Artillery, who has kindly drawn my attention to many valuable details bearing upon it. I trust that the present work may be found to supply a want, and to prove of interest to those whose residence in Malta leads them to desire information on the subject of its history.

# MALTA AND ITS KNIGHTS.

## CHAPTER I.

Foundation of the Hospital of St. John—Conversion into a Military Order—Establishment of the Knights Templars—Loss of Jerusalem—Expulsion from Acre—Suppression of the Knights Templars.

THE advantages which the island of Malta possesses with regard to its position and configuration, seem to point it out as the natural site for a vast insular fortress and naval station. Lying, as it does, midway between Sicily and the north coast of Africa on the one hand, and Gibraltar and the Levant on the other, its situation renders it the most convenient and accessible depôt for the vast commerce which flows along the Mediterranean. The capacious and sheltered harbours, formed by the indentations of its north-eastern coast, are capable of containing the largest fleets; and the soft rock of which it is composed affords ample material for the construction of such works of fortification as appear necessary for its security.

The traveller who enters for the first time the grand harbour of Valetta, and sees the accumulation of parapets and batteries which frown upon him, will naturally be struck by the reflection that such a gigantic mass of works could only have been reared in a country where building material was most abundant, and the cost of labour but trifling. The island being throughout its extent one vast quarry of stone, easily raised and readily worked, it required but the labour necessary to sink the ditches of the fortress to provide an ample supply of material for the raising of its escarps, in those places where the precipitous character of the natural rock did not altogether supersede the necessity for artificial revetments. Labour was at the same time, during the residence of the Order of St. John in Malta, remarkably cheap and abundant. In fact, most of the work was executed by the slaves, who were retained in vast numbers upon the island, and who, when not toiling at the oar on board the galleys, were employed on shore, either in the dockyard or upon the numerous works of defence which were ever in progress.

As regards the utility of many of these works, little can be said. It must, however, be borne in mind that when the first lines for the protection of the proposed city of Valetta were traced, the art of fortification upon modern principles was still in its infancy, and the means at the disposal of the Order very limited compared with the magnitude of the object aimed at. As time wore on, improvements were by degrees carried out in all directions to remedy the original defects and omissions. The fortress, therefore, cannot be looked at as one vast and comprehensive design, the offspring of a single mind, but as an aggregate of successive ideas accumulated through a period of upwards of two hundred years. Still, with all its defects, the fortress of Malta must take rank as one of the most powerful strongholds in the world, and will ever remain an undying record and proud memorial of that illustrious fraternity under whose rule it was reared.

It will be well, before entering upon a history of its construction, to sketch briefly some of the antecedents of that fraternity.

The new doctrines of Islamism, which, within the space of fifty years from the first appearance of Mahomet as a prophet, had spread over all the countries bordering upon Arabia, were not long in reaching the effete province of Judea, which from that time fell under the sway of the caliphs of Egypt. These rulers were far too keen-sighted and politic to prohibit entirely the annual influx of pilgrims, who had for ages past poured forth from every country in Europe with the pious object of visiting the soil rendered sacred by the ministry and passion of our Lord. They were, however, by no means unwilling to extort from the wanderers an ample tribute in return for their complaisance. Many hardships consequently fell to the lot of those whose worldly means were not sufficient to meet the rapacious demands of the new lords of the soil, and the pilgrim not unfrequently found himself at the close of his journey utterly bereft of the means either of present sustenance or of future return to his home.

Under these circumstances, some charitable merchants of Amalfi (then an important commercial city of Italy), whose avocations had thrown them into frequent and friendly intercourse with the caliph Monstaser Billah, obtained his sanction, in the year 1050, to the erection of a hospital, to be devoted to the shelter and support of such pilgrims of the Christian faith as might require assistance or maintenance whilst in the holy city. The benefits conferred by this establishment soon became so celebrated, and were so loudly and universally lauded by the grateful pilgrims who had enjoyed its seasonable hospitality, that contributions rapidly poured in from all quarters, and the hospital of St. John gradually extended its sphere of usefulness until it became an institution of no little importance. It was at first placed under the patronage of St. John the Almoner, but this dedication was before long changed to that of St. John the Baptist, who continued the patron saint of the Order throughout its existence.

Many as were the hardships which the Christian pilgrims of Europe had been called upon to endure under the sway of the Egyptian caliphs, they were as nothing compared to those imposed upon them after the irruption of the Turcomans, who, towards the latter end of the eleventh century, overran the province of Judea. Extortion and robbery of every description, too frequently accompanied by murder, awaited the wretched palmer in the city of his devotion; and the tales of wrongs endured and cruelties suffered, which were narrated by such of them as had made good their escape from the scene of their miseries, aroused the religious enthusiasm of Europe to a pitch of frantic vehemence. The efforts of Peter the Hermit to organise this popular ferment ended in that gigantic expedition known as the First Crusade, in which a torrent of European chivalry was poured upon the coasts of Asia. After a fearful loss of life, these warriors succeeded in rescuing the city of Jerusalem and some of the neighbouring provinces from the hands of the Turks, and in establishing a Latin kingdom, under the sway of the noble Godfrey of Bouillon, the chief who had led the expedition to its successful issue.

The hospital of St. John was at this time under the

control of Peter Gerard, who presided over the institution
under the title of Rector. No sooner had the crusaders
forced their way into the city than the portals of the hospital
were at once thrown open for the reception of the sick and
wounded of the conquering army. Godfrey and the other
leaders were so impressed with the benefits thus conferred
upon their followers, that they hastened to testify their
gratitude by endowing the institution with numerous manors
in every part of Europe.* The wealth of the hospital having
thus received a vast augmentation, its rector became desirous
of placing it upon a more permanent and solid basis. He
demanded, therefore, and received the papal sanction for the
formation of an order upon a strictly religious footing, the
members of which should assume the three monastic
obligations of chastity, poverty, and obedience, and should
be distinguished by a regular habit, consisting of a black
cloak bearing a white cross of eight points on the
shoulder. Many of the crusaders whose religious fervour
had been stimulated by the success of their late efforts on
behalf of their faith, abjured the world and enrolled themselves as members of the newly organised fraternity, and
as the changes introduced by Gerard became more generally
known throughout Europe, the institution rapidly increased
both in numbers and wealth.

The death of Gerard, in the year 1118, caused another and
most important change to be introduced into the organisation
of the fraternity. Hitherto, it had merely assumed a
religious aspect, and in most respects differed but little from
the numerous monastic institutions of Europe. The new
rector, Raymond du Puy, was, however, a man of a very

* The act of donation by Godfrey, of the manor of Montboise, in Brabant,
is still preserved in the library of the Vatican.

different character and temperament from the pious and saintly Gerard, and found many amongst the members of his convent whose hearts were not so deadened to the martial enthusiasm of the age as their profession required. The ranks of the community had been largely recruited from amongst the crusaders of Godfrey's army, men whose lives had been spent in scenes of strife, and to whom the excitement and glory of a martial career were absolute necessaries of existence. A very short term of seclusion amidst the calm and monotony of the hospital of St. John had been sufficient to engender a feeling of lassitude and a craving for exertion in the hearts of these neophytes, and, happily for them, the spirit of their new chief was in thorough accordance with them.

The infant kingdom of Jerusalem was still in a very precarious position. Consisting merely of isolated cities with the territories immediately adjacent, most of the intervening country was in the hands of an inimical population, and the communication between the various strongholds of the Christian power was dangerous and frequently intercepted. Under these circumstances, Raymond du Puy proposed to convert his peaceful fraternity into a band of warrior monks, who, without abandoning either the vows or the principles of their original institution, should add thereto the further obligation of combating on behalf of their faith. This suggestion was received with as much eagerness by the king of Jerusalem, as it was greeted with joyful enthusiasm by the members of the convent. The change was, indeed, a great one, converting the peaceful and indolent churchman once more into the eager and zealous warrior, and supplanting the quiet and solitude of the cloister by the excitement of the battle-field. Nothing could have been devised more strictly in accordance with the spirit of the age and of the feeling which had originally prompted the organisation of the Crusade. Papal sanction was speedily obtained for the contemplated change, and before many years had passed the white cross banner of the Order of St. John had waved over many a field of strife, and had spread terror and dismay amidst the ranks of many an infidel host.

Under the new organisation of the community, its members were divided into three classes, first of whom, in rank and position, were the Knights of Justice. Admission to this grade was only granted to those who could produce satisfactory proofs of the nobility of their descent. Every candidate must have already received the accolade of knighthood from secular hands, before he could be enrolled as a Knight of Justice in the Order of St. John.* The second class comprised the strictly ecclesiastical portion of the convent, and at a somewhat later period was subdivided into two distinct grades; the conventual chaplains, who performed all the religious functions of the Order within the convent and hospital at Jerusalem, and the Priests of Obedience, who performed similar duties at the various stations which were gradually established throughout Europe for the due superintendence and management of the property held by the Order. The third class were denominated serving brothers, and were also subdivided into servants-at-arms or esquires, and servants-at-office. The servants-at-arms performed the duties of esquires under the Knights of Justice,. and if they were eligible, became in due time enrolled amongst their number. The servants-at-office were

* Hence the term Knight of *Justice*, signifying that the postulant, having fulfilled certain conditions, could claim, as a matter of justice and not of favour, admission into the ranks of this branch of the fraternity.

men in a menial capacity, who performed all the duties of domestics within the convent. This class, though without the dignities and position of their nobler brethren, possessed numerous privileges and emoluments, which rendered admission into the Order, even in this grade, very advantageous to men of the lower ranks of society.

As the new duties of the Order of St. John enabled them to render frequent and most seasonable assistance to the struggling kingdom of Jerusalem, the fame of their exploits soon filled the Christian world, and recruits from the noblest families of every country flocked to their standard. Wealth also rapidly poured into their coffers, it being considered by those who were unable or unwilling to take up arms personally in behalf of their religion, that they were contributing their quota to the good work by assisting in the support of a fraternity whose sole duty it was to maintain the integrity of the Christian cause in the East. In order to ensure the due and economical administration of their vast property, preceptories were formed, afterwards termed commanderies, wherever their territorial possessions were sufficiently extensive to require such a foundation. In these branch establishments the interests of the fraternity in the immediate locality were duly protected; and eventually it was decreed that novices might be professed into the Order, within their limits, without the necessity of a previous visit to the *chef lieu* of the convent. At the head of each commandery was a member of the Order, who presided over the institution with the title of commander, and who might be either a knight chaplain or serving brother; by far the larger proportion, however, being of the former class. A certain number of the commanderies in each country were clustered together into priories, over which presided a dignitary under the title of Grand Prior, who watched over the interests of the district confided to his charge. There were often several of these priories within the limits of each kingdom; the greater number being in France, where the Order was possessed of very extensive property.

Within a very few years of the establishment of the Order of St. John upon a military basis, a rival fraternity sprang into existence under the title of Knights Templars, and as the former had adopted the distinctive badge of a white cross upon a black ground, the latter selected for themselves a red cross upon a white ground; hence the rival fraternities were commonly distinguished as the White Cross Knights and the Red Cross Knights. A similarity of design and a rapidly accumulating revenue in the treasuries of both orders, gradually led to the engendering of a fatal spirit of jealousy between them. So long as this jealousy only displayed itself in the honourable emulation of the battle-field, and the sole superiority sought for was the honour of bearing the banners of their respective Orders furthest into the heart of the opposing hosts, all was well, and the feeble kingdom realized much benefit from their support. By degrees, however, this spirit became embittered, and at the very time when the hold of the Christians over the drooping kingdom was relaxing more and more, and when consequently it was more than ever necessary that a perfect feeling of unity should be preserved between the only two powers capable of rendering any real aid, their broils and disputes broke out into open strife. It would doubtless have been impossible for the military orders unaided to have ultimately preserved the Holy Land as a Christian kingdom, even had they remained in the strictest amity with each other; but the fatal moment would probably have been considerably retarded, and it cannot be denied that the loss of Jerusalem itself was greatly owing to their ill-timed strife, which was with difficulty appeased even by the vehement remonstrances of the Pontiff, the common superior of both orders.

It is needless to follow the career of the Order through the various struggles which marked the twelfth century. The precarious hold which the Latins maintained over the city of Jerusalem, the principalities of Antioch, Edessa, and the various other minor points where they had gained a temporary footing, gradually gave way to the increasing power of the Saracens, who, as they became better acquainted with the European tactics of war, were enabled to maintain themselves upon a greater footing of equality, and to derive more certain advantage from their enormous numerical superiority. Towards the close of that century, the Saracen power was consolidated under the sway of one well able to use it with the utmost effect, and the rise of Saladin sounded the death-knell to the Christian kingdom. Advancing from victory to victory, this heroic chief found himself gradually drawing nearer and nearer to the great object of his ambition, the recovery of Jerusalem; and this event, so fatal to the cause of Christianity in the East, was unfortunately hurried forward by the determination on the part of Guy de Lusignan, the feeble and unworthy king of Jerusalem, to stake his all on the issue of a single field. The disastrous result of the battle of Tiberias, fought in 1187, decided the fate of Jerusalem. The Christian forces, after a most desperate and protracted conflict, were utterly routed. The King, the Grand Master of the Templars, and a host of other dignitaries, fell into the hands of the enemy, and Garnier di Napoli, the eighth Grand Master of the Order of St. John, and one of the few Englishmen who have ever held that dignity, fell nobly upon the field of battle.

The Christian host being thus annihilated, the road to Jerusalem was open to the advance of the victorious Saracen army. Saladin was not the man to neglect the advantage thus presented to him, and in a brief space of time he secured all that the most skilful generalship could give him as the result of the successful issue of the battle. Jerusalem itself was one of the first cities to capitulate upon the approach of the enemy. After a short resistance, protracted for fourteen days, more through the desperation of its few defenders than from any hope of ultimate success, the town passed into the hands of Saladin, and was for ever lost to Christianity. This melancholy result of a strife which had raged for nearly an entire century, took place on the 2nd October, 1187. Well was it for the inhabitants that their conqueror, Saladin, was endued with nobler feelings of clemency than had been displayed by the crusading army, which, ninety years before, had made their successful entry into the city. Then its streets and mosques had been deluged with blood, and a cruel massacre of the unoffending inhabitants, without regard to age or sex, had disgraced the Christian arms, and had cast a foul stain upon the holy cause in which they were engaged. Saladin, however, sought no bloody revenge for this scene of carnage; the transfer of the city was effected peaceably; and he even carried his clemency so far as to permit ten members of the Order of St. John to remain for twelve months within the city, to continue their care of the sick, with whom the hospital was then, as it always had been, crowded.

The loss of Jerusalem created a general excitement scarcely inferior to that popular ferment which had produced the first crusade; and before long the chivalry of Europe was once more wending its way eastward to recapture the holy city. This expedition, known as the Second Crusade, boasted of the presence of no less than four reigning monarchs—the kings of England and France, the Emperor of Germany, and the Duke of Austria, having all joined its ranks. The history of this crusade is too well known to need much detail here. The King of Jerusalem, Guy de Lusignan, had been taken prisoner at the battle of Tiberias, and his release had been purchased by the surrender of the powerful city of Ascalon, one of the few remaining bulwarks of Christianity in the East. When the first panic consequent on that fatal battle had in some degree subsided, Guy collected under his standard the shattered relics of his army, and being joined by the forces of the military Orders, also much reduced by the late war, he laid siege to Acre, one of the cities which had, during the panic, opened its gates to Saladin almost without resistance. Whilst engaged in this operation, he was gradually joined by the various forces composing the crusade; and after a protracted struggle of upwards of two years, during which the Christians lost more than one hundred thousand men, the recapture of the city was effected in 1191, principally owing to the gallantry and energy of the heroic Richard of England.

From this date until the kingdom of Jerusalem was finally lost, the city of Acre became the capital and stronghold of the Christian power, and the Hospitallers, who, after the loss of Jerusalem, had temporarily established their *chef lieu* at Margat, now transferred it to Acre, which continued the head-quarters of the convent until the ultimate loss of that city. Here they continued to practise those hospitaller duties from whence they derived their name, and which formed one of the fundamental principles of their institution.

The success of the second crusade ended with the capture of Acre; for in spite of the zeal of Richard Cœur de Lion, he was so impeded in his progress by the reduction of his forces from disease and climate, and by the desertion of his allies, that he was unable to bring to a successful issue the object he held so dearly at heart, the rescue of the sacred city itself. After many futile attempts at an advance, one of which actually brought him within sight of Jerusalem, he was forced to retire, and, re-embarking his troops, abandon the enterprise, he himself falling a prisoner into the hands of the Duke of Austria as he was making his way homewards in disguise through the dominions of that treacherous ally. The siege of Acre may be further noted for the formation of another military order, which, during its progress, was called into existence. This fraternity, which received the name of the Teutonic Order, was composed exclusively of Germans. Their dress consisted of a white mantle with a black cross embroidered in gold, and the rules of their governance were in close approximation to those of the Hospitallers and Templars. It may here be mentioned that a fourth order of chivalry was also in existence, its original institution, as a monastic order, having been of greater antiquity than even the hospital of St. John. It was entitled the Order of St. Lazarus. They themselves claimed their foundation as far back as the first century. The earliest date, however, at which it can with any certainty be fixed, is the year 370, when a large hospital was established in the suburbs of Cæsarea, under the auspices of St. Basil, for the reception of such as were suffering from the loathsome plague of leprosy. Similar establishments gradually sprang up elsewhere, and

as they all placed themselves under the protection o
St. Lazarus, their hospitals became known as Lazarettes.
They were originally only a religious fraternity following
the rule of St. Augustin. However, shortly after the
Hospitallers and Templars had established themselves on
a military footing, the monks of St. Lazarus in their turn
donned the coat of mail. For this purpose they divided
themselves into two separate bodies. Those amongst them
who were afflicted with leprosy, amongst whom was their
Grand-Master, he being by their rules always a leper, carried
on the peaceful duties of the hospital. The remainder being
in a condition to bear arms, joined the ranks of the King of
Jerusalem, whenever called on for the defence of the country.
The cross upon their mantles was green.

The thirteenth century was marked by a succession of
crusades, all equally useless in fulfilling the objects for which
they were undertaken. The Emperor Frederic did, indeed,
succeed in extorting by treaty the re-transfer of Jerusalem
to the Christians, but the boon being coupled with the
condition that no fortifications were to be raised, the gift was
of no value, and was soon lost. King Louis IX. of France,
canonised as St. Louis, also led two crusades for the
recovery of the Holy Land. The first was brought to an
untimely end in the marshes of Egypt, near the city of
Massoura, where he fell a prisoner into the hands of the
Saracens. He was only rescued by the payment of an
enormous ransom, a large portion of which was contributed
from the coffers of the hospital of St. John. His second
expedition, which was diverted from its original destination
into an attack on Tunis, likewise failed utterly, and the
king himself fell a victim to the pestilence which was
decimating his army. Another expedition made itself

## Description of Acre.

master of Constantinople, and having annihilated the effete Greek empire, erected a Latin kingdom in its place. Little benefit, however, occurred to the Christian cause in the East from this change. Year by year the prospect of recovering the holy city became more faint, and the hold of the Christians upon the other strongholds in Syria more feeble. Indeed, but for the zealous and unintermitting exertions of the military orders, the kingdom must long since have been utterly lost. Even their united efforts, strenuous though they were, could not avert, though they succeeded in postponing, the impending catastrophe. Step by step the Saracens, under the leadership of the Sultans Keladun and Mansour, advanced upon their enemies and reduced the limits of the kingdom within an ever-narrowing space, until at last the city of Acre became the one only stronghold remaining.

This city, which, ever since its recovery during the second crusade, had become the capital of the Christian power in Syria, was much strengthened by the various fortifications which during that time had been added to it, and at this period justly ranked as the noblest fortress in the East. Crowded with a vast population from every nation in Europe, and containing within its area the whole remaining wealth and aristocracy of the kingdom, the luxury of Acre had reached an almost fabulous pitch. Ancient chroniclers have exhausted their powers of invention in their endeavours to portray in glowing colours the extraordinary accumulation of wealth and grandeur which was gathered within the city. Glass, which at that time was almost unknown in Europe, was here in common use, and silken awnings are said to have stretched from side to side across the streets to screen the passers-by from the fierce noon-day blaze of the almost tropical sun of Syria. Its harbour was the depôt for the vast commerce which even then had begun to stream between Europe and the Levant. Vice and immorality of every description stalked rampant through the city, and the frail beauties who lived on the traffic of their charms swarmed in countless numbers within its precincts. The city was under the government of no less than seventeen municipalities of the various nations composing its population. The control thus exercised was miserably inefficient, and a general spirit of licence prevailed unchecked everywhere. To this discreditable condition had the Latin kingdom of Jerusalem dwindled within less than two centuries from its original foundation; and now even this last stronghold was doomed to pass into the hands of the infidel.

In 1291, the Sultan Khalil, with an army of 60,000 cavalry and 140,000 infantry, appeared before the city, determined once and for ever to drive the last remnant of Christianity from Syria. John de Villiers was at this time Grand Master of the Order of St. John, the twenty-first in succession from Raymond du Puy. William de Beaujeu was, at the same time, the Grand Master of the Templars. Under these gallant and daring spirits, the knights of the two orders maintained a long and energetic resistance, aided by a reinforcement brought to the city by the King of Cyprus in person. Their valour and devotion were, however, vainly exerted to the utmost against the overwhelming force of the enemy, and at length Henry of Cyprus, with his auxiliaries, in despair, abandoned the city to its fate. The greater number of its knightly defenders having succumbed from wounds and disease, the strength of the garrison became too much reduced to maintain their works, and the Saracens at length succeeded in penetrating within the walls.

A frightful scene of carnage and licence now ensued. Neither age nor sex was spared, and the power of Christianity in the East was extinguished, amidst the despairing shrieks and dying groans of the thousands who fell victims in the massacre. The Grand Master of the Temple fell at his post on the last day of the siege; the chief of the Hospital was more fortunate. In the general scene of confusion which ensued on the capture of the fortress, he succeeded in embarking the slender relics of his Order, and thus rescued them from the fate which befell all who were unable to escape from the doomed city.

Saddened and dispirited, the reduced band of warriors who still owned allegiance to the white cross banner wended their way towards the island of Cyprus, where they were received with every hospitality by the king, who was anxious to atone, as far as possible, for his abandonment of Acre. Here the convent was again established, and a hospital opened in which the brethren were enabled to continue the peaceful functions of their profession, although the power of combating for their faith was for the time lost to them.

They were not, indeed, without hope that they might again be enabled to establish themselves in the land of their adoption by the assistance of a new crusade from Europe. Great efforts were made once more to arouse the religious enthusiasm and the chivalric ardour of Europe, but in vain. The spirit which had prompted the universal rush of the kingdoms of the West to the rescue of the Holy Land had now died out. So many unsuccessful expeditions had exhausted the fervour of Christian zeal, and quenched the ardent aspirations of its chivalry; and now that the Holy Land was fairly lost, there was no desire evinced to join in any further efforts for its recovery.

The Knights of St. John being thus baulked in their efforts to renew the struggle to which, by their profession, they had devoted themselves upon the sacred soil of Palestine, turned their attention to the establishment of their *chef lieu* in some spot whence they could continue to maintain the warfare which had become hereditary between themselves and the Ottoman Empire, and where they would no longer feel themselves in the dependent position to which their residence in Cyprus subjected them. William de Villaret, the twenty-third Grand Master of the Order, in the commencement of the fourteenth century, turned his eyes towards the island of Rhodes, as being well adapted for the future home of the community, and gradually made his preparations for its conquest. Death, however, intervened to prevent the accomplishment of his design, but his brother Fulk, who was raised to the vacant dignity, completed the organization of the expedition, and in 1308 landed in the island. The struggle for its possession lasted during a period of two years, during which time the forces of the Order underwent extraordinary hardships, and but for the dogged determination of their chief, would more than once have abandoned the attempt.

The island of Rhodes had originally formed a dependence of the Empire of Constantinople. At the time when that effete power fell into the hands of the Latin crusaders, it became the prey of the Genoese, in whose possession it remained unchallenged until Vatiens, one of the most talented princes of the age, succeeded in expelling the intruders, and restoring it to the empire from which it had been torn. Gradually, however, its governors established themselves as independent princes of the island, and in order to make good their pretensions against the emperor, they opened their ports for the reception of all the Ottoman traders who chose to make it their home. The corsairs also, who had now for a long period been the terror of the Levant, were always sure of a hearty welcome and a safe shelter within its harbours. To repel this noxious swarm, and to destroy their nest, was no light undertaking, and it was not until the 5th August, 1310, that the white cross banner of the Order waved over the ramparts of Rhodes.

Encouraged by this great success, Villaret had no sooner settled himself in his new home than he commenced assembling a fleet of galleys for the protection of Christian commerce from the depredations of the corsairs whom he had so lately driven from their lair. Unable longer to act up to the letter of their profession in the manner contemplated by their founder, the Knights of St. John were still determined not to abandon the good cause, but to continue their protection of the interests of Christianity in any manner in which they could still make it available. Before long the flag of St. John, waving over a powerful fleet of galleys, became as much an object of terror to the infidel in the waters of the Levant, as it had been for the two previous centuries to his brethren on the sandy plains of Palestine. This period may, therefore, be marked as the epoch when first arose that naval superiority on the part of the Order which they continued to preserve until the commencement of the eighteenth century, and which rendered them the scourge of the Moslem and the bulwark of Christianity throughout the Mediterranean. It was at this time, also, that the Order was first regularly divided into *langues*. Hitherto the natives of the various countries who comprised the fraternity had known no other division that of the three classes of knights, chaplains, and serving brothers. Now, however, it was found advisable to create a new classification upon the principle of nationality, in addition to, and without disturbing the distinctive organization which already existed. The Order was, therefore, divided into the seven languages of Provence, France, Auvergne, Italy, Aragon, Germany, and England. To these seven an eighth was subsequently added, to increase the Spanish influence in the fraternity. The language of Aragon was subdivided, one-half retaining the original title, and the remainder being termed the language of Castile and Portugal. Whilst on this subject, it may be added that the Reformation in England having annihilated that language, it remained practically dormant until, in the middle of the eighteenth century, a new language was formed in Bavaria, which was coupled with that of England, under the title of Anglo-Bavarian.

It has already been stated that throughout the last century of Christian rule in Palestine, frequent and bitter animosities had broken out between the rival fraternities of the Hospital and the Temple. On one occasion this spirit of antagonism had been carried so far that a regular combat took place, in which the Order of the Temple was almost annihilated. The historians who have recorded these events have been so greatly biassed by their respective partialities, that it is very difficult to decide on which side to lay the greatest share of blame in this suicidal conflict.

The difference, however, in the conduct of the two Orders subsequent to their expulsion from the Holy Land is so marked, that it requires no great perspicuity to decide between the rival factions. Whilst the Hospitallers, eager to carry on the duties of their profession, hastened to establish themselves as near the former scene of action as possible, and to continue that warfare to the maintenance of which they, in common with the other military orders, stood pledged, the Templars, on the other hand, abandoning all ideas of further contest with the Ottoman power, hurried home to their European preceptories. Here, by their idle ostentation and haughty turbulence, they soon created for themselves a host of powerful enemies. The monarchs of the respective countries in which these preceptories were situated were naturally inimical to them. Their avarice was aroused by the vast wealth which was diverted from the ordinary channels into the coffers of the Order, and their jealousy was excited by the bands of armed men who had established themselves throughout their dominions, and who claimed exemption from all the ordinary duties and imposts of their fellow-subjects.

The result of this injudicious conduct was soon manifested, and it was not long before the fraternity of the Temple had bitter reason to regret their abandonment of the holy cause, which by the laws of their profession they should still have aided in maintaining. A conspiracy for their destruction was hatched between Philip the Fair, king of France, and Pope Clement V., who had owed his elevation to the papal chair almost entirely to the king's interest, and who became in consequence his most obsequious tool. This plot aimed at nothing short of the complete annihilation of the Order, and the confiscation of their revenues. The details of this melancholy story do not pertain to the present narrative. The scenes that were enacted throughout France, ending in the martyrdom, for so it may be justly called, of the heroic Jacques de Molay, the last Grand Master of the doomed Order, rank amongst the most touching and heartrending of the age. In England and in other countries their destruction was effected in a milder but equally complete manner; and a general scramble at once ensued for the enormous revenues thus left without an owner. The kings and nobility of the various countries in which the fraternity had flourished, hastened to secure for themselves a rich booty out of the prey thus abandoned to their power. The loss of such a vast amount of wealth from the control of ecclesiastical authority did not at all suit the views of the Pontiff. Although he had yielded implicitly to the dictation of Philip so long as his demands only involved the persecution and destruction of a body of men whom he himself regarded with much jealousy and dislike, he was not prepared to remain a mute spectator whilst so much wealth, originally dedicated by pious donors to ecclesiastical purposes, was being confiscated and diverted to swell the revenues of the lay nobility. By dint of much exertion, and after the promulgation of several bulls, he ultimately succeeded in rescuing a portion of the coveted property, with which, after due deliberation, the Order of St. John was endowed, it being considered that that Order had shown by their continued stay in the East, and recent establishment at Rhodes, a most praiseworthy determination to preserve inviolate the character of their profession.

The causes assigned by Philip and his party, in exculpation of the cruel persecution to which the unfortunate Templars had been subjected, were foully calumnious, and at the same time childishly absurd. The hideous orgies with which they were accused of celebrating their ceremonials, and the foul blasphemies and utter infidelity with which they were charged, are the mere inventions of the bitterest malice, only supported by the evidence of two reprobates, both, at the time when they were suborned by Philip, under sentence of perpetual imprisonment, and only one of them a member of the Order. Such absurd charges require no refutation on the part of their defenders, who, with much truth, ascribe the entire transaction to the rapacious avarice of the king. The secrecy with which the various ceremonials of the Order were conducted, combined, as it is generally supposed they were, with the mystic fraternity of Freemasonry, presented a wide contrast to the public and perfectly open manner in which everything connected with the Order of St John was performed, and thus aided Philip greatly in impressing upon the ignorant people an idea that this mystery was a cloak to every kind of horror and abomination. By these means, at the hour of their greatest need, he utterly deprived them of the support of public sympathy.

There can, however, be no doubt that the conduct of the Red Cross Knights had been such as of itself to create them many enemies, and to alienate many who would otherwise have stood their warm friends in adversity. Their pride, luxury, and licentiousness, coupled with the total abandonment of the cause they had espoused, and for the defence of which they had originally been endowed with that wealth which they now lavished on such widely different objects, marked them as fit subjects for suppression. Had that suppression been effected everywhere, as it was in England, without cruelty, and had due provision been made for the support of such members of the extinct Order as were dependent on its revenues for the means of subsistence, little could have been urged against the justice of the measure; but the needless barbarity and relentless ferocity with which they were hunted down, have combined to arouse a very different feeling in the hearts of all who peruse the melancholy tale.

At the same time, the fact that the Order of the Hospital had created for itself a very different reputation, may be plainly seen by the contrast in their respective fates. Whilst the one community was annihilated, the other was not only left uninjured, but was actually endowed with much of the wealth of its unfortunate rival, as a testimony of the zeal which it continued to manifest in the good cause. For many years, however, the gift was more nominal than real, and it was long before the coffers of the hospital were swelled by any considerable contributions from the forfeited lands of the Temple fraternity.

# CHAPTER II.

Establishment of the Order in Rhodes—Formation of a Fleet of Galleys—Description of Rhodes—Enmity of the Turks—First Siege of Rhodes—Its successful Defence—Arrival of Zizim—His ultimate Fate—Second Siege of Rhodes—Expulsion of the Order from the Island.

VILLARET, having succeeded in establishing himself in undisputed possession of the island of Rhodes, lost no time in taking steps to secure his position by restoring the shattered fortifications of the town; at the same time he made such arrangements with the islands surrounding his stronghold as their close proximity seemed to render advisable. Upon the principal of these, then named Cos, now known as Stanchio, a strong castle was erected, to render it secure from a *coup de main*. The other islands which fell under the domination of the Order, owing to their proximity to Rhodes, were Calamos, Leros, Symia, Nisyrus, and Patmos. This latter was assigned as the private domain of the Grand Master. The Order having settled themselves in their new home, lost no time in organizing a fleet of galleys which should enable them to sweep the Levant, and restrain the excesses from which the commerce of Europe suffered at the hands of the infidel corsairs who swarmed in those seas.

Year by year as it passed away left the fraternity more

powerful, and their successes upon this new element more brilliant. Fronting the enemy as an advanced post of Christianity, they performed duties in its behalf which could hardly have been looked for from any other source, and all the maritime nations of Europe rang with the applause bestowed upon them. The Ottoman power, which had established itself in the place of the Saracens, had now become a very formidable foe to Christianity. It was no longer a question of wresting Palestine from its hands, or of maintaining a Christian kingdom in the East. The Ottomans, secure beyond dispute within their own limits, had dreams of ambition which tended westward, and throughout the fourteenth, fifteenth, and sixteenth centuries the advance of the Crescent was a permanent source of uneasiness to Europe.

In all the struggles consequent on this state of things, the Order bore their part most gallantly, both by sea and land, and, whilst extorting the praise of Europe, rendered themselves more and more obnoxious to their enemies. At length the feelings of the Ottoman nation became so embittered against them, that an earnest cry for revenge arose throughout the empire. It was no longer to be tolerated that a mere handful of men, a band of armed monks, whose sole principality was a group of small islands in the Levant, should presume to exist so close to the confines of the ever-expanding empire, and to harass by their constant enterprises the navy and commerce of the East. Mohamed II., who ascended the throne in 1452, had done more than all his predecessors in the consolidation and extension of the empire, and eventually determined to throw a lustre over the last years of his reign by achieving the annihilation of the Order of St. John, and the rescue of the lovely island of Rhodes from their power. He had, in the year 1470, succeeded in capturing Negropont

## Description of Rhodes. 27

from the Venetians, and encouraged by this success, he commenced the organization of a vast force, consisting of a fleet of 160 vessels, and an army of upwards of 80,000 men, which was appointed to rendezvous at the port of Phisco, in Lycia, in the early part of the year 1480.

Peter D'Aubusson was at this time Grand Master, the thirty-eighth from Raymond du Puy who had been invested with that dignity. Well was it for the Order that their fortunes were at this critical moment swayed by one so preeminently fitted for the arduous post. Long before he had become elevated to the dignity he now held, D'Aubusson had rendered such services to the Order, and the public confidence in him had been raised to such a pitch, that his followers were prepared to yield him the blindest obedience. The city, moreover, was now in a very different condition from what it had been when first torn from the hands of the Turk. Since that period the Order had lavished its treasures partly in the construction of works as perfect as the state of the art of fortification admitted, and partly in the erection of magnificent buildings, the ruins of which yet remain to attest their grandeur. The town was situated on the seashore, embracing within its circuit the two harbours known as the outer and inner port. The outer port was formed by a long strip of land running in a northerly direction, and jutting into the sea so as to enclose between it and the shoreline an anchorage sheltered from all but northerly winds. On the rock at the extremity of this neck of land stood the tower of St. Nicholas, erected only a few years previously by the Grand Master, Zacosta. This tower, the first object which greeted the mariner on nearing the shores of Rhodes, was justly considered the most important point in the defences. Surrounded almost entirely by sea, it was difficult to attack under any circumstances, and from a sudden surprise it might be considered perfectly secure. The inner port was enclosed by two moles running respectively in a northerly and easterly direction, so as to enclose an expanse of water segmental in form, the circumference being formed by the town, and the radii by the two moles. At their extremities stood two other towers, St. Michael and St. John.

The land defences of the city consisted of a double rampart subdivided by thirteen towers. Its form, thus encircled, partook very much of that of a crescent, in the upper horn of which dwelt the aristocracy. As is the case in all Eastern cities, the Jews were settled in a corner allotted to them at the south-eastern extremity of the town.

The amazing fertility and luxuriant vegetation of the island had converted the country outside the walls into one vast garden. Here and there on every side the ground was clothed with chapels, summer-houses, and other rustic buildings, adding much to the picturesqueness of the scenery, but unfortunately highly detrimental to the defence of the town. D'Aubusson had, it is true, exerted his power with no sparing hand to sweep away the most obnoxious of these buildings; still, however, much remained to afford cover to an advancing foe. To quote the quaint language of Mary Dupuis, himself a member of the Order, who, although not actually engaged in the siege, arrived there shortly afterwards, and wrote a history of it:—

"Around the city of Rhodes lay the most admirable country in the world for carrying on a siege, for all around the said town there were numerous gardens filled with little churches and Greek chapels with old walls and stones and rocks, behind which cover could always be found against the

garrison to such an extent that if all the artillery in the
world had been inside the town it could do no harm to those
that were without, provided they did not approach too
close."

The western side of the town was overlooked by the
dominant hill of St. Stephen, but the power of artillery was
as yet too little developed for the disadvantages of this spot
to have become properly appreciated by the defenders. Such
was the town, and such the general aspect of its surround-
ings, when, after having been kept for nearly forty years in a
state of perturbation and alarm, it was destined to undergo
a siege supported by the utmost strength of the Ottoman
Empire.

On the 23rd of May, 1480, the Turkish force, under the
command of Paleologus Pasha, disembarked upon the island
of Rhodes, and encamped at the foot of St. Stephen's Hill.

The importance of the tower of St. Nicholas being evident,
it was decided to throw the whole weight of the attack at
once upon that point. For this purpose a battery was
commenced within the gardens of the church of St. Anthony,
a convenient spot for the purpose; and although the knights
strove their utmost to impede the progress of the work, it
gradually increased its proportions, and on completion was
armed with three huge basilisks. These basilisks, of which
sixteen had accompanied the Turkish army, were of such
stupendous dimensions that their very appearance might well
spread dismay amongst the ranks of the garrison. They
were eighteen feet in length, and were designed to cast stone
balls of from twenty-four to twenty-seven inches in diameter.
These enormous guns were fired with comparatively small
charges of powder; their range was consequently very limited.
Apparently, they trusted more to the weight of the missile

than to its velocity for the desired effect; still, it could have been by no means a reassuring incident to the defenders of St. Nicholas to be battered with such gigantic artillery.

The result soon manifested itself. Before long a gaping breach on the land face marked the effect of the battery. On this breach an assault was delivered on the 9th of June, and maintained with all the force of the besiegers for several hours. The difficulty of approach, and the narrow strip of land over which the assailants were forced to advance, aided D'Aubusson, who was throughout the day conducting the defence of the fort in person, in successfully resisting the onset. At length, a number of fire-ships having been brought to bear successfully against the galleys on board which the assailants had been conveyed to the mole, they were forced to retire. The attack of the fire-ships was accompanied by a vigorous sally on the part of the defenders, the ladders were overturned, and such of the enemy as had gained a footing on the breach were hurled to the bottom. The batteries which had been constructed to bear upon this point were now opened against the confused and disordered mass huddled together on the mole. Most of the galleys which had borne them to the scene of action had been either destroyed by the fire-ships, or had retired. The assailants were therefore compelled to make their way to the mainland by swimming, and a vast number lost their lives in the attempt.

The pasha, however, was not a man to despond at the first failure. Conceiving that the knights were probably straining every nerve for the protection of this point, he determined to break ground in a new direction, and for this purpose moved his heavy battering train to the southern side of the city. The Jews'.quarter was selected as the new point of attack. The ramparts at this place were of extreme thickness, but at the same time of great age, and therefore ill suited to resist the fearful battering to which they were now exposed. The pasha was not content to confine his efforts to a single point, but harassed the garrison by a general bombardment on all sides. From the mortars which formed a part of his siege train he hurled into the city gigantic fragments of rock and other ponderous missiles. He also poured a vast quantity of fire-balls and other combustibles into the town. Against these various dangers, D'Aubusson's ready genius was enabled to provide a remedy. He created shelter for such of the inhabitants as were not required in the defence, by the erection of large sheds, constructed of sloping timbers built against the walls, in such sites as were least exposed to fire. Others took refuge within the vaults of the churches and similar places of security, so that the effects of the bombardment were comparatively but little felt. True, that as Mary Dupuis records, one shot struck the vaulted roof of the refectory in the Grand Master's palace, and after descending through the stone floor into the cellar, it there destroyed a hogshead of good wine, a loss which seems to have struck the annalist with the liveliest regret; but it was not by such casualties as these that the surrender of Rhodes was to be compelled. The danger of fire was averted by an organized band, whose sole duty it was to watch the flaming projectiles in their descent and quench them promptly. This duty was rendered the easier from the incombustible character of the town, which was built entirely of stone. It is recorded that the roar of the bombardment was heard distinctly in the island of Lango, a hundred miles westward of Rhodes, and in that of Château Roux, the same distance eastward.

The state of the ramparts in front of the Jews' quarter soon became such as to render prompt measures necessary for the safety of that point. D'Aubusson, therefore, directed the construction of a retrenchment which should cover the breach. For this purpose he levelled the houses in rear of it, sank a deep ditch with a semicircular trace, and behind this obstacle he raised a brick wall supported by a terreplein of sufficient thickness and solidity to resist the battering of the enemy. The Grand Master himself set the example, not only by giving directions, but by taking his own turn at the manual labour. The effect of this good example was not lost. Not only did the knights and upper classes amongst the Rhodians join in the work, but also women and children; nay, even the secluded inmates of the convents, casting off the ordinary restrictions imposed upon them by their profession, joined, at this perilous crisis, in the universal enthusiasm, and performed the tasks of ordinary workmen. The new barrier was, consequently, soon raised, and the pasha, after having succeeded in the demolition of the Jews' rampart, found himself opposed by a fresh obstacle of a still more formidable character, and which rendered futile all the efforts he had made and the ammunition he had expended.

Disheartened by this ill success, Paleologus returned once more to his first point of attack at the tower of St. Nicholas. To facilitate the approach of the assaulting columns, he constructed a floating bridge, sufficiently wide to carry six men abreast, which was to stretch from the shore beneath the church of St. Anthony to the rocks at the foot of the tower. Under cover of the darkness, a Turk succeeded in fixing a large anchor under water at the end of the mole, through the ring of which he passed a rope, intending thereby to warp the bridge across the inlet to its destination. This cunning device, however, had been espied by an English sailor, called

Roger Gervase (for so history has preserved his name, though it was probably really Jervis). He quietly awaited the departure of the Turk, and as soon as the coast was clear detached the rope from the anchor, and leaving the former loose in the water, carried the latter in triumph to the Grand Master. D'Aubusson was so pleased with the intelligence and promptitude of Jervis, as he stood radiant and dripping before him, with his ponderous trophy still in his grasp, that he rewarded him with a present of 200 golden crowns.

The Turks having completed the construction of the bridge, made their arrangements for a new attack. The former assault had been undertaken in broad daylight; now they determined to try the effect of a night surprise. The 19th of June was the date selected for the important attempt, and at about midnight their various detachments were set in motion. It had been arranged that whilst the bridge was being warped into its position, a large body of troops, shipped for the purpose on board some of their smaller craft, should approach the mole and make a sudden dash at the breach, in the hope of taking the garrison unawares. The incident of the anchor had, however, forewarned D'Aubusson; every step, therefore, that prudence could suggest or engineering skill could devise had been taken to meet the attack. The first strain upon the rope, by which the pasha had hoped to warp his bridge across the creek, showed that the device of the anchor had been discovered. Unwilling, however, to forego the advantages of his preparations, Paleologus decided, notwithstanding this failure, upon proceeding with his attack. He directed that the bridge should be towed to its destination by boats, and whilst this operation was being carried on he gave the signal for the advance of the troops embarked. The garrison was on the alert, and the alarm being promptly given, a desperate fire was opened upon them from all sides. Secrecy being no longer possible, the Turks hurried from their boats and dashed boldly at the breach. The struggle was carried on by both parties with equal obstinacy and determination. The fire ships of the garrison were once more let loose upon the enemy's fleet, towards which they drifted in a column of flame, bearing panic and confusion in their course. The early light of a summer's dawn broke upon this scene of strife before success had declared itself on either side. Guided, however, by the rapidly increasing light, the artillery of the garrison were enabled to direct their fire with greater accuracy, and soon destroyed the bridge, which had hitherto been most useful to the Turks in bringing up their supports. This loss, by which not only was the advance of fresh troops rendered difficult, but the retreat of those already on the mole much imperilled, decided the fortunes of the day; the breach was abandoned, the creek was once again covered with drowning men, and the routed relics of the pasha's army left to find their way back to their camp as best they could.

The dismay caused by this new failure was such that for some time the Turkish army remained apparently paralyzed, and the garrison were permitted to repair damages almost without let or hindrance. At length, however, Paleologus once more roused himself from the despondency into which he had been plunged, and decided upon making another and still more strenuous effort against the Jews' quarter. Taught by his previous ill-success that he could not hope to overcome his enemies in the rough-and-ready manner he had hitherto adopted, he now opened his approaches in a more methodical and scientific order, and driving galleries underground he gradually reached the edge of the ditch. From these points he caused to be poured into the ditch such a vast accumulation of *débris* that at length he succeeded in establishing a roadway across it. Meanwhile, his batteries, planted very near the edge of the counterscarp, maintained an incessant fire upon the breach, and when all was in readiness for the assault, this fire was redoubled in intensity. Quailing beneath the pitiless storm thus hurled against them, the garrison had been driven to seek shelter, and when the assailants rushed through the breach, about an hour after sunrise on the morning of the 27th July, they found themselves unopposed. Before the alarm could be given, the Turkish standard was waving on the rampart, and their troops pouring in through the undefended gap.

In this disastrous conjuncture a general panic seized the defenders. Men ran to and fro, scarcely knowing where to bend their steps, or how to resist the storm. A few minutes more of this perilous confusion, and all must have been lost. D'Aubusson, however, was equal to the emergency, and rushing to the spot, by his mere presence restored order and decision. He instantly dashed at the rampart, the summit of which could only be gained by means of ladders, and the first to ascend, sword in hand, was the Grand Master.

At this moment was seen the unusual spectacle of the garrison converted into assailants, and endeavouring to recover by escalade, the ramparts now crowded by a victorious foe. Twice was D'Aubusson hurled from the ladder, each time severely wounded; and yet again he returned to the assault. Unless the fatal breach were recovered, he felt that all was lost, and so rallying his followers for a final effort, he at length succeeded in establishing himself on the rampart, where he was speedily joined by a considerable number of his followers. The Turks were so crowded together that they found it impossible to act with vigour upon the narrow space. Swaying to and fro before the fierce attack of the knights, they were eventually driven backwards over the breach. This was the turning point in the struggle—the panic having once established itself, spread with rapidity. Flying from their enemy, they found the causeway blocked by the troops marched thither for their support. In this predicament, friend was not distinguished from foe, and the most eager of the fugitives hewed for themselves a pathway by the indiscriminate slaughter of their comrades. Meanwhile, a deadly fire was kept up on the dense mass from every available point of the adjacent ramparts, and as each shot told, the slaughter was fearful. The fight now degenerated into a massacre. Pursued by the excited and victorious garrison, they were driven like sheep; nor was safety to be found even within the limits of their camp, from whence they were speedily driven, the great banner of the pasha, which was planted in front of his pavilion, falling into the hands of the knights.

Rhodes was now saved. The Turkish troops were so demoralized that all further efforts on their part were manifestly useless, and they were embarked, in tumultuous haste, on board their galleys, so that before the sun of that eventful day was set, the island was freed from its invaders. This glorious issue was not purchased without severe loss on the part of the garrison, and D'Aubusson himself received no less than five wounds, one of which, it was at first feared, might prove fatal. He, however, eventually recovered, and lived many years to enjoy the triumph which his gallant deeds and those of his brethren had achieved. The Pope presented him with a cardinal's hat, in token of his admiration, and the fame of the Order rose throughout Europe, even to a higher pitch than it had yet attained. Mohammed, on the other hand, was so overwhelmed with the disastrous issue of the enterprise, in which his army had suffered a loss of nine thousand killed and fifteen thousand wounded, that he sank under the disgrace. He died in the following year, directing that the only epitaph to be inscribed on his tomb should be, "I designed to conquer Rhodes and subdue Italy."

His death brought with it a most seasonable period of repose to the Order, whose resources had been greatly exhausted by the fearful conflict in which they had been engaged, and which, notwithstanding its successful issue, had caused them most extensive losses. The vacant Ottoman throne was disputed between the two sons of Mohammed, Bajazet and Zizim. The former having succeeded in making good his claim, the latter was compelled to fly from the vengeance of his brother, and sought refuge at Rhodes. D'Aubusson was overjoyed at finding himself the negotiator in a matter so nearly affecting the internal peace of the Ottoman Empire. The power he obtained by the presence at Rhodes of a rival to the throne, whose claims he might at any moment support in opposition to those of the Emperor, was used by him to obtain terms such as freed the Order from all fear of further invasion on the part of Bajazet. That monarch not only paid them an annual subsidy for the maintenance of Zizim in a position suited to his imperial birth, but even condescended to make them a large compensation for the injuries inflicted by his father during the siege.

Until the death of Zizim, which occurred several years later from poison administered to him by Pope Alexander

VI., profound peace reigned between the Order of St. John and the Turkish Empire; and although after that event, when Bajazet had nothing further to dread from the fraternity, war once more broke out, it was confined to naval encounters, so that the island had ample opportunity afforded to it of recovering from the effects of the devastation caused by the army of Paleologus.

This state of peace and prosperity was, however, brought to a close upon the accession to the Ottoman throne of Solyman II., afterwards called the Magnificent. This prince determined to mark the commencement of his reign by the successful prosecution of an enterprise which had proved beyond the powers of his great ancestor Mohammed; and having, as a preliminary exploit, besieged and taken the powerful fortress of Belgrade, he commenced earnest preparation for his new attempt.

In the previous year, Philip Villiers de l'Isle Adam had succeeded to the government of the fraternity as their forty-second Grand Master. He lost no time in preparing his island for resistance to the storm destined so soon to break over it. Every effort was made to swell the numbers of his garrison, and the members of the community were summoned on all sides from their various European Commanderies to aid in the defence of the Convent. When all had arrived, it was found that they mustered about 600 knights and 4,500 other troops, a slender force with which to resist the gigantic host then being organized by Solyman for the capture of the island.

A general description of the fortress and harbour of Rhodes has already been given, but during the forty years which had elapsed since the former siege, many important additions and improvements had been effected. All the buildings which had been left standing at the time of D'Aubusson, and which had afforded so much cover to the besiegers, were now cleared away, and the country left completely open to the guns of the town, which enfiladed it in every direction. The main port was closed with a double chain, whilst the outer port, since termed the port of the galleys, was blocked, by sinking at its mouth boats laden with stones. To the double *enceinte*, which completely encircled the town, was added in the most exposed parts a third line of rampart. Five of the thirteen towers flanking the line were enclosed in bastions, of which they became the keep; so that these five points were capable of a separate and isolated resistance, even should the intermediate rampart be forced. They were called respectively the bastions of Provence, Auvergne, England, Spain, and Italy, and their defence was entrusted to knights of those several *langues*—who were expressly nominated for the purpose, and under whose orders were placed select detachments of their different nations. The general *enceinte* was divided, according to custom, into eight portions, each of which was confided to the care of a separate *langue*. The corps of reserve was divided into four portions, at the head of which were placed respectively the Chancellor d'Amaral, who was to support the quarters of Auvergne and Germany; the English Turcopolier, John Buck, for Spain and England; the Grand Prior of France, for France and Castile; and the Grand Prior of Navarre, for Provence and Italy. The tower of St. Nicholas was placed under the command of Guyot de Castellan, a knight of Provence, the garrison consisting of 20 knights and 300 men.

Whilst these preparations were making for the defence, Solyman was on his side gathering together his forces, in readiness for the attack. He selected Mustapha Pasha as the leader of the army, and Curtoglu as the admiral of the fleet. The army numbered 140,000 men, in addition to whom were 60,000 peasants from Wallachia and Bosnia, who were brought there to execute such field works and mining operations as their skill in husbandry would enable them to perform with greater facility than the Turkish soldiers. These unfortunate wretches had been torn from their homes, and compelled, against their will, to take part in an enterprise for which they could have no possible sympathy. The ruthless manner in which they were worked like beasts of burden, and driven to labour under the most deadly fire, was such that in spite of their vast number, scarcely a man survived to witness the conclusion of the siege.

The naval armament by which this enormous force was transported, together with all its material and provisions, numbered nearly 400 sail, of different descriptions, of which upwards of 100 were galleys and vessels of considerable magnitude. An advanced detachment, consisting of thirty vessels, piloted the way to the scene of action, and pouring upon the smaller islands, the defence of which had been abandoned, carried fire and sword in every direction. In the island of Lango, however, where a small force had been left, they met with a decided repulse. The governor, a French knight, named Prejan de Bidoux, at the head of his little garrison, dashed at the disembarking marauders, and drove them back in confusion to their ships. Overawed by this act of determination, they sheered off, and bore away for Rhodes.

Early on the morning of the 26th June, 1522, a signal from St. Stephen's Hill conveyed intelligence into the city that the Turkish fleet was in sight. It was during the octave of the festival of St. John, at which time it had been an invariable custom at Rhodes for a procession to pass daily through the streets of the town. L'Isle Adam, desirous, as far as possible, to reassure the people, directed that the procession should be formed as usual, although the hostile fleet was at that moment studding the horizon. The procession over, high mass was performed in the cathedral, and at its conclusion the Grand Master mounted the steps of the altar, and put up a prayer to God on behalf of the people committed to his charge, that He would deign to give them fortitude to defend His holy religion, and that the slaughter and rapine with which they were menaced might be averted from them. L'Isle Adam, who was recognised as one of the leading soldiers of the day, was equally eminent for the fervour of his piety. When, therefore, he thus consecrated his cause to Heaven, and appealed to the Most High for protection against the foe, his hearers felt that under the leadership of such a man they were in good hands, and that if it were the will of Heaven that they should prosper, none could better carry that decree into effect.

The religious ceremony concluded, the doors of the church were closed, and the garrison directed to repair to their respective posts. Not a man, woman, or child on that eventful morning remained within doors, but every point of view from whence the movements of the hostile fleets could be observed was crowded with anxious gazers. Many there were within that mingled crowd who, looking back through a long vista of years, could call to mind a scene very similar to the present, when their seas had once before been covered by an enemy's fleet. Then they had triumphed gloriously, and the God of battles had fought on their side. He had aided them to hurl back the ruthless invader from their soil, and even now the bones of thousands who had once mustered in that proud array lay whitened beneath their soil. The husbandman still turned up relics that reminded him of that strife which he justly esteemed his country's glory; and amidst those plains of verdure with which the city was surrounded, many a patch of green, more brilliant than the rest, was pointed out as the spot where lay one of those numerous masses of slain, placed there in huddled confusion on the retreat of their fellows.

With all these memorials of their former victory before their eyes, and with the knowledge that the Rhodes of their day was far more capable of resistance than it had been when it maintained itself successfully forty years before—with the strains of martial music filling the air and exhilarating their hearts—with the summer sun flashing upon many a knightly helm and many a broidered pennon, it was but natural that the general feeling should be one of confidence, and even of exultation. Some there were, however, who, in spite of all these brilliant prospects, shook their heads in doubt. They knew but too well that the power of Mohammed, even at its zenith, was far inferior to that of Solyman. The career of this latter prince had so far been one unbroken succession of triumphs; no power had as yet been able to withstand his attacks; the army which was now about to land on their island exceeded that which they had before overcome, not only in numbers but in every branch of its equipment, and was led by generals who had been trained to victory under the eye of their sultan himself. With such fearful odds to contend against, it might well prove that the constancy and bravery of the garrison might, after all, be unavailing, and that the fair island in which they had so long dwelt with honour might be torn from their grasp.

The disembarkation of the besieging army, which extended over several days, proceeded without interruption from the garrison. In fact, the main difficulty against which L'Isle Adam had to contend was the smallness of his force. He was therefore obliged to forego numerous promising opportunities of attack, as every such attempt must have involved a certain amount of loss, and no minor advantage could compensate for the most trifling diminution of his resources. The Turkish army was therefore permitted to complete all its preliminaries without interference. At length they commenced the construction of their trenches, with the aid of the Wallachian peasants who had been brought for the purpose. Then L'Isle Adam considered that it was necessary to assume the offensive, and harassed the working parties by constant sorties, in which the garrison gained great advantages. These incessant checks greatly impeded the progress of the trenches, and vast numbers of the defenceless pioneers were slain.

Disaffection soon commenced to show itself in the Turkish army, caused by the ill-success of their first efforts. Murmurs and remonstrances arose in all directions, and it was at last with difficulty that the troops could be induced to advance to what they considered certain destruction. Pyrrhus Pasha, an aged counsellor, in whom Solyman reposed the utmost confidence, and who accompanied the army rather as an adviser than a general, deemed it necessary to report the disaffection of the janissaries to his master, informing him that nothing short of his actual presence would control them. Solyman had staked too much on the issue of the contest to permit of its miscarriage. Hastily assembling an additional force of 15,000 men, he hurried to the scene of action, where, by a judicious mixture of clemency and severity, he rapidly restored the spirit of his army, and the late mutineers, ashamed in the presence of their sultan of the insubordination they had shown, became fired with an ardent desire to efface the memory of their cowardice.

The lines of the besiegers stretched in a complete arc round the ramparts of the city, their flanks resting on the water's edge on either side. The fleet stretched across from flank to flank, so that the town was completely surrounded both by land and water. The battering train included six 10-inch, and fifteen 16-inch brass cannon, twelve large 30-inch, and two 33-inch mortars. Bourbon records that from this gigantic artillery they discharged 1,713 stone shot, and eight brass balls filled with artificial fire. These latter were probably the first attempt at the use of shells on record.

The main points selected for attack were two in number; one in front of the bastion of Italy, the other between the posts of Spain and Auvergne; and in order to dominate over these ramparts two huge cavaliers were raised. Every battery which could be brought to bear played unceasingly upon these works whilst in process of construction, and the slaughter of the pioneers was prodigious. Heaps of slain marked the advance of the structures; but as Solyman held the lives of the unfortunate peasants in no esteem, the labour was pushed on in spite of everything, and at length rose to a height which enabled the besiegers to command the ramparts in' their front.

Meanwhile a division was made in the Turkish camp. In order to attack the city on all sides, Mustapha Pasha directed that against the English quarter, Pyrrhus Pasha against the Italians, Achmet Pasha against Spain and Auvergne, the Beglier Bey of Natolia against Provence, and the Beglier Bey of Roumania from the gardens of St. Anthony against the Germans in the tower of St. Nicholas.

For a whole month the air resounded with the constant roar of artillery. The bastions of England and Italy soon showed signs of weakness. At the former spot, a new rampart had been constructed but a short time before the siege, and this speedily gave way. The older ramparts proved a better defence, and resisted the enemy's artillery long after the other had crumbled away. The unflagging energy of the garrison enabled them to repair these damages as rapidly as they were caused, by the construction of retrenchments in rear of the vulnerable points. Solyman soon perceived that with antagonists such as these a simple war of artillery might last for ever; he determined, therefore, to change his mode of attack, and commenced approaches by mining.

Gabriel Martinigo, a celebrated Venetian engineer, had enlisted in the service of the Order when it had first become apparent that Rhodes was to undergo a second siege, and he had been placed by L'Isle Adam at the head of the engineering branch of the defence. No sooner had he discovered Solyman's new mode of attack than he commenced to countermine, and for a while the struggle between the two forces appeared to have been entirely transferred below ground. For a long time he succeeded in keeping back the approaches of the besiegers. Two galleries, however, which had been driven beneath the bastion of England, unfortunately eluded his vigilance, and the first warning given of their construction was conveyed by their explosion, and the consequent overthrow of the entire salient. A sudden rush was immediately made by a battalion of Turks, who succeeded during the confusion in obtaining possession of the bastion. At this critical juncture the Grand Master made his appearance on the scene, accompanied by his body guard. The alarm had reached him whilst attending mass in the chapel of St. Mary of Victory. The officiating priest had just intoned the prayer, "Deus in adjutorium meum intende." "I accept the augury," cried he. "Come, my brethren, let us exchange the sacrifice of our prayers for that of our lives in defence of our religion." Roused to enthusiasm, they rushed to the point of attack, hurled themselves into the midst of the struggle, and soon carried all before them. Foremost in the fray stood L'Isle Adam, his gigantic and burly frame conspicuous above them all, as, armed with a short pike, he dashed at the assailants, and by word and deed encouraged his followers to drive them back. A few moments sufficed to attest the moral and physical superiority of the defenders. The Turks, unable not only to advance, but even to maintain themselves upon the ground already won, gave way, and were gradually driven back in confusion through the breach they had so shortly before entered in triumph. Mustapha Pasha had been watching the fortunes of the day from the advanced trenches, and his fury, as he beheld his troops pouring back from the breach, exceeded all bounds. Hastily drawing his scimitar, he rushed upon the fugitives, and cut down several with his own hand. Then, leading the remainder in person, he forced them once more to mount the breach and renew the struggle. It was now, however, too late; the garrison had been thoroughly alarmed, and had crowded to the spot in sufficient numbers to resist all his efforts, and he was at length compelled to call off his forces, and retire in despair to his trenches.

It would prove an almost endless task to describe the constant succession of assaults that followed this first attempt. Indeed, the history of the siege during the month of September would consist of a series of scenes similar to that already depicted. The sudden alarm, caused either by the explosion of a mine, or a dash of the enemy upon one of the numerous breaches, the hasty call to arms, the rush of the assailants, the firm stand of the defenders, the war-cries shouted on either side, the war of artillery, the rattle of small arms, the flashing of Greek fire, and the hissing of the seething pitch poured upon the assailants, such were the details that made up the picture presented during these scenes of strife. The results were invariably the same. Though the assaulting columns were numbered by thousands, and those the flower of Solyman's army, whilst the defenders were scarcely as many hundreds, harassed and exhausted by their previous efforts, still upon each successive occasion the Turk was forced to recoil from the impassable barrier of Christian steel.

The most furious attacks were made upon the 13th, 17th, and 24th of September; that of the 13th upon the Italian quarter, and that of the 17th upon the English bastion, the celebrated English commander the Turcopolier, John Buck, falling on this occasion at the head of his *langue*. Upon the 24th the attack was directed simultaneously upon every point where a practicable breach had been established; the bastions of Spain, Italy, Auvergne, and England were all attempted at the same moment, but even this gigantic effort of superior force failed.

The rage of Solyman now knew no bounds. His two lieutenants, Mustapha and Pyrrhus were banished the camp, and the admiral, Curtoglu, was forced to undergo the indignity of corporal punishment on the poop of his own galley, upon the charge of having neglected to support the attacks of the land forces by means of a naval diversion.

Whilst these successes were inspiriting the garrison, the first symptoms of those disastrous results which eventually led to the loss of the town had commenced to show themselves. Although, prior to the commencement of the siege, it had been reported to L'Isle Adam by the commissioners appointed for the purpose that the quantity of powder stored in their magazines was sufficient for a siege of a year's duration, yet a month had barely elapsed before it was manifest that the supply was running short. It became, therefore, necessary to practise the most rigid economy in the expenditure of ammunition, and the efforts of the garrison were much impeded by this vital want. It is not surprising that under these circumstances men should lend a ready ear to tales of treason. Whilst the ferment was at its height, a servant of the Chancellor d'Amaral, named Blaise Diaz, was detected on the bastion of Auvergne with a bow in his hand. As this was not the first time that he had been seen under similar circumstances, he was arrested and brought before the Grand Master. By his order the man was interrogated before the judges of the Castellany, and when placed under the torture he averred that he had been employed by his master to discharge treasonable correspondence into the enemy's camp with an arrow. D'Amaral was at once arrested and confronted with his accuser. He was a man whose haughty temper and unbounded ambition had created for him many enemies in every sphere of life, and no sooner had his name been connected with the suspicion of treason than numbers rushed forward eager to add corroborative testimony in support of the accusation. A Greek priest deposed that he had seen the Chancellor with Diaz upon the bastion of Auvergne,

## Execution of the Chancellor D'Amaral.

and that the latter had discharged an arrow with a letter attached to it from the rampart. Other evidence was also adduced to prove that on the election of L'Isle Adam, D'Amaral, who on that occasion had been a candidate for the office, and was much disappointed at his non-election, had asserted that there would be no more Grand Masters of Rhodes.

He was submitted to torture without eliciting any confession. His firmness, however, did not avail to save him from those who now clamoured for his death. He was sentenced to be beheaded. Prior to his execution, it was necessary that he should be stripped of the habit of his Order, which ceremony was carried into effect in the church of St. John, on the 7th of November, and on the following day he suffered the last penalty of the law in the public square with the same dignity and firmness that had characterized the whole of his conduct from the first moment of his arrest.

Of the two contemporary writers who have recorded this event, one, the Chevalier de Bourbon, asserts the guilt of the chancellor without hesitation, and may fairly be taken as the exponent of the general opinion within the city. The other, however, Fontanus, who was one of the judges appointed to investigate the charge, is far more obscure in the matter, and it may fairly be gathered from his writings that he had detected no satisfactory proof of guilt. Never, perhaps, was man condemned on weaker evidence. The deposition of his own servant, who had been detected in a treasonable act, and might naturally wish to save himself by fixing the guilt upon another, should have been received with great caution. The evidence of the Greek priest was absolutely worthless. Why, if he had really witnessed the transmission of treasonable correspondence, had he not denounced the criminal before? The explanation which D'Amaral gave of this man's evidence was probably correct—that it was an act of revenge, owing to the chancellor having frequently had occasion to find fault with the looseness of his life.

Curiously enough, the most important evidence against the chancellor only came to light in the year 1846, when a violent earthquake destroyed a great number of buildings in Rhodes. It has been stated that the supplies of gunpowder had, at a very early period of the siege, been found running short, although a commissioner, appointed by the Grand Master, had reported an ample store to have existed. The control of these supplies was undoubtedly vested in D'Amaral and his subordinates, and suspicion was at the time aroused that considerable quantities of powder had, in some manner, been made away with. Nothing, however, could be traced, and all search was unavailing. At the time of the earthquake above alluded to, the cathedral of Rhodes was utterly destroyed by an explosion of powder which took place in the vaults beneath. No one in the town knew anything whatever of the existence of this magazine, and the opinion of the Turkish Government has always been that it dated from the time of the knights. If so, it must have been a concealed store, probably walled up, or it could never have escaped detection for so long a time. Its presence in such a position would tally accurately with what is known of the events of this siege, and would go far to convict D'Amaral of the treason he was accused of. Still the evidence, although strong in proof of treason somewhere, hardly points sufficiently clearly to him. A man in his position would probably leave much of the details of his charge in the hands of subordinates, and it is with one or more of these probably that the onus really rests. Be that as it may, the explosion of 1846 strengthens the suspicion, that the loss of Rhodes in 1522 was in a great degree to be attributed to treason, and that but for this the defence might have terminated as gloriously for the knights as it did in 1480.

The discovery of treason and the fatal scarcity of ammunition soon told upon the spirits and energy of the defenders, and as the sultan was kept well acquainted with the state of affairs within the walls, he deemed the time appropriate to suggest a capitulation. For this purpose he despatched a Genoese, named Monilio, for a parley. In reply, he was informed that the Knights of St. John only treated with the infidel sword in hand. A second attempt met with no better result, the Grand Master having determined to cling to the defence of the city to the very end.

Had the town contained within its limits none but members of the Order, this resolution would probably have been adhered to. It no sooner, however, became known to the townspeople that terms of capitulation had been offered, than a cabal arose to press its acceptance. The principal citizens commissioned their metropolitan to urge upon the Grand Master the necessity of treating with the enemy. L'Isle Adam soon saw that without the concurrence of the townspeople it would be impossible to protract the defence. He therefore summoned a council to deliberate on the matter, and called upon the engineer, Martinigo, to report upon the state of the fortifications. Thereupon Martinigo rose and asserted upon his honour and conscience that he considered the place no longer tenable. The slaves and others employed as pioneers had all been either killed or wounded, they had therefore not sufficient labour even to move a piece of artillery from one battery to another; all further repairs

and reconstructions had become impossible; their ammu:
tion and stores were nearly all consumed; the enemy w(
already established upon two very vital points, and in ]
opinion the town was therefore lost.

The council was long and stormy; many there were wl
like the Grand Master, were desirous of emulating the se:
devotion of their predecessors, and of burying themselv
beneath the ruins of Rhodes. Others, however, were n
wanting who perceived that in passing this sentence of doo
upon themselves, they were also drawing down destructic
upon the citizens, who, having faithfully stood by the:
throughout the struggle, were entitled to consideration <
their hands.

It was, therefore, ultimately decided that the next offer <
parley should be accepted, and that the Grand Master shoul
be authorized to yield to the best terms he could obtain. Th
leaders of Solyman's army were too desirous of putting ;
stop to the fearful effusion of blood which had now beer
going on for six months, and of obtaining possession, upor
almost any terms, of that city which seemed as it were t
recede from their advance, to keep the garrison waiting lon{
for an opportunity of negotiation. Upon the 10th or
December a white flag was observed waving from the top of
a church standing within the limits of the Turkish position,
and this was at once answered by another hoisted upon a
windmill near the Cosquino gate. Two Turks then
advanced from the trenches, for the purpose of holding a
parley, and were met at the gate by Martinigo and the Prior
of St. Gilles. They handed in a letter containing the
conditions offered by the sultan.

In consideration of the instant surrender of the town, he
was prepared to permit the Grand Master, with all the

members of his Order, together with such of the citizens as chose to follow them, to depart unmolested with all their personal property. Those, on the other hand, who preferred to remain, were guaranteed in the undisturbed exercise of their religion, and were to be free of tribute for five years, the churches were to be respected, and all property, public and private, protected from pillage. Whilst these terms were under the consideration of the council, an unfortunate collision took place between a portion of the garrison and the Turks, in which several of the latter lost their lives. This so complicated matters that a whole week was lost, and hostilities recommenced. The loss of the Spanish bastion, which was captured after a severe struggle on the 18th of December, completed the dismay of the inhabitants, and they urged L'Isle Adam to reopen the negotiation.

Envoys were therefore dispatched to Solyman, with *carte blanche* to surrender the town upon the best terms they could obtain. Solyman received the ambassadors in his pavilion, in all the splendour of his imperial majesty, surrounded by the janissaries of his guard. He consented to renew the terms he had previously offered. These conditions were immediately accepted, and it was decided, in order to ensure the due execution of the treaty, that the Turkish army should be withdrawn from the vicinity of the city, and only a select body of 4,000 janissaries be permitted to enter. In return for this clemency, so unusual in those days of sanguinary warfare, the knights agreed to yield up peaceable possession, not only of Rhodes, but also of all the dependent islands. Twenty-five knights of the Order, including two Grand Crosses, and the same number of citizens, were to be given as hostages for the due execution of the treaty, and as soon as they made their appearance in the

Turkish camp, the aga of the janissaries, with the specific number of troops, entered the town, and took formal possession of it on behalf of the sultan.

To the nations of Europe the loss of Rhodes was a deep disgrace. Apathy and indifference were displayed on all sides whilst this struggle between Christianity and Infidelity was going forward, and its unfortunate issue must ever remain a blot upon the history of the sixteenth century. To the Knights of Rhodes, however, no such disgrace can attach itself. The gallantry which had so long withstood such desperate odds was warmly recognised and enthusiastically hailed by admiring nations. As the struggle progressed, and its ultimate issue became more and more certain, men gazed with amazement upon that touching scene of heroism and endurance; and when at length, driven from their homes, feeble in number and shattered in prospects the relics of that gallant band wandered westward in search of a new resting-place, they were everywhere greeted with rapturous enthusiasm. The feeling of Europe generally was aptly expressed by Charles V., who, upon hearing of the disastrous issue of the siege, turned to his courtiers and exclaimed, "There has been nothing so well lost in the world as Rhodes!"

## CHAPTER III.

Offer of Malta to the Order—Its Acceptance—Its previous History—Description of the Island—Gozo—Attempt against Modon—Final determination to settle in Malta—Loss of Tripoli—Additions to the Fortifications—Accession of La Valette.

On the 1st of January, 1523, L'Isle Adam, with the entire body of the Order, quitted Rhodes, accompanied by 4,000 citizens, who preferred to follow them rather than remain in the island under its new *régime*. For seven years they led a wandering and homeless life; Candia, Messina, Cumæ, and Viterbo, being visited in succession. Their diminished revenues were drained by the expense of providing for their Rhodian followers, who received support from the public treasury under the name of "the bread of Rhodes."

Meanwhile, L'Isle Adam exerted himself on all sides to procure such aid as should enable him to reconquer his old home, or, failing that, to secure the establishment of his fraternity in some new and convenient locality. The Order had performed such gallant services in protecting the commerce of Europe, and checking the advance of the Turkish empire, that a general desire manifested itself that they should not abandon the scene of their former exploits,

but should be furnished with a new home within the lim
of the Mediterranean Sea.

Charles V., King of Spain and Emperor of Germany, w
at this time at war with France. The French monarc
Francis I., had fallen into his hands after the battle
Pavia, and was being retained a prisoner at Madrid. L'I؛
Adam visited the Spanish court in that city, partly
negotiate between the two monarchs, at the request of tl
regent of France, and partly to endeavour to obta
assistance for the recovery of Rhodes, a project for whic
undertaking being at that time under consideration. In bot
of these objects he was perfectly successful. He receive
liberal promises of support from the two princes, an
Charles V. further offered him the sovereignty of the island
of Malta and Gozo, and the city of Tripoli for the Order c
St. John, in case he should fail in his attempt agains
Rhodes.

The design in question had been suggested by no less ؛
person than Achmet Pasha, on whom, after the degradatioɪ
of Mustapha, the command of the Turkish army hac
devolved. This general, after establishing himself in Egypt
had renounced his allegiance to the sultan, and assumed the
position of a sovereign prince. To support him in his
attempt he addressed himself to L'Isle Adam, informing him
that he had it in his power to restore the island of Rhodes to
the Order. The new commandant of the tower of St.
Nicholas was a renegade Christian, and a tool in his hands,
who, if an adequate force were landed in the island, would
surrender his post and join the invaders. The plot, however,
fell through, having been discovered by Solyman. Achmet
Pasha was assassinated, and all hopes of success in that
quarter came to an end.

Nothing remained, therefore, but to fall back upon the offer of Charles V., and commissioners were despatched to examine and report upon the islands of Malta and Gozo. Many difficulties occurred before their acceptance was finally determined on, as Charles had coupled with his offer several conditions which could not be entertained. The Pope, however, who had himself been a Knight of St. John, and had abandoned the Order to pursue that ecclesiastical career which raised him to the papal chair under the title of Clement VII., exerted his influence and obtained a mitigation of the terms by which the emperor had shackled his gift.

Matters were at last arranged to the satisfaction of all parties, and in the year 1530, Charles signed a deed in which he made over to the Order of St. John, in perpetual sovereignty, the islands of Malta and Gozo with their dependencies, coupled with the city of Tripoli, upon the condition of an annual payment of a falcon as a recognition of the feudal tenure of the gift.* The Order further agreed that they should never make war against the emperor or the kingdom of Sicily; that the nomination to the bishopric of Malta should rest with the emperor from amongst three candidates, to be selected by the fraternity, one of whom was always to be a Spaniard; and that the sovereignty of the islands should not be transferred to other hands without his sanction being previously obtained. The deed was dated on the 24th March, 1530.

The donation of the emperor was promptly confirmed by a

* This document is still preserved in the Armoury of the Palace at Malta. It is a square of parchment written in Latin, and signed in the emperor's own hand, "Yo el Rey." A seal is attached, bearing the impress of the emperor on horseback brandishing a sword.

papal bull, upon the receipt of which L'Isle Adam sen Grand Crosses to Sicily to receive a formal investiture c territory from the viceroy. After this ceremony had completed, they proceeded to take possession of their acquisition, and to place members of the fraternit command of the various posts surrendered to them.

The day upon which the Grand Master, with his c arrived at Malta, was the 26th October, 1530, and he at assumed sovereignty over the islands. At the entrance ¡ of the Citta Notabile, a small town upon the summit of a in the centre of the island, surrounded by a feeble forti tion, he was stopped until he had sworn upon the holy c the symbol of his religion, that he would preserve privileges of the inhabitants, and govern them in accord with their ancient laws. The keys of the town were t presented to him, and he made his entry amidst the accla tions of the people.

The early history of Malta is somewhat difficult to tr A race of giants, termed Phœacians, are traditionally s posed to have originally peopled the island; but, be this it may, there is no question that it was colonized at a v early period by the Phœnicians; and in many parts it rich in remains of that people. About 755 B.C., the Gree returning from the siege of Troy, overran the Mediterrane founded some cities in Calabria, and amongst other acqui tions established themselves in Malta, driving out t Phœnicians. Prior to this event, the island had been knov by the name of Ogygia; it was now, however, changed that of Melitas. It remained in the possession of the Gree for two hundred years, at the expiration of which period tl Carthaginians disputed the sovereignty of the island wi them, and eventually succeeded in wresting it from the

hands. In the second Punic war, Sempronius established the dominion of Rome in Malta, driving out its Carthaginian inhabitants. The Greeks, however, were allowed to remain, and their laws and customs were not interfered with. The island was attached to the government of Sicily, and was ruled by a pro-prætor dependent on that province.

Whilst under their sway, Malta attained to a very high pitch of civilization and refinement. Situated in the centre of the Mediterranean, within a few days' sail from the shores of three continents, it speedily became a thriving mart for much of the commerce of Rome. Its manufactures of cotton, and its public buildings, principally temples erected in honour of its tutelary deities, were celebrated throughout the Mediterranean; and the Maltese themselves were esteemed the most hardy mariners in Europe. On the division of the Roman Empire, the island of Malta fell to the lot of Constantine, and from that period its decadence may be first dated. In the fifth century it was seized on successively by the Vandals and Goths, and although in the sixth century Belisarius, the general of Justinian, drove out the barbarians, and once more established the Roman power, the island never re-attained its former prosperity.

The rapid spread of Mahometanism in the eight and ninth centuries brought Malta under the sway of the Saracens, who, in the early portion of the latter century, exterminated the Greek population, and established a government in the island, dependent on the Emir of Sicily. Much that is Saracenic, both in building and language, still remains to mark this period of occupation, and, indeed, the Maltese may be said as a race to partake more of the Arabic than of the Italian type to this day.

At the close of the eleventh century, the Saracens were expelled by Count Roger, the Norman, who established a

principality in Sicily and Malta, which was converted i[n]
monarchy under his grandson. It subsequently becam[e]
appanage of the German emperors, in whose han[ds]
remained until Charles of Anjou, who was invested wit[h]
government by the Pope, re-annexed it to the kingdo[m]
Sicily, and with that kingdom it fell into the possessio[n]
Spain after the tragedy of the Sicilian Vespers.

Its decadence during these successive ages had [been]
continuous, and the thriving aspect of the island whilst u[nder]
the Roman sway was now utterly lost. With great nat[ural]
capabilities for the formation of a powerful naval statio[n]
was at this time little more than an arid rock about twe[nty]
miles in length by twelve in breadth, and presented a so[me]
what uninviting appearance to L'Isle Adam when he [first]
landed to assume its sovereignty. In fact, the only poin[t of]
attraction to the Order was the magnificent port which [lay]
on its eastern coast, and which afforded capacious [and]
sheltered anchorage where the largest fleets might ride [in]
security.

This harbour is divided into two main portions [by]
a promontory of land jutting out from the inner side [of]
the bay in a north-easterly direction, termed Mou[nt]
Sceberras. The eastern port, called the great or gra[nd]
harbour, by far the most capacious of the two, is, in [its]
turn, subdivided by the indentions of its eastern coa[st,]
which, by the projection of two other promontories in [a]
north-westerly direction, forms three inner harbours. T[he]
western port, called the Marsa Muscetto, though small[er]
than the other, is still of considerable capacity, and bein[g]
sheltered from the north-east wind, always very prevale[nt]
in the Mediterranean, and in winter extremely violent, is [of]
considerable service for the commerce of the island. I[t]

accommodation, however, is much reduced by a large island which lies in its midst.

The only protection of which Malta boasted at the time of its transfer to the Order, was a fort constructed on one of the promontories jutting out into the great harbour, and called the Castle of St. Angelo, around the foot of which was clustered a small group of houses. This hamlet was termed the Bourg. The chief town, called the Citta Notabile, lay in the centre of the island, and was of far more importance than the Bourg. Situated at the extremity of a hill which stands forth with great boldness, and terminates almost precipitously, it was further secured by a rampart, and here all that remained of the wealth and prosperity of Malta was collected. The rest of the island lay completely open to the piratical incursions of the corsairs, who swarmed on the northern shores of Africa, and nothing could have protected it from their ravages but the poverty of the inhabitants. The soil, which is both scanty and ungrateful, did not suffice for the wants of the population, and they were, to a great extent, dependent upon Sicily for the importation of grain. The principal article of culture was cotton, which thrives well in Malta, and the manufacture of which has always been one of the staple industries of the people. Scarcely a tree was to be seen, with the exception of a few caroubas and shumacks dotting the landscape here and there. The eye roamed in vain for a patch of green to relieve the glare of the white rock when reflecting the blaze of the summer sun.

In addition to the Citta Notabile, there were several small villages, called casals, dotted over the island; the total population, however, did not exceed twelve thousand persons.

The island of Gozo is divided from Malta by a channel of about four miles in width, in the midst of which lie two

smaller islands, Comino and Cominetto. It is far more f[
in its soil than Malta, but utterly destitute of harbours.
extent is rather less than eight miles either way, an
inhabitants, numbering about five thousand at the time
transfer to the Order, dwelt in small casals like thos
Malta.

With regard to the city of Tripoli, the other gift which
annexed to that of Malta and Gozo, and with which
Order would gladly have dispensed, had its acceptance
been insisted on by the Emperor, it will not be neces
here to enter into any description. This town remaine
their possession only twenty years, at the expiration of w
time that fate befell it which had been foreseen from
first. The Order were expelled after a long siege, in wl
notwithstanding the obloquy which his capitulation ɪ
unjustly threw upon his name, the commandant, the Mar
La Vallier, greatly distinguished himself.

The practised eye of L'Isle Adam was not long in ]
ceiving the advantages of the position of Mount Sceber
dominating, as it did, over both harbours, and owing to
formation, easily rendered secure from attack, except on
land side. Here, therefore, he first contemplated
establishment of the convent, and the erection of works
sufficient magnitude to secure it from insult. Unfortunate
the funds necessary for such an undertaking were not for
coming. The migratory life which the Order had led for ɪ
preceding eight years, accompanied as they were by a laɪ
colony of Rhodians, who, to the number of four thousaɪ
had subsisted mainly on the charity of the Order, h
exhausted the treasury. L'Isle Adam consequently fou
himself absolutely unable to undertake any work of magɪ
tude, even though of the most vital necessity. He, theɪ

fore, decided upon establishing himself in the fort of St. Angelo as a temporary measure, and on fixing the convent of the Order in the surrounding Bourg. Such additions to the slender defences of the fort as his means permitted, were at once constructed, and a line of entrenchment was traced across the head of the promontory to enclose the Bourg, and to cover it as far as practicable from the surrounding eminences.

The Grand Master was at this time the less disposed to undertake any work of magnitude at Malta, because he still entertained hopes of establishing his convent in a more advantageous position elsewhere. At the time when Achmet Pasha had opened negotiations for the surrender of Rhodes, L'Isle Adam had despatched the commander, Bosio, to visit that island in disguise, with a view to ascertaining the feasibility of the project. Bosio had, whilst thus engaged, opened negotiations with certain persons in the town of Modon, a port in the Morea, which had been captured by the Turks some years prior to Rhodes. The position of this city rendered it well adapted for maritime enterprise, and L'Isle Adam was the more anxious to obtain possession of it, since its proximity to Rhodes would enable him to seize upon the first favourable opportunity for repossessing himself of his old home. Two renegades, one the commandant of the fort, the other the chief of the custom-house, had notified to Bosio their willingness to enter into the views of the Order, and to assist them in seizing on the town, provided a sufficient force were despatched to ensure success.

On the 17th August, 1531, L'Isle Adam sent a fleet of eight galleys, under the command of Salviati, Prior of Rome, to attempt the enterprise. On arriving near Modon, Salviati hid his fleet in a retired creek in the island of

Sapienza, which lies off the mouth of the harbour, smuggled into the port two brigantines, ostensibly l with timber, beneath which, however, lay concealed a ] of soldiers. The renegades, faithful to their pro admitted these vessels, and the commandant of the in order to facilitate the seizure of the town, plied janissaries under his command with wine, till they reduced to a most helpless state of intoxication. A gun then fired, as a signal for the fleet to enter the harb and follow up the advantage which had been gained, b contrary wind prevented Salviati from hearing it, so many hours were lost before any support arrived. M while, the governor of the city, recovering from his panic, and perceiving the slenderness of the force by wh he was attacked, collected the townspeople together, an desperate encounter ensued. The knights were well-n overpowered, when Salviati, having been summoned fr his place of concealment, by a boat sent to him for purpose, at length made his appearance, and turned fortunes of the day. The Turks were driven into the citad and the rest of the town fell into the hands of the knigh Unfortunately, however, a body of 6,000 Turks lay camped within a few miles of Modon, and a summo having been forwarded to them for assistance by t governor, the knights were ultimately forced to aband the enterprise. The fleet returned to Malta, carrying 8 Turkish prisoners, mostly women and children, with a lar amount of plunder. The latter, however, falling to the sha of the individual adventurers, constituted no reimbursemer to the exhausted treasury for the outlay caused by t expedition.

The failure of this enterprise destroyed the last hope

which L'Isle Adam had entertained of removing his convent to a more favourable situation than Malta. Nothing, therefore, remained but to take such measures as should best ensure security in their new home. Many additions were made to both the fortifications and armament of the castle of St. Angelo. The ramparts which enclosed the Bourg, now rapidly rising into a considerable town, were much strengthened. The fortifications of the Citta Notabile were restored and improved, and an ample garrison allotted for its defence. At Tripoli similar precautions were taken, and a vessel having arrived from England, laden with artillery, the present of Henry VIII. to the Order, this seasonable acquisition was at once despatched thither, to add to the armament of that exposed point.

On the 22nd August, 1534, the Grand Master, L'Isle Adam, aged upwards of seventy years, died, to the great grief of the fraternity. The heroism and grandeur of L'Isle Adam's character were such that the clouds of adversity only set it forth in brighter lustre. The loss of Rhodes, the greatest disaster which had befallen the Order since that of Jerusalem, has connected itself so imperishably with his name that he has gained a higher renown for his conduct in that calamity than other men have achieved by the most brilliant victories. As the establisher of his Order in the island of Malta, and the prime agent in its resuscitation after its late desperate losses, he may be looked upon as its third parent and founder. Raymond du Puy has associated his name with the original foundation of the institution. It was to Fulk de Villaret that the Order were indebted for their establishment in their lovely island home at Rhodes; and it is to L'Isle Adam that the merit is due of having guided their fortunes to that rocky island in the centre of

F

the Mediterranean, where for upwards of two centuries
a half the banner of St. John waved proudly, an honou[r]
Christianity and a terror to the infidel.

During the absence of Peter du Pont, who upon the d[eath]
of L'Isle Adam had been elected to the vacant dignity,
who at the time of his elevation was residing at Calab[ria]
the Grand Prior of Toulouse, acting as his lieuten[ant]
continued to strengthen the Castle of St. Angelo, [and]
excavated its ditch from sea to sea, so as completely [to]
isolate the fort by water.

In 1541 the Grand Master, John d'Omedes, called in [the]
chief engineer of the Emperor, named Caramolin, in or[der]
to receive his opinion as to the proper steps to be taken [for]
the due security of the fort and the improvement of [the]
existing works. That officer at once condemned both [the]
Bourg and St. Angelo, as being incapable of maintaini[ng]
any serious or protracted defence; nor did he consider [it]
advisable to make any great outlay for their addition[al]
security, deeming that their situation, overlooked as they we[re]
by neighbouring heights,* within a very easy distance, w[as]
radically defective and untenable. He proposed, therefor[e,]
as a more efficient measure, to fortify the promontory whi[ch]
divided the two harbours called Mount Sceberras.

Although this work was not executed in accordance wit[h]
the suggestions of Caramolin, the credit is undoubtedly du[e]
to him of being the first to point out the advisability an[d]
necessity of occupying that most important point. Th[e]
dread of the expense and other causes prevented his desig[n]
from being then carried out, and the knights contente[d]

* The heights here alluded to are those of Mount Salvator and the pro[-]
montory of Senglea, which have long since been embraced within th[e]
fortifications.

themselves with still further deepening the ditches of the Bourg, and raising a cavalier in the Castle of St. Anzelo, which should dominate over all the neighbouring ground. It has been already stated that the finances of the Order were at this time in a very impoverished condition. Now a fresh blow was struck, which still further weakened their resources.

The commencement of the quarrel between Henry VIII. and the Pope had already assumed a most threatening aspect prior to the death of L'Isle Adam, and his fears for the security and permanence of the English *langue* had embittered the last moments of that venerable chief. Since then matters had rapidly reached their culminating point, and the Reformation soon developed itself in England. An institution like that of the Order of St. John, still maintaining obedience to the Pope, was not likely to remain long undisturbed under the new *régime*. Henry VIII. had, prior to his renunciation of papal domination, displayed a desire to interfere in the affairs of the Order in England on more than one occasion, and now the moment was come when he determined to crush them altogether.

There exists amongst the archives of Malta a document assuming the form of letters patent, bearing date, Westminster, 7th July, 1538, which commences by entitling Henry the supreme head of the Anglican Church, and the protector of the Order of St. John of Jerusalem. It then goes on to declare, first, that for himself and his successors he gives licence to Brother William West, Grand Prior of England, to confer the habit and receive the profession requisite to admit such English subjects as may desire to enter the Order, under the usual conditions, provided that such postulant shall have previously taken an oath of allegiance to the said monarch; secondly, that any pe nominated by the Grand Master in Council to a commanc in England shall obtain confirmation of his appointn from the king. He will be required to pay the first ye revenues of his commandery into the king's treasu thirdly, it shall not be lawful for the Order of St. Joh1 make eleemosynary collections* within the realm of Engla unless in virtue of a royal warrant, which warrant sl contain the express clause that such collection was not m in virtue of any bull from the Roman Pontiff, but un letters patent emanating from the King of Englar fourthly, those brethren holding, or hereafter promoted commanderies within the realm of England, shall not rec nise, support, or promote the jurisdiction, authority, rank, title of the Bishop of Rome; fifthly, those brethren holdi1 or hereafter promoted to, commanderies within the realm England, shall, after payment of the first year's revent into the king's treasury, transfer those of the second year the treasury of the Order, for the general maintenance a1 support of the convent, with the reservation of such annu tithes as the king retains to himself from all the comman eries within his kingdom; sixthly and lastly, that every ye a chapter of the Priory shall be held, in which all crim committed by the fraternity within the realm of Englan shall be examined into and duly punished, and if any of tl offending brethren shall consider himself aggrieved by tl sentence of the chapter, he shall appeal either to the vicar the king or to the conservator of the privileges of the Ordc of St. John, duly appointed by the king.

\* These collections had hitherto been frequently made under the sanctio of Papal authority, and formed a considerable source of revenue under th title of " confraria."

A very cursory glance at these clauses will mark the subtlety and rapacity of those who drew them up. The fourth clause was of itself amply sufficient to prevent any member of the Roman Catholic religion from holding office or emolument within the kingdom of England; but, as if the monarch feared lest the members of the Order might be possessed of consciences sufficiently elastic to take the oath, he secures for himself an ample provision from the revenues of the commanderies, payment of which would be enforced even upon the most compliant of the fraternity. Had the Order of St. John been in the habit of paying to the See of Rome any annual tithes or contributions, it would have appeared but natural that the King of England, when assuming to himself the papal functions within his realm, should also have transferred to his own treasury all such payments, but this had never been the case. From the earliest period of its institution, the Order had been exempted by papal authority from the payment of all ecclesiastical tithes or contributions, and this exemption had been continued and confirmed from time to time ever since. Henry, therefore, in demanding the payment of tithes was arrogating a privilege such as had never been assumed by the pontiffs of Rome, even in the days of their most dictatorial authority. One of the great sources of revenue enjoyed by the treasury of the Order was the payment of the first year's income by the successor to a vacant commandery. It was this revenue, of which Henry contemplated the spoliation, and by the substitution for the benefit of the treasury of a second year's payment he mulcted the unfortunate commanders by so much additional taxation.

It is much to the credit of the English *langue* that they did not permit the natural desire of retaining their large

possessions in England to outweigh their sense of relig
duty. Hard as were the terms imposed by Henry, t
were such as many men would have deemed far prefer:
to absolute confiscation, but the Order of St. John was
prepared to admit of any compromise between its duty
its interests. It had been reared in the bosom of the Chu
of Rome; it had been nurtured by the protection of e
successive pontiff, and now that a storm had burst over
head of the father of the Church, which bid fair to dep:
him of the spiritual allegiance of a vast proportion of
flock, the Order were not prepared to abandon his cause, e
for the sake of retaining their worldly advantages. ]
terms offered by Henry were peremptorily declined, &
the *langue* of England, which, for many years, had be
considered one of the brightest adjuncts of the Order, and
whom the historian Bosio, himself an Italian, and, therefo
an unprejudiced witness, has recorded, "*cosi ricco nobile
principal membro come sempre era stata la venerabile ling
d'Inghilterra*" was lost for ever to the fraternity. A gene:
sequestration of their property in England took pla
accompanied by much persecution. Some perished on t
scaffold, others lingered long in prison, and the remaind
homeless, destitute and penniless, found their way to Malt
where they were received with all brotherly kindness a:
Christian consideration. The loss thus sustained by t]
treasury of the Order, at the time of its greatest need, w
severely felt in Malta, and went far towards preventing t]
construction of the most important works, although imper:
tively demanded for the security of the island.

The dangerous position in which the garrison of Tripc
was placed had, from the first occupation of that post by tl
Order, been a subject of great anxiety, and many appea

had been made to the Emperor to aid in an expedition for its support. The northern coasts of Africa, abutting upon the Mediterranean, had first been occupied by the Arabians during the latter portion of the seventh century. The country had gradually become subdivided into several kingdoms, of which Morocco, Algiers, and Tunis were the most important. These principalities were inhabited by a mixed race, comprised of the original Arabian conquerors, the negroes, who had spread themselves over the country from the more southern provinces, and the Moors, who had been driven thither from Spain during the preceding two centuries. Until the commencement of the sixteenth century these petty kingdoms interfered but seldom in the politics of Europe, and their very existence was but little known and as little cared for.

Then, however, a revolution took place, which materially altered their position. Two of the four sons of a Turk resident at Mitylene, named Horuc and Hayradin, prompted by a spirit of daring, abandoned their father's home, and joined a crew of corsairs. Their boldness and skill soon raised them to the command of the band, and they gradually augmented their forces, until they had assembled a fleet of twelve galleys, besides other smaller vessels. Calling themselves friends of the sea, and enemies of all who sailed thereon, they scoured the Mediterranean, and rendered their names terrible in every part of its waters. They were both known by the surname of Barbarossa, from the red colour of their beards, and whilst Horuc Barbarossa was recognised as the supreme chief, the authority of Hayradin Barbarossa was but little inferior. Increasing in ambition as their power extended, they at length sought the acquisition of a port from whence they might carry on their buccaneering expeditions in security.

An opportunity was not long in presenting itself. C[n] in by the king of Algiers to support him in a war wi[t] neighbouring chief, Horuc succeeded in dethroning murdering that monarch, and in establishing himself in place as king of Algiers. To render his position the m[ore] secure he placed himself under the protection of the sul[tan] of Turkey, to whom he tendered the homage of a tribut[ary] prince. That monarch, with whose ambitious views it w[ell] accorded to add these extensive provinces to his empi[re] accepted the proffered homage, and promised his support [to] Horuc.

In the year 1518 Horuc was killed in action, and ] brother Hayradin assumed the vacant sceptre. The fame his naval exploits in this new dignity having reached Co[n]stantinople, the sultan appointed him to the supreme co[m]mand of the Turkish fleets. Armed with this new powe[r] it was not long before he made himself master of Tuni[s] which he purposed to add to his kingdom of Algiers. [At] this conjuncture Charles V. thought it high time to interfe[re] to prevent the establishment of a piratical power, which, permitted to consolidate itself unchecked, might eventuall[y] prove most disastrous to Europe. He therefore led a[n] expedition in person against Tunis, in which he was aide[d] by the entire naval strength of the Order. This expeditio[n] was thoroughly successful in its object—Tunis was rescue[d] from the hands of Barbarossa, and restored to its legitimat[e] monarch. Inflated by this success, a second expedition wa[s] subsequently undertaken against Algiers by the emperor, but failed utterly, owing to the foolhardiness of Charles, who persisted in the undertaking against the advice of his celebrated admiral, Doria.

This failure rendered the position of Tripoli more pre-

# PLAN OF THE
# FORTRESS OF MALTA

at the time of the Siege by the Turks in 1565

The Positions of the Turkish Batteries are coloured Green

## Expedition against Mehedia.

carious than ever, and in the crisis the Grand Master and council selected for the onerous post of its governor a Provençal knight, afterwards destined to render his name one of the most illustrious in the annals of his Order, John Parisot de la Valette. Even at this time La Valette had distinguished himself by his bravery and skill in numerous cruises against the Turks. He had never quitted Malta from the day of his admission into the Order, except when undertaking these cruises, and had risen from rank to rank, until he now stood forth one of the foremost men of the fraternity.

The fate of Tripoli was destined, however, to be postponed for awhile. Barbarossa having died at Constantinople, was succeeded in the command of the Turkish fleet by his lieutenant, Dragut. This man had attained a notoriety in the Mediterranean only second to that of the Barbarossas, and his assumption of command was followed by prompt and decisive measures on his part. He possessed himself of the town of Mehedia, a port situated midway between Tunis and Tripoli, and here he established a naval depôt in the most dangerous contiguity to the latter stronghold. Against this new danger a third expedition was formed, under the command of Doria, the contingent of the Order, consisting of 140 knights and 500 men, being under the command of the Bailiff, De la Sangle. The siege of Mehedia commenced at the end of June, 1550, and after a desperate resistance the town was captured by Doria. As it was not contemplated that the place should be retained, the fortifications were razed, and the post abandoned.

This success, in which the knights had borne a gallant part, so enraged the Turkish sultan that he at once commenced preparations for a gigantic armament against Malta.

Neither time nor means were available for D'Omedes
was at that time the Grand Master, to place his island
proper state of defence, and when, on the 16th of July,
the Turkish fleet, under the command of Dragut, and
in the Marsa Muscetto, but few additions had been ma
the feeble fortifications with which the Bourg was prot
The commanders of the Turkish armament landed
Mount Sceberras, and from that point reconnoitred th
of St. Angelo. Fortunately for the Order the great str
of the work daunted the Turkish leaders, and they aban
the idea of an assault at that point, preferring to com
operations against the Citta Notabile. The troops
therefore disembarked, and marched directly into the in
of the island, taking with them a sufficient power of art
to enable them to prosecute the siege of the town. F
as its defences were against the powerful force which
peared before it, the garrison stoutly maintained
resistance, and, fortunately for them, intimation re
Dragut that Doria had set sail for the relief of Malta
a large fleet. This intelligence, which was completely
so far terrified him that he decided upon abandoning
attempt on Malta, and re-embarked his troops with
utmost expedition. As a last effort he made a descent
the defenceless island of Gozo, which he ravaged with
punity.

The attack on Malta having thus signally failed, Dr
directed his course towards the city of Tripoli, with a
determination of accomplishing its capture. At this
the governor of Tripoli was Gaspard La Vallier, who
relieved La Valette in the post. To the summons of
Turk he replied with the most disdainful pride, and the
was commenced in due form. Treachery within the t

aided those in its front, and eventually La Vallier was forced to treat for a capitulation. The most honourable terms were granted, but when the time arrived for their execution they were basely violated, and the garrison, together with a considerable number of the citizens, were made prisoners.

The general feeling in Malta at the loss of Tripoli was very bitter. The Grand Master, D'Omedes, feeling that he was himself not without blame, in having neglected to provide assistance for the threatened city, was anxious to divert the popular wrath into another channel, and caused La Vallier to be arrested, with three of his companions in arms. Never was innocent man more basely sacrificed to popular clamour, and La Vallier, than whom a braver man or more skilful commander did not exist within the ranks of the Order, was stripped of his habit and imprisoned.

The panic created by these events brought the question of the construction of further defences for Malta prominently forward, and in spite of financial difficulties, it was felt on all sides that something must be done, *coûte que coûte*. Counsels, however, differed as to what steps should be taken, and whilst these deliberations were pending the convent remained in a most critical state of insecurity.

In this conjuncture, the Prior of Capua, who was sufficiently clear-sighted to perceive how great a risk the Order was running by their constant delays, brought forward in council a clear statement of the position in which they stood, and the measures which he considered most suited to the circumstances of the case. A vehement debate ensued, but he succeeded in carrying his point, and his project was adopted by a large majority. This design, in addition to a further increase in the works of the Bourg and St. Angelo, contemplated the occupation of the point of land which jutted out from the

eastern coast of the grand harbour, parallel to that on wl
St. Angelo stood, with a work to be called St. Michael,
also the extremity of Mount Sceberras with another to
named St. Elmo.

In order to carry out these additions with the gre
vigour, three commissaries were named, one for each p
who, assisted by the knights and other members of the Or
pushed forward their respective works with the utn
rapidity, and stimulated the workmen with their const
presence. Don Pedro Pardo, a celebrated Spanish engin
designed the new forts and the other works, to the ra
execution of which each one devoted his utmost energies.
Bailiffs and other Grand Crosses contributed the gold cha
from which the insignia of their rank were suspended,
also a large portion of their plate; the other knights follov
their example, subscribing liberally from their private me
for the use of the public treasury, to enable the great expe
consequent on these works to be punctually defrayed.
galleys were also retained in port instead of performing th
accustomed cruises, or caravans as they were termed, in or
that their crews, who were principally composed of slav
might be employed on the rising works.

The result of these exertions was so satisfactory, that
the month of May of the following year, 1553, the forts
St. Michael and St. Elmo, and the bastions traced at
head of the Bourg, were completed and armed, whilst
ditches, although not quite finished, were in a very advan
state.

At the latter end of this year the Grand Master D'Ome
died, and was succeeded by a French knight, named Clau
de la Sangle, who, at the time of his nomination, was residi
at Rome. He hurried at once to Malta, and on inspection

the works as they then stood, was so far from feeling content that he determined at once upon enclosing the entire of St. Michael's Mount on the side of the Coradin Hill which dominated over it on the west. In pursuance of this project, he commenced in the following year the construction of a bastioned line along the entire side of the promontory, next that hill within which he founded a town under the protection of his newly-raised ramparts, and which, in honour of him, received the name of La Sangle, afterwards corrupted into Senglea.

La Sangle was succeeded in the government of the Order by John Parisot de la Valette in the year 1557, and under his rule the fraternity were destined to achieve the most glorious success that had ever attended their arms. The first design of the new chief was to occupy the entire peninsula of Mount Sceberras with a line of ramparts similar to that constructed at Senglea, and for this purpose he invited Quinsan de Montalin, an engineer of high reputation, to visit the island and report upon his project. After a minute inspection of the locality, it was decided that although the measure would undoubtedly be most advisable, and would add greatly to the general security of the works, more especially at the Bourg, which still continued the head-quarters of the convent, yet, that owing to the great drain which former constructions had caused upon their treasury, means no longer existed for carrying the design into effect.

As, however, the Grand Master had been warned by his emissaries in Constantinople that an expedition was preparing for the subjugation of Malta, he determined at once to make such additions to the fortress as his limited means permitted. The front of Senglea on the land side was greatly improved, terrepleins were added to the ramparts, and the ditches of the

Bourg were completed. He also constructed a small batt[ery]
for three guns beneath the fort of St. Angelo, nearly o[n a]
level with the water's edge to flank the fort of St. Mich[ael,]
which, during the siege then impending, proved a worl[d of]
the utmost importance at a very critical moment. A giga[nt]
chain was fixed at the entrance to the port of the galleys,
extremity of which was secured on the platform of rock be[low]
St. Angelo, and the other at the point of Senglea.

So anxious was La Valette to hurry these works and
ensure their completion before the arrival of the enemy, t[hat]
he and his knights laboured themselves constantly at th[em,]
and it is recorded that the Grand Master and the o[ther]
dignitaries of the Order took their places amongst the l[ong]
file of labourers who were carrying materials to the rampa[rts.]
The Viceroy of Sicily, Don Garcia de Toledo, having at [that]
time paid a visit to Malta to arrange with La Valette a[s to]
the measures of defence to be adopted, it was proposed [by]
him that a ravelin should be constructed at Fort St. E[lmo]
on the side nearest the Marsa Muscetto, and this design
at once carried into effect.

Such was the state of the fortifications of Malta at [the]
time when that storm burst over the island which had b[een]
so long brewing, and which had for so many months k[ept]
the arsenals of Constantinople in a state of the utm[ost]
activity. From the moment that the Order had first e[sta]-
blished themselves at Malta, and had recommenced th[ose]
naval expeditions which had rendered their flag redou[bt]-
able during their occupation of Rhodes, Solyman had p[on]-
dered over the design of once more attacking his
enemies and driving them from Malta as he had done fr[om]
Rhodes.

Various causes, however, had hitherto interfered to prev[ent] the accomplishment of his purpose, and the Order had used their utmost exertions in taking advantage of the respite thus obtained to add to their security. The fortifications of Malta, though still very feeble, were widely different from what they had been thirty years previously, when the small fort of St. Angelo with its two guns was the only defence of the Bourg; and the garrison, fired with the hope of avenging the calamities brought upon them by the capture of their beloved island of Rhodes, burned for the opportunity of once more crossing swords with their infidel foe.

Not content with adding their quota on the occasion of the three expeditions directed against the Barbarossas by Charles V., the Maltese galleys had frequently taken the sea on their own account, and in numerous isolated engagements had succeeded in humbling the Ottoman flag. More and more irate did the powerful and now aged sultan become as news of these successes reached his ears, but the event which filled the vial of his wrath to overflowing was the capture in the Adriatic of a large and richly laden Turkish galleon after a desperate conflict of five hours' duration. Most of the valuable cargo on board this galleon was the property of some of the ladies of the sultan's harem, and the fair odalisques were aroused to a state of indignation at the loss they had thus sustained. All the power of the seraglio was therefore exerted to induce Solyman to avenge the affront by a signal chastisement, and the capture of Malta, when pleaded for by bright eyes and rosy lips, was at length decreed by the amorous sultan.

A vast armament was promptly prepared, the command of which was entrusted to Mustapha Pasha, whilst the fleet was placed under the orders of Piali. The sultan, however, strictly enjoined both of these officers to receive the corsair,

Dragut, into their counsels, that celebrated freebooter havi pledged himself to join the expedition at Malta with reinforcement of Algerines.

Whilst these preparations were making at Constantinoj La Valette was on his side by no means dilatory in prepar to meet the storm. A general call was made for all knig and other members of the Order whose age did not precl their taking part in active warfare, to hurry at once to defence of their convent, and to swell the ranks of its garri at this critical moment. He also petitioned all the courts Europe for assistance in a war in which the interests of were engaged. His appeal, however, met with only a sca response. Spain, indeed, did contribute a small body troops, and the Pope a trifling sum of money, but the ot powers held aloof, and watched the struggle without int ference. The Viceroy of Sicily had, as we have already se paid a visit to the island, and had pledged himself to co to their assistance with a powerful reinforcement in case t were really attacked. He also left his son under charge La Valette, in order that the youth might win his sp under so renowned a commander, and flesh his maiden sw in so honourable a conflict. With these exceptions Order was left to sustain the shock of Ottoman invas unaided.

Undaunted by this prospect, La Valette continued preparations with unabated zeal, and was met with { utmost ardour by the members of his community. From quarters they flocked in eager haste to Malta, and once m ranged themselves beneath that banner which had so lo waved in triumph above them. In order to ascertain t every one was properly equipped, a general parade of t *langues* was held, when each was inspected by two knigl

## Garrison of Malta. 81

selected from some other *langue*. At this parade the following numbers were present:—

|  | Knights. | Servants-at-arms. |
|---|---|---|
| Provence | 61 | 15 |
| Auvergne | 25 | 14 |
| France | 57 | 24 |
| Italy | 164 | 5 |
| Aragon | 85 | 2 |
| *England | 1 | 0 |
| Germany | 13 | 1 |
| Castile | 68 | 6 |

making a total of 474 knights and 67 servants-at-arms. There were in addition several conventual chaplains; but as their profession prevented them from taking any active share in the defence, they cannot be included in the garrison. Great pains had been taken by La Valette to train the militia of the island, and they had been duly organized into battalions for that purpose. The same measures had been adopted with the crews of the galleys, and so it was found, on a general muster of the garrison, that it numbered the following strength, in addition to the 541 members of the Order before mentioned, viz.:—

### REGULAR FORCES.

| | |
|---|---|
| Hired Spanish troops | 800 |
| Garrisons of St. Elmo and St. Angelo | 150 |
| Household and Guard of the Grand Master | 150 |
| Artillery | 120 |

* The solitary English knight present at this siege was Sir Oliver Starkey, Latin secretary to La Valette, and author of the inscription on the tomb of that Grand Master, by the side of whom his own remains are laid, in the crypt of St. John's Church.

G

MILITIA AND OTHER FORCES.

| | |
|---|---:|
| Militia of the Bourg | 500 |
| Ditto of Burmola* and Senglea | 300 |
| Ditto of remainder of Island | 4,560 |
| Crews of the galleys | 700 |
| Volunteers from Italy, Sicily, Genoa, Piedmont, &c. | 875 |
| Total | 8,155 |

so that, including the Order, La Valette might count up a force of rather less than 9,000 men for the defence of ] island. His next step was to appoint to each his prop post on the ramparts, and, in accordance with ancient usa; this was done by *langues*. The land port of the Bourg, th considered the most important and dangerous post, w allotted to the three French *langues*. The line from ther to St. Angelo, facing the sea, was garrisoned by th( of Castile and Germany; whilst the inner line, faci Senglea (since destroyed), was the post of the Spaniar The defence of Senglea was entrusted to the Italians, un( the command of the Admiral De Monte, who in after ye became Grand Master. St. Angelo itself was under the i mediate command of La Valette, with a force contribu1 from all the *langues*, and with a due proportion of soldiery.

The ordinary garrison of St. Elmo had hitherto b( composed of only sixty men, under the command of an a; knight named De Broglio; but in the present emergei

---

* After the foundation of Senglea by the Grand Master De la Sang] suburb had gradually formed itself between that town and the Bourg, w out the fortifications, which was called Burmola. The three towns of Bourg, Burmola, and Senglea are now commonly known as the three ci in contradistinction to Valetta.

it was deemed necessary considerably to augment this slender force, and a reinforcement of sixty knights, with a company of infantry, under the command of a Spanish knight named La Cerda, were directed to place themselves under the orders of De Broglio. A more difficult matter appeared to be the appointment of a commander less aged and infirm than that veteran, a step which appeared absolutely necessary, yet one which La Valette was very indisposed to take. A compromise was at length effected by the appointment of D'Eguoras, the Bailiff of Negropont, a commander of tried valour and experience, as auxiliary captain, equivalent to the rank of lieutenant-governor; thus, without displacing De Broglio, the benefit of more youthful energy and activity was ensured to the garrison.

There yet remained the Citta Notabile and the island of Gozo to protect. Opinions were much divided in the council as to the proper measures to be adopted in these cases. Some were for abandoning both points, and withdrawing their garrisons to increase the defenders of the Bourg, as the most important point; others, again, whilst anxious to abandon Gozo, deemed it prudent to retain possession of the Citta Notabile, which would act as a diversion, and either cause a most seasonable delay should the Turks undertake its siege, or else prove a constant annoyance to their rear should they at once sit down before the Bourg. La Valette ultimately determined upon retaining both of these posts, in order, if possible, to distract the enemy from their main attack, and thus to afford time for the arrival of succour, as promised by the Viceroy of Sicily. Their garrisons were therefore reinforced, and placed under the command of knights in whose courage and constancy he could confide, and who, he felt sure, would maintain their posts to the last.

Everything was thus organized upon the best footing, a
the distribution of the available force equalized as far
possible. La Valette, conscious that he could carry his p
cautions no farther, and that he must now trust the issue
God, his own strong arm, and the anticipation of succo
made a spirited harangue to his troops, in which he recall
to their memory the long list of victories the Order had,
ages past, gained over the infidel with numbers still m
disproportioned than at present, and further urged upon the
that as true soldiers of the Cross they were bound, if call
upon, to seal their faith with their blood, and to deem the
selves highly favoured if by death in the defence of th
religion and their convent they could attain to the honou
of martyrdom.

This inspiriting harangue was succeeded by a ceremor
yet more calculated to arouse all the religious fervour
their hearts. The entire body of the fraternity wend
their way in solemn procession to the conventual church
San Lorenzo, and there, after confession and absolutio
partook of the Holy Eucharist, and once more consecrat
their weapons to the preservation of their faith and of the
convent home.

## CHAPTER IV.

Arrival of the Turkish Expedition—Its Composition—The Janissaries—Attack on St. Elmo commenced—Arrival of Dragut—Repeated Assaults—The Fort cut off from succour—Its Fall—Massacre of the Garrison.

ON the morning of the 18th May, 1565, a signal gun from the castle of St. Angelo, answered from the forts of St. Michael and St. Elmo, announced to the garrison of Malta that the enemy was in sight. The Turkish fleet consisted of 130 galleys, 50 vessels of smaller size, and a number of transports laden with stores for the army. The military force numbered 30,000 men, of whom 5,000 were janissaries.

It may be well here to say a few words upon the subject of this redoubtable body, for so many years the chief bulwark of the Turkish empire. Once in every five years a general conscription was levied upon the children of all Christians resident within the empire between the ages of seven and twelve years. Such as displayed any pre-eminence, either of mind or body, were carried away to Constantinople, and from that moment were lost to their parents for ever. Those of them who exhibited the greatest promise of bodily strength, were chosen for the corps of janissaries. Every effort was made from the moment of their selection to endue them

with the martial spirit of their calling. Marriage was strict
forbidden; they had, therefore, no family ties to divide th[eir]
affections. The *esprit de corps* thus fostered increased wi[th]
their age, and they formed a body of troops upon whom t[he]
strictest reliance could be placed in the most desper[ate]
emergency. Such were the men who composed an importa[nt]
portion of the force which Solyman had despatched agai[nst]
Malta.

After some little cruising backwards and forwards t[he]
Turks eventually disembarked, partly in the Marsa Siroc[co]
and partly in St. Thomas's Bay. A small body of knigh[ts]
had been sent out under Marshal Coppier to watch t[he]
proceedings of the enemy, and to intercept stragglers. O[ne]
of the knights, named De la Rivière, fell into the hands [of]
the Turks, and was taken before Mustapha, who directed th[at]
he should be subjected to torture to compel him to disclo[se]
the resources of the place. De la Rivière, pretending to yie[ld]
to his fears, made a statement to the pasha to the effect th[at]
the weakest point in the fortifications was the post of Casti[le]
in the land front of the Bourg. Relying on this informatio[n]
Mustapha advanced upon the town, determined to make [an]
immediate attack at that point. On reaching Mount Calcar[a]
however, a considerable eminence to the south-east of t[he]
Bourg, he perceived at a glance that his prisoner h[ad]
deceived him, and that the point indicated was in truth t[he]
most impregnable part of the works. The unfortuna[te]
knight fell a victim to his constancy, as Mustapha imm[e]
diately directed him to be put to death.

Counsels were now divided in the Turkish camp as to t[he]
course to be pursued. Dragut, the Pasha of Tripoli, had n[ot]
yet arrived, and in his absence Piali was of opinion that n[o]
steps should be taken beyond intrenching the arm[y]

Mustapha, on the other hand, dreading to lose valuable time, and to give opportunities for a fleet of succour to arrive, urged proceeding with the siege at once. He pointed out that the fleet lay at present in a very exposed situation, and that it would be of the greatest possible advantage if they could obtain possession of the Marsa Muscetto, within which they would be sheltered from the easterly winds then prevalent. For this purpose it was necessary that they should capture Fort St. Elmo, by which the entrance to that harbour was commanded, and this operation he proposed undertaking at once, leaving to Dragut the responsibility of deciding after his arrival upon their future measures. These views ultimately prevailed, and the siege of St. Elmo was commenced.*

Mount Sceberras being but a bare rock, the Turkish engineers were unable to open their trenches in the ordinary manner. Gabions, fascines, and even earth had all to be conveyed from a distance, a task of enormous labour, but by dint of perseverance and at a great sacrifice of life, from the galling and incessant fire of the defenders, the work was at length accomplished. The siege operations at this point were most unskilfully planned. In order to shelter themselves from the fire of St. Angelo they kept their trenches on the reverse side of the hill, and thereby left the communication

* The general trace of this fort approached in form what is technically termed a star fort. It consisted of four salients. The land front was broken into a bastioned form, by the addition of small rounded flanks, and on the sea side arose a cavalier, which dominated over the remainder of the work. This cavalier, which is now embraced within the main work, was then separated from it by a ditch. On the side of the Marsa Muscetto was a small ravelin, upon the ground now occupied by the military prison and adjacent buildings. In other respects the trace of the work still remains much what it then was.

between that fortress and St. Elmo quite free. This err
led to a protracted and bloody siege before a fort whi
should have been taken in a few days.

The trenches being at length completed, a battery w
constructed to bear against the point selected for attack at
distance of 180 yards from the fort. It was armed with t
guns throwing 80lb. shot, three columbrines for 60lb. sh
and one huge basilisk for 160lb. shot. The guns a
columbrines were mounted on wheels, but the basili
required complicated machinery to enable it to be point
and to check its recoil. The Turks in those days ma
greater use of artillery than any other nation, and their gu
were of enormous calibre. The labour of placing them
position was consequently very great, and the fire was by
means rapid; still, at short ranges, their battering power w
terrific. The result speedily manifested itself in the walls
St. Elmo. Three breaches were formed, in the raveli
cavalier, and fort itself, and the ditches were choked with tl
*débris* of the crumbling walls.

The slender force which garrisoned the fort was plain
insufficient to maintain it in its present state. D'Eguara
therefore, despatched an envoy to the Grand Master deman
ing further aid, and the Spanish knight De la Cerda w
selected for the office. A worse choice could scarcely ha
been made. In a garrison where nearly every man was
hero, the slightest taint of cowardice became doubly apparen
and unfortunately La Cerda was not free from this weaknes
Exaggerating the injuries which the fort had sustained, l
pressed strenuously for immediate reinforcement, an
further announced, in open council, that even under tl
most favourable circumstances they could not hold out mo
than a few days. La Valette was justly irritated with tl

injudicious envoy, who was thus publishing before the whole council what, at all events, he should have reserved for the private ear of his chief. He was also much disappointed at this speedy demand for succour, before a single assault had been delivered. He had counted upon the delay which the attack on St. Elmo must occasion as the salvation of the island, since it would enable the Sicilian Viceroy to redeem his pledge, and to hurry to the rescue. If, however, as La Cerda proclaimed, the fort could only be held for a few days more, he might expect to see the siege of the Bourg opened long before Don Garcia could possibly arrive. He hastened, therefore, to comply with the demand of D'Eguaras, and reinforced their garrison with 50 knights and 200 men, under the command of Gonzales de Medrano, a gallant knight, in whom he placed the most implicit confidence.

Medrano had no sooner entered the fort than he proposed a sortie to destroy the besiegers' trenches, and headed the operation in person. At first the attack was completely successful, the Turks were routed, their parapets overthrown, and the result of much labour destroyed. As, however, they speedily rallied, and returned to the attack in overwhelming numbers, Medrano was compelled to draw off his slender force, and to retreat into the fort. The wind, which at the time was southerly, had blown the smoke in the direction of St. Elmo, and concealed the movements of the Turks from the view of the garrison. What was their dismay when it cleared away to perceive that the besiegers had advanced unnoticed, and had taken possession of the covered way within which they were rapidly engaged in intrenching themselves. A heavy fire was at once opened on them, but in vain, the covered way was irrevocably lost, and from that

time became embraced in the general scheme of the Turk
advance, which was thus brought close to the walls.

A few days later a gross act of carelessness on the part
the garrison, caused the loss of the ravelin itself. So
Turkish engineers were engaged, under cover of the nig
in making a reconnoissance of the opposing works from t
ditch, to which, since the capture of the covered way, th
had free access. Anxious to discover the nature of t
defences in the ravelin, one of their officers had the har
hood to climb into an embrasure, trusting to the darkness
the night to elude the vigilance of the sentinels. To
amazement he found the ravelin apparently untenant
and certainly unguarded. He at once hastened back
camp, informed Mustapha of what he had discovered, a
offered to lead a party to the instant attack of the unprotec
post. In an incredibly short space of time a chosen band
janissaries was selected, who, led by the engineer, silen
stole into the work. The defenders were taken complet
by surprise, and unable to offer any effective resistan
Driven back by the fierce onset of the excited janissaries, th
gave way, and were forced to seek refuge in the fort, whit
they were hotly pursued by the Turks. But for the her
efforts of one of the Spanish officers, of an inferior gra
who standing at the entrance of the drawbridge, withsto
for some moments, almost singly, the onset of the enen
and maintained his post like Horatius, in the Roman sto
until support was brought him from within, St. Elmo wor
on that day have fallen. D'Eguaras, Medrano, and oth
knights had, however, upon the first sound of the tumu
hurried to the scene of action, and by their exertions succeed
in preventing the enemy from penetrating into the fo
The most powerful efforts were made on both sides—

## Attempt at Escalade.

knights striving to retake the ravelin, the Turks to push their advantage still further. Both were, however unsuccessful. In spite of the most desperate sallies, aided by the fire of two guns which were brought to bear upon the outwork, the Turks succeeded in establishing a lodgment in the ravelin, and maintained themselves behind it with pertinacious gallantry.

They were so stimulated by this success that, hoping to end the whole siege whilst the garrison were suffering from the depression consequent on their loss, they determined upon the bold measure of an attack by escalade. This was an operation not likely to succeed against such men as those who were maintaining St. Elmo. Their ladders, moreover, were too short to reach to the crest, yet still they struggled on with the most invincible resolution to effect an entrance. Here and there a Turk, more daring and more agile than his fellows, would obtain a momentary footing upon the parapet, but before his comrades could come to his assistance he was invariable hurled headlong downwards. Boiling pitch and wildfire streamed upon the mass congregated within the ditch. Huge rocks were hurled upon them, and all the savage ferocity of war was let loose throughout that eventful day. The Castle of St. Angelo was thronged with anxious spectators, eagerly straining their eyes to discover the issue of the fight. Amidst the roar of artillery, the volleys of arquebuses, the screams, shouts, and yells of the combatants, little could be distinguished to mark how turned the tide of battle. A dense canopy of smoke hung over the devoted fort, rent at intervals by the flash of guns, and it was not until the sun had declined far towards the west that they were enabled to discover the real state of things. The Turkish banner was then seen waving over the

captured ravelin, whilst on the other hand the white cr
banner still floated proudly over the fort and cavalier.

Finding all their efforts at accomplishing the capture
the fort unavailing, a retreat was sounded, and the Tu
sullenly retired into their trenches. The capture of
ravelin, was, however, an immense advantage to
besiegers, and though this success was purchased at
cost of 2,000 men, Mustapha had good cause for c
gratulation. The loss of the garrison did not exceed 1
men, but of these twenty were knights, whose scanty nu
bers could ill afford so large a sacrifice.

Much recrimination ensued touching the loss of
ravelin. After careful inquiry it at length became
general opinion that the sentry on the exposed point v
either asleep on his post or had been killed by a chai
shot, without attracting the notice of the guard. In eit!
case, the latter cannot be acquitted of neglect, and dea
did the devoted garrison subsequently pay for the want
vigilance. At this juncture Dragut made his long expect
appearance from Tripoli, with a fleet of thirteen galle
He was greeted with the utmost enthusiasm by the Tur
his reputation in all matters, military as well as nav
deservedly standing very high. He at once condemned t
course adopted by Mustapha, of attacking St. Elmo.
his opinion the island of Gozo should first have be
secured, and after that the Citta Notabile. By the
measures the garrison would have been cut off from
communication, and would have been prevented fro
receiving assistance in the way of either men or provisio
The rear of the besieging army would have been secu
instead of being, as it then was, liable to be harassed '
constant attacks from the Citta Notabile. The landing

a relieving force from Sicily would also have been rendered far more difficult. As, however, the attack on St. Elmo had been commenced, he did not think it consonant with the dignity of the sultan to abandon the enterprise, and he, therefore, proposed to push it forward with increased vigour.

Under his direction a second battery, still more formidable than the first, was erected upon the most elevated point of Mount Sceberras, which could play either upon St. Elmo or St. Angelo. He also caused a small battery of four guns to be constructed on the point of land directly opposite St. Elmo, and forming with it the entrance to the Marsa Muscetto. This battery played with great effect upon both the fort and cavalier, and the point has in consequence received the name of Point Dragut.

After the late attack La Valette had removed the wounded from the garrison of St. Elmo, amounting to nearly 100 men, and had reinforced them with an equivalent number of fresh troops commanded by the Chevalier de Miranda, who had recently arrived at the Bourg from Sicily. During one of the first days of the siege, whilst the batteries and trenches were in the course of formation, the Turkish Admiral Piali had been struck by a fragment of rock. The wound, though not mortal, was sufficiently severe to spread consternation among the besiegers, and La Valette taking advantage of the confusion which ensued when the intelligence of this calamity became spread abroad, succeeded in despatching an envoy to Sicily to urge the viceroy to forward instant succours. The envoy returned with a pledge from the viceroy that he would arrive at Malta in the middle of June, provided La Valette would send him the fleet of galleys then cooped up in compulsory idleness in the grand harbour. It was in company with the bearer of this mes-

sage that Miranda arrived at Malta. He instantly volu
teered his services to join the defenders of St. Elmo, as bei
the post of the greatest danger, and consequently of 1
highest honour. This knight had already achieved a hi
reputation for military genius and courage, and La Vale
immediately acceded to a request which added to the defend
of that post such an experienced soldier.

The Grand Master was deeply disappointed at the con
tion with which the viceroy had hampered his proffers of a
In order to despatch the galleys which were thus demande
it would be necessary to man them with slaves whose servic
at that moment were most urgently required within t
fortress. They must also have been accompanied by a gua
from the garrison to prevent a mutiny on board, which tl
proximity of the Turkish fleet would otherwise have rendere
inevitable. This diminution of his already too scanty for
could not for one moment be thought of, and La Valet
once again appealed to the viceroy for unconditions
assistance.

Meanwhile, he spared no effort to prolong the defence
St. Elmo. Fresh troops were every night forwarded thither t
replace casualties. D'Eguaras and De Broglio had bot
been severely wounded in the last assault, and La Valett
had directed their immediate return to the convent. It ha
been recorded in all previous accounts of the siege that bot
of these knights sturdily refused to abandon their post. Witl
respect to D'Eguaras, there is no doubt that such was th
case, as his name appears in the list of killed; but th
evidence as regards De Broglio is different. In the firs
place, there is no record of his death, as there would have
been had he remained in the fort; but the strongest and
most conclusive evidence that he availed himself of La

Valette's permission to retire into the Bourg is the fact that, on the 13th of June, the Grand Master and Council appointed Don Melchior de Montserrat governor of the fort, which could hardly have been done had not De Broglio resigned the post.* The Spanish knight La Cerda, who had previously exhibited signs of cowardice, took this opportunity of returning to the Bourg amongst the other wounded, although he was suffering from a scar of so trivial a nature that it could in no way have incapacitated him from remaining at his post. The Grand Master was so irritated against him for this second exhibition of cowardice that he caused him to be imprisoned. Before the close of the siege, however, La Cerda had, by an honourable death in the face of the enemy, wiped out the stain thus cast upon his fame. Being released from his confinement, he joined valiantly in the defence of the Bourg, and fell during one of the numerous assaults delivered at that point.

Now that both the covered way and ravelin had fallen into the possession of the besiegers, on the latter of which two guns had been mounted that completely swept the fort, it was impossible for the garrison to find shelter from the pitiless storm of missiles constantly rained upon them. The large batteries which played upon their exposed scarps from the summit of Mount Sceberras, aided by the fire from that on Point Dragut, as well as from some Turkish galleys, at long range, from the entrance of the harbour, speedily reduced the whole work to a mass of ruin. The bravest of

* This appointment has only lately been discovered by the author in a manuscript book entitled "Decreti provisionali del Ven. Conseglio in materia di guerra et altre diligenze fatte da Ven. Commis. delle Fortific. Agozzini Reali Cap<sup>ae</sup>. d'armi di queste Citta & altri Offic<sup>li</sup>. militari in esec<sup>ne</sup>. delli d<sup>i</sup>. decreti del V. Conseglio, dal 1554 fin al 1645."

the garrison now felt that all had been done that w
possible, to retard the capture of the fort, and that the ti
had arrived when, unless they were to be buried within
ruins of their post, they should be at once withdrawn, a
the fort abandoned.

The Chevalier de Medrano, a knight whose establish
reputation would render his report free from all suspicion
cowardice, was selected to explain to La Valette the desper
straits to which the garrison were reduced, and to urge th
immediate recall into the Bourg. La Valette could not in
heart deny that all had been done which human ingenu
could devise to protract the defence, and that the fort h
been maintained against the most overwhelming odds with
constancy and devotion worthy of the highest praise, a
that if the lives of these gallant men were not to be d
liberately sacrificed they should be at once recalled. Still,
could not bring himself to direct the abandonment of t
post. By its maintenance the siege of the Bourg w
being deferred, and the time prolonged during which t
succours expected from the Viceroy of Sicily might arriv
Toledo had indeed, in his last communication to La Valett
insisted on the retention of St. Elmo as an essenti
condition of his support. Unless, he said, that point we
maintained he should not feel justified in hazarding tl
emperor's fleet in any attempt to raise the siege. La Valet
felt, therefore, so much hanging upon the issue of tl
struggle, that he determined at all costs to maintain S
Elmo until it should be wrested from him by sheer force.

He directed Medrano to return to his post, and point or
to his comrades the absolute necessity of their holding out t
the last extremity. When this stern decree became known
the garrison perceived that they were doomed to be sacrifice

## Insubordination of the Defenders.

for the general safety. Many amongst them, particularly those who, having grown grey in the service of the Order, felt perhaps the more ready to lay down their lives at the will of their chief, prepared at once to obey the mandate, and to prolong their resistance to the utmost. Others, however, there were of the younger knights by no means so willing to await in calm obedience the fate to which the decree of the Grand Master had doomed them. They were ready and willing to brave an honourable death in the face of the enemy, with the prospect of striking one last blow in the good cause before they fell, but the present was a very different case. They conceived that they were being needlessly sacrificed, merely to prolong the resistance of the fort for a few days. Loud murmurs of astonishment and indignation arose, therefore, amongst their ranks when the message of La Valette was communicated to them by Medrano.

This insubordination did not find vent merely in idle murmurs. That same evening a petition was forwarded to the Grand Master signed by fifty-three of their number, urging him to relieve them instantly from their untenable post, and threatening, in case of refusal, to sally forth and meet an honourable death in open fight rather than suffer themselves to be buried like dogs beneath the ruins of St. Elmo. La Valette was highly incensed at the insubordinate tone of this document. He informed the bearer that, in his opinion, the vows of the Order imposed on its members the obligation, not only of laying down their lives when necessary for its defence, but further, of doing so in such a manner and at such a time as he, their Grand Master, might see fit to appoint. Fearful, however, lest the garrison might be driven to desperation, and in reality execute the threat they had held forth, and being, moreover, anxious to prolong, if

H

only for a few hours, the retention of the fort, he despatch
three commissioners to inspect and report upon its conditi
and power of further resistance.

The arrival of these knights was hailed by the garris
with the most lively satisfaction, as they deemed it a p
liminary step to their being withdrawn into the Bourg. ]
deed, they had already commenced making preparations
that event, and when the commissioners arrived were engag
in throwing their shot into the wells, to prevent th
being useful to the enemy. They pointed out the shatter
state of the ramparts, and appealed to them with confider
for a justification of their conduct. Two of the co
missioners decided unhesitatingly that the place was
longer tenable. The third, however, an Italian, nam
De Castriot, was of a different opinion. He stated th
although the fortifications were ruined, and the whole inter
of the work was exposed to the fire of the enemy, still it w
feasible, by means of further retrenchments, to maintain t
place. This unsupported opinion appeared to the malconter
little better than an insult, and high words ensued.
Castriot asserted that he was prepared to back his opini
by personally undertaking to conduct the defence of the fo
This offer raised their feelings of indignation so strong
against him that a general tumult seemed about to bre
forth. The governor, however, with great presence of mi
caused the alarm to be sounded, when every knight i
stantly rushed to his post, and the irritating conference w
brought to a close.

The commissioners returned to the Bourg, and De Castr
still maintained the views he had already put forth. ]
requested the permission of the Grand Master to raise a bo
of volunteers, with whose aid he guaranteed to maint

St. Elmo against any odds. This offer met the views of La Valette, as he foresaw the result that would inevitably follow. Permission was granted to De Castriot to raise his corps of volunteers, and there were so many applicants that numbers were of necessity rejected. Meanwhile a most cold and sarcastic letter was forwarded by the Grand Master to the garrison of St. Elmo, informing them of the steps that were being taken, and stating that they would shortly be relieved from their post.

The consternation caused by this letter was great. Each one felt that it would be impossible to accept the offer of safety thus ignominiously tendered. They had requested permission to abandon the fort, but they were not prepared to yield their place in so honourable a struggle to others. An earnest letter was therefore instantly forwarded to the Bourg, imploring pardon for their previous rebellious conduct, and begging to be permitted still to retain the post of honour. This was the result which La Valette had foreseen, but he did not deem it prudent to accept their submission too promptly; he therefore coldly declined their offer, and once more directed them to prepare for relief. This refusal increased the general dismay, and a still more pressing request was forwarded, once more imploring that they might have an opportunity of wiping out the memory of what had passed in their blood. They pledged themselves, should they be permitted to remain at their post, to hold the fort to the very last.

This was all that La Valette had desired. The garrison was now roused to such a pitch of enthusiasm that the defence of the fort could with safety be entrusted to them. Contenting himself, therefore, with despatching such reinforcements as the constantly occurring casualties demanded, he

prepared to await the issue. This was not long in arrivi
The incessant cannonade of the besiegers had destroy
nearly every vestige of defence, and at length instructic
were given by Mustapha for a general assault. On t
whole of the 15th of June their artillery played so inc
santly that the garrison were unable to repair any of t
damages. This furious cannonade was towards evening i
creased by fire opened from the fleet. Mustapha, confide
of carrying the work on the following day, had direct
his ships to be in readiness to force the entrance of t
Marsa Muscetto as soon as the assault commenced, and
was for this purpose that they had arrived from Mar
Sirocco that afternoon.

These and other unmistakeable symptoms warned t
garrison of the attack which was awaiting them. The
therefore took every precaution which their limited men
permitted to resist it to the death. Huge piles of rock we
placed around on the parapets to be hurled upon tl
besieging columns. The knights were so placed that one
them stood between every three men for support ar
guidance. Three small bodies were kept in reserve
render assistance at any point which might be hard presse
and a few who, from wounds or age were considered le
available than their comrades for active duty, were told off 1
convey ammunition and refreshment to the combatants,
that they might on no account be called upon to leave the
posts. Various descriptions of fireworks were provider
Pots of earthenware, so baked as to break with great facility
were filled with wildfire. They were of a size that admitte
of their being thrown by hand from twenty to thirty yards
and had a narrow orifice closed with linen or thick pape
secured by cords dipped in sulphur. Before throwing th

missile these cords were lighted, and on falling the earthenware broke in pieces, and the contents at once became ignited. This wildfire was composed of saltpetre, ammoniacal salt, pounded sulphur, camphor, varnish, and pitch. It burnt with the utmost fury, clinging to the bodies of those with whom it came in contact, and in most cases causing death in the greatest torture. The same material was also placed in hollow cylinders of wood, called trumps, which when lighted poured forth a stream of flame. These trumps attached to the ends of halberds or partisans, became a most formidable obstacle to the advance of a storming party. Another missile used with great effect at this siege, was a hoop or circle of fire of considerable diameter, which when hurled from above into the midst of a body of men, often enclosed several in its fiery embrace, and easily succeeded in igniting their clothes, which, in accordance with Eastern custom, were flowing and of light material.

Before dawn on the morning of the 16th of June, the garrison detected the sounds of a religious ceremonial, which they rightly judged was the precursor to an assault. Mustapha's first step was to line his trenches with arquebusiers to the number of 4,000. These men had already displayed their skill as marksmen, and during this day's struggle they were of the greatest use in checking the defenders from exposing themselves on the parapets. At the appointed signal, given by Mustapha himself, a body of janissaries, the leaders of the assault, rushed into the ditch at a point where a yawning breach promised the greatest facilities for ascent. During the interval, brief as it was, whilst they were crossing the open ground, the guns of St. Angelo, directed by the watchful La Valette himself, opened with great steadiness and effect upon their dense columns. Indeed, throughout the day the artillery of S[t] Angelo rendered the most efficient assistance to the garriso[n] of St. Elmo, by raking the flank and rear of the Turkis[h] forces, which in their advance to the attack became muc[h] exposed and suffered considerably in consequence. That [the] St. Elmo itself was no less vigorously served. From th[e] instant that the enemy first showed himself, its guns opene[d] upon the advancing battalions, and before the foot of t[he] breach was reached many a turbaned head had been laid lo[w.]

The janissaries, however, were not troops to be diverte[d] even by this deadly fire. With yells of defiance, and shout[-] ing the war-cry of their religion, they dashed forward wit[h] reckless intrepidity, and as the iron hail ploughed dee[p] furrows in their ranks, they closed up with the mo[st] invincible steadiness, still pushing their way towards th[e] breach. Here, however, they met with fresh obstacles and new foe. The summit of the breach was crowned with me[n] who had despaired of saving their lives, and who stood ther[e] prepared to sell them as dearly as possible. Against thi[s] impenetrable phalanx, to which the force of desperation ha[d] added yet greater strength, it was in vain even for th[e] redoubtable janissaries to attempt an entrance. Though the[y] hurled themselves again and again upon the enemy, the[y] were as often forced to recoil, and the mass of killed an[d] wounded with which the breach lay strewn, marked at onc[e] the vigour of the attack and the desperate gallantry of th[e] defence.

Whilst this main attack was going forward on the lan[d] front, two other attempts were being made to carry the for[t] by escalade, one on the side of the Marsa Muscetto, the other on that of the grand harbour. The first was repulse[d] without much difficulty. The huge fragments of rock whic[h] the defenders hurled from the parapet broke several of the scaling ladders, and the assailants were thrown backwards into the ditch, many of them being crushed to death. On the grand harbour side, however, the attack was led by a forlorn hope of thirty men, who, with a fanaticism not unusual to their nation and creed, had bound themselves by a solemn oath either to carry the fort or to perish in the attempt. They made their rush at the rampart in full view of St. Angelo, and succeeded in planting their ladders. The defenders were, in truth, taken somewhat by surprise, never having contemplated that a spot so open to the fire of St. Angelo could be selected for attack. The determined fanatics, followed by a column of janissaries, had well-nigh effected a footing on the works, when the guns of St. Angelo opened upon them. La Valette, who had been watching the conflict from his post of observation, soon perceived the desperate character of the attempt, and at once prepared to render assistance to the defenders. The first shot was, however, most unfortunate, for instead of falling amongst the assailants it raked the parapet itself, and killed or wounded eight of the garrison. Subsequent discharges were more effectual; the assailants were thrown into confusion, and their fanatical leaders having all met that fate which they themselves had decreed should be the consequence of failure, the remainder abandoned the attempt, and returned to their trenches. Still the main attack continued to rage with unabated violence. Fresh battalions were hurried in succession to the foot of the breach by the determined Mustapha, and as constantly driven back with great slaughter by the garrison. Ever and anon shouts of encouragement and admiration were borne across the water from the anxious spectators who crowded the ramparts of St. Angelo, and as

these cheering sounds reached the harassed combatants
St. Elmo, they were nerved to redouble their efforts, and
continue stedfast in their resistance. They felt, inde
that their recent insubordination had to a certain exte
lowered them in the eyes of their comrades, and th
rejoiced in thus having the opportunity of restoring the
selves to their good opinion. For six hours was the atta
sustained, and yet the assailants had failed to penetrate
any one point of the enceinte. At length the intoleral
heat, combined with the exhaustion of so lengthened
struggle, rendered further efforts impossible, and Mustap
was reluctantly compelled to sound a general retreat. A lo
shout of victory rose from the midst of that heroic band, w
had thus, for a short time longer, averted the fate impendi
over them, and a responsive echo came floating over t
waters from their brethren in the Bourg.

Great, however, as had been their success, it had bee
dearly purchased, seventeen knights and three hundred me
having fallen in the defence. Chief among the former w
the gallant Medrano, who was killed in the act of wrenchin
a standard from the grasp of a Turkish officer. His corps
was removed with all due honour into the Bourg, where
was interred in a vault of St. Leonard's Church set aside fo
the dignitaries of the Order. The loss of the Turks wa
never ascertained, but it must have reached a very hig
figure. Raked as they had been throughout the day b
the artillery from St. Angelo, and exposed to the incessan
fire of St. Elmo, it is impossible that the struggle could hav
been maintained for so many hours without swelling the lis
enormously.

Night had no sooner set in than boats were despatched
from the Bourg to bring in the wounded. The gallant

D'Eguaras was again amongst the number, but he still refused to leave his post. A most generous rivalry had sprung up in the garrison of the Bourg, each one striving to form one of the reinforcing detachment. Although it was clear to the meanest capacity that the post they sought was one of almost certain death, the brave volunteers crowded forward, and La Valette's only difficulty was whom to select where all appeared so eager. The choice was however made, and the fort once more placed in as favourable a position for defence as its desperate condition permitted.

In the Turkish camp anxious consultations were held as to the steps to be taken to bring this protracted siege to a conclusion. Dragut, who appears to have been the only commander in the Turkish army of any real talent, pointed out that so long as the garrison of the Bourg were permitted to keep up a communication with St. Elmo, and to pour in fresh bodies of troops after every assault, they would never succeed in carrying the fort. Under his advice, therefore, the headland opposite Point Dragut, forming with it the entrance to the harbour, was occupied by the Turks, and a battery constructed on it. He also extended the trenches in front of St. Elmo down to the water's edge opposite St. Angelo, and here he constructed a small battery which effectually precluded the possibility of any boat landing at the fort from the Bourg.

The construction of the works was attended with great difficulty and much loss of life, the workmen being completely exposed to the fire of St. Angelo. Amongst those who suffered in consequence, was Dragut himself, who was struck in the head by a splinter and conveyed mortally wounded to his tent. By dint of perseverance, however, the work was at length finished, and on the 19th of the month

the investment was completed, and the garrison cut off
all further reinforcement.

For three days more an incessant fire was kept up
thirty-six guns in the Turkish batteries. Had the ram
of St. Elmo been constructed entirely of masonry they
have been almost swept away by the effect of this
whelming fire, but in many parts they were formed of
solid rock, of which the peninsula is composed, and
portions remained invulnerable. From the same caus
attempt could be made at mining, and thus the garrison
the satisfaction of knowing that they had only an open f
contend with, and that no invisible labour was undermi
their defences.

With the earliest dawn of the 22nd, a fresh assault l
upon St. Elmo. Exhausted as they were with cons
watching, short of ammunition, and exposed on their ru
ramparts to the deadly fire of the Turkish arquebusiers,
still met their foe with the same indomitable resolutio
before. Three times was the assault renewed, and as o
successfully repulsed, but on each occasion that gallant l
band became more and more reduced, and the prospec
further resistance more and more hopeless. In breath
suspense La Valette, from his post of observation, watc
the scene of strife, and great was his exultation when c
again he heard the sound of retreat issuing from the Turl
host. Again had the Moslem recoiled in defeat from t
blood-stained rock. Still was its white cross banner wav
defiantly; and the slender relics of its noble garrison o
more raised a feeble shout of victory. It was, however, tl
last expiring effort. Begirt by foes on every side, cut
from all assistance, and reduced to little more than half tl
original number, they felt that their last triumph had b

## The Beginning of the End.

gained, and that the morrow's sun would see the banner of the infidel waving over the ruins of St. Elmo.

In this desperate emergency, an expert swimmer contrived to carry a message to La Valette conveying intelligence of the truth of which he was, alas! too well assured. All that human effort could accomplish had been done to save that vital point. Its defence had been protracted far beyond the period which even the most sanguine could have anticipated, and now there remained not the shadow of a doubt that it wanted but the light of another day to ensure its destruction. La Valette felt that the moment had now arrived when, if it were not too late, the remnant of the garrison should be withdrawn into the Bourg, and the ruins of St. Elmo abandoned to the enemy. For this purpose he despatched five large boats conveying a body of volunteers who were even then willing to share the fate of their comrades, and with this succour he forwarded a message to the governor, leaving to him the option of abandoning the fort, and retiring with the whole garrison into the Bourg. The permission, alas! came too late; La Valette had sternly refused all suggestions of surrender whilst the road for a retreat yet lay open, but now it was closed for ever. In vain did the relieving force attempt to approach undetected the rocky point where the ruined fort still loomed indistinctly in the darkness of the night. The wary Turk too surely suspected that a last effort would be made to save the victims whom he had at last securely enclosed within his grasp, and his watchful sentries gave speedy notification of the approach of the boats. The alarm was instantly given, and the battery which Dragut had constructed for that purpose opened with deadly precision. Thus discovered, it was useless to persevere in the attempt, and with heavy hearts the relieving force were compelled to return to the Bourg, leaving their comrades to their fate.

Anxiously had the attempt been watched by the garrison and when the opening of the Turkish battery told them that it had been discovered and foiled, they felt that all was over Silently and solemnly they assembled in the little chapel o: the fort, and there once more confessed their sins, and par took of the Holy Eucharist for the last time on earth. I was a sad and touching sight that midnight gathering around the little altar of St. Elmo's chapel. Scarred with many a wound, exhausted with days of strife and nights o vigil, every hope of rescue driven to the winds, that littl band of heroes stood once again, and for the last time consecrating themselves, their swords, and their lives t the defence of their faith.

The religious ceremony concluded, they proceeded to tak such measures as were still in their power to sell their live dearly, and to retain their post to the last moment. Suc of their number, and they were by no means a small pro portion, as were too severely wounded to be able to stan unsupported, caused themselves to be conveyed in chairs t the breach, where, sword in hand, and with their face to tl foe, they prepared to meet their fate.

With the first blush of dawn the Turks, who had bee anxiously awaiting its appearance to pounce upon the prey, rushed fiercely at the breach, with frantic shouts hatred and exultation. Baffled in so many previous attempt their rage had increased with every new disaster, and no every passion in their hearts was aroused to avenge t fearful losses they had sustained. For four hours the str raged wildly around that fated spot, and though ea moment lessened the number of the defenders, the daui less remnant still stood firm. At length, incredible as it may seem, the Turkish force, exhausted with its efforts, once more suspended the assault. No shout of triumph at this unexpected respite arose from the ranks of the defenders, nor did any encouraging voice find its way across the waters from St. Angelo. Only sixty wounded men remained to dispute the entrance of the foe, and to their imperishable renown, be it told, that it was from the almost exhausted efforts of these sixty men that the Turkish army had recoiled.

The garrison took advantage of the interval to bind their wounds, and prepare for a renewal of the conflict. The governor, who perceived that the handful remaining within the fort must be overwhelmed by the first rush of the enemy, recalled the defenders of the cavalier, to reinforce the slender remnant, trusting that his abandonment of that dominating point might remain unperceived for some time at least. But in this he under-estimated the vigilance of Mustapha. That chief had been too often worsted in his attempts upon St. Elmo not to maintain a watchful eye upon all that was passing amidst its ruins. He detected the movement, and at once despatched a body of janissaries to occupy the abandoned work, which, from its dominant position, commanded the whole interior of the fort. At the same moment he gave the signal for a renewal of the assault. The defenders were taken by surprise at the suddenness of the onset, and before they could rally themselves the fort was lost. All combined action was now over, and it only remained that the last scene of that sad tragedy should be enacted which has cast such melancholy interest over the name of St. Elmo.

No quarter was asked or given, and desultory combats in

various parts of the enclosure ensued, until the last
garrison had fallen. A few of the Maltese soldiery,
as now, expert in the art of swimming and d
succeeded, amidst a storm of missiles, in making
their escape to St. Angelo. Another body of nine
but whether members of the Order or soldiers is not
clear, were saved from death, by falling into the har
Dragut's corsairs. These pirates realizing the fact t
live Christian was a more valuable article of mercha
than a dead one, and being actuated by a love of gain
than by such fanaticism as stimulated the Turks to w
sale slaughter, preserved the nine prisoners whom they
captured, for the purpose of making them galley s
The tattered banner of St. John was torn ignominiously
its post, and on the 23rd June, the eve of its patron s
festival, the flag of the Moslem was raised in its place.

The native ferocity of Mustapha's character had
aroused to the utmost by the desperate resistance he
encountered. Even the senseless and bleeding corpses c
enemy were not sacred from his revengeful malice.
directed that the bodies of the knights should be sele
from amongst the piles of slain, that their heads shoul
struck off, and erected upon poles looking towards
Angelo. The trunks were then fastened on planks, exter
in the form of a cross, the same emblem being also de
gashed upon their breasts. Thus mutilated, they were
floating into the harbour, and the action of the str
carrying them across to St. Angelo, the garrison of that
were aroused to a frenzy of indignation by the sad spect
thus presented to their view. By La Valette's order
bodies were reverently raised from their floating bed, and
it was impossible in their then condition that they co

be recognised, they were all solemnly buried together in the conventual church of the Bourg.

The revenge taken by La Valette for this act was unworthy of his character as a Christian soldier. He caused all his Turkish prisoners to be beheaded, and their heads to be fired from the guns of St. Angelo. Repulsive as this act seems to modern notions, it was too much in accordance with the spirit of the age to have been regarded with disapprobation by the chroniclers of the time.

The intelligence of the capture of St. Elmo was promptly conveyed to the wounded Dragut, who lay in the agonies of death in the Turkish camp. A gleam of satisfaction passed over the wan countenance of the dying man, and as though he had lingered on earth only to assure himself of the success he had so materially aided to gain, he no sooner heard the news than he breathed his last. His loss, which in itself was a great blow to the Turks, was by no means the only price they had to pay for the purchase of St. Elmo. No less than 8,000 Turks fell in the siege from first to last. The loss of the Christians amounted to 1,500, of whom 130 were members of the Order.

Thus, after a siege of upwards of a month, fell that ruined bulwark, shedding even in its loss, a greater glory over its heroic garrison than many a more successful defence has done elsewhere. Though Mustapha had achieved his object, yet much precious time had been sacrificed, and there can be no doubt that the protracted defence of St. Elmo was the main cause of the ultimate failure of his enterprise. The losses the Turkish army had sustained, severe as they were, counted but little in Mustapha's eyes when compared with this great and unexpected sacrifice of time. He had been thus taught the resistance he might expect in every subse-

quent stage of the undertaking, and even his bold
quailed at the difficulties with which his path was still
Well might the aged chief, standing upon the ruins of
fort he had gained at such a sacrifice, and gazing a
lofty ramparts of St. Angelo, whose rising tiers of batt
were still crowned at their summit with the white
banner of St. John, exclaim in an agony of doubt
perplexity, "What will not the parent cost us when
child has been purchased at so fearful a price!"

## CHAPTER V.

Siege of Malta continued—Arrival of the first Reinforcement—Investment of the Bourg—Attack on Senglea—Its signal Failure—Combined Attack on the Bourg and Senglea—Repeated Attempts on both Points—Exhaustion of the Garrison—Arrival of a Succouring Force from Sicily—Close of the Siege.

THE festival of St. John the Baptist on the 24th June, 1565, was celebrated by the inhabitants of the Bourg with very gloomy feelings. A cry of anguish had arisen whilst the sad tragedy was being enacted at St. Elmo, and the horrifying spectacle of the headless and mutilated trunks which greeted their sight on the first dawn of their patron saint's day increased the general despondency. To overcome this feeling La Valette exerted all his eloquence, and in a public address which he on that day delivered, he aroused them rather to emulate the deeds of the heroes of St. Elmo than to mourn their fate. "What," said he, "could a true knight desire more ardently than to die in arms? And what could be a more fitting fate for a member of the Order of St. John, than to lay down his life in defence of his faith? Both of these precious boons have been vouchsafed to our brethren: why then should we mourn for them? Rather should we rejoice at the prospect of the glorious futurity which they have earned. They have gained a mar-

tyr's crown, and they will reap a martyr's reward. V
too, should we be dismayed because the Moslem has at le:
succeeded in planting his accursed standard on the ru
battlements of St. Elmo? Have we not taught him a le
which must strike dismay throughout his whole army?
poor, weak, insignificant St. Elmo were able to withstand
most powerful efforts for upwards of a month, how can
expect to succeed against the stronger works and n
numerous garrison of the Bourg? With us must be
victory. Let us then, on this sacred day, before the altai
God, once more renew those vows of constancy which ‹
slaughtered brethren have so nobly accomplished."

After this stimulating address a procession was formed
the conventual church of San Lorenzo, and there the sai
solemn scene of consecration was re-enacted which has be
already described.

Whilst these ceremonies marked the festival on the part
the Christians, the Turkish camp was, on its side, filled wit
sounds of rejoicing at their victory. The Marsa Muscett
was now open to their fleet, and a long line of galleys, gail
decorated, and with the strains of martial music resoundin
from their poops, rounded the Point Dragut triumphantly, an
came streaming in succession into their newly acquired haven.
The works of St. Elmo were dismantled, and the guns captured on its ramparts despatched at once to Constantinople,
as a token of the success which had been achieved.

Mustapha now turned his attention towards the new and
far more formidable undertaking which still awaited him.
The two peninsulas which jutted out into the main harbour
had been, as already stated, fortified as strongly as time and
means would permit. The month which had been expended by the Turks before St. Elmo, had not been passed in

idleness by La Valette; wherever new works could be made to impart additional security to his enceinte, he had carried them out. Men and women, high and low, the noble and the peasant, the knight and the private soldier, all laboured with energy and good-will at the important work. A floating-bridge was constructed across the inlet between the two peninsulas, and thus free communication was established between the Bourg and Senglea. The garrison of the Citta Notabile was reduced by five companies of soldiers, who were called in to aid in the defence of the Bourg, and all private stores and provisions were seized for the public use, the owners being duly compensated from the treasury. It was decreed that no further prisoners should be made, and thus a war à outrance was declared; no quarter being either asked or given.

When these instructions reached Citta Notabile, where the garrison from their position in the rear of the besiegers had constant facilities for cutting off stragglers, the practice was established of hanging a prisoner every day; and this was continued without intermission till the close of the siege.

Mustapha, now that Mount Sceberras was in his possession, at once moved the greater portion of his army round, so as to enclose the two peninsulas. The outline of the grand harbour of Malta shows two bold promontories of very high land, which jut out one on either side; that on the south being Mount Corradin, and the other, Bighi. The trenches of the Turks were constructed so as to stretch from one of these hills to the other, and when they were completed La Valette and his garrison were altogether isolated from succour.

Before this was accomplished, however, four galleys, under

the command of Don Juan de Cardona, had reached Ma
and landed their force on the north of the island. T
reinforcement consisted of forty-two knights, twenty gen
men volunteers from Spain, eleven from Italy, three fr
Germany, two from England (whose names have b
recorded as John Smith and Edward Stanley), fifty
gunners, and a body of six hundred imperial infantry un
the command of the Chevalier de Robles.

Taking advantage of a thick mist which most fortunat
overspread the island (an event very unusual at this per
of the year), Robles succeeded in passing the Turkish li
in safety with his little force, and joined his brethren in
Bourg on the 29th June. This reinforcement, slender a
was, greatly raised the spirits of all; the more so, as the n
comers brought the intelligence that a far more efficient fo
was being assembled in Sicily, which would shortly make
appearance in the island. In proportion as the spirits
the garrison were raised, those of the Turkish army w
depressed.

They soon learnt that fresh troops had entered the Bou
and their fears greatly exaggerated the number. Rumo
also reached them of the large preparations going forward
Sicily, so that Mustapha, dreading an interruption, and w
but little confidence in the stanchness of his troops, deem
it advisable to attempt negotiation. For this purpose,
selected as an envoy a Greek slave, whom he despatch
under a flag of truce, as the bearer of most liberal ter
should the Grand Master consent to capitulate. The
terms included all that had been granted on the surren
of Rhodes, and the Order were guaranteed security both
life and property.

To La Valette this mission was most unacceptable. I

had, from the first, determined either to succeed in his defence or to bury himself and his Order beneath the ruins of his fortress. His eloquent exhortations and his own example had roused a similar feeling in the minds of all the garrison, and he was most unwilling that their firmness should be shaken by the offer of such alluring terms as those proffered by the Pasha. In order, therefore, to prevent the repetition of such messages he at once directed the envoy to be hanged. The unfortunate Greek implored mercy on the ground that he had been compelled to undertake the office, and with difficulty procured a reversion of the sentence. At length La Valette relented, and pointing to the ditches surrounding St. Angelo, bade him inform his master that there lay the only ground within the island of Malta which he was prepared to surrender, and that only as a grave for the Turkish army.

This defiant reply showed Mustapha that he had nothing to gain by negotiation; and that if Malta were to be won it must be by force of arms alone. He therefore pushed forward his siege works with the utmost vigour, and early in July had completely surrounded both the Bourg and Senglea. The latter, surmounted at its extremity by the fort of St. Michael, was the object of his first attack, and he opened batteries upon it from every available point. From Mount Sceberras and the Corradin a tremendous fire was brought to bear upon that portion of the fort which it had been determined to breach. The point selected was called the Spur bastion, and formed the extremity of the fort, touching the harbour. It was therefore open to attack by sea as well as by land. As it was impossible for Mustapha to bring his galleys to the attack of this work by the ordinary channel, without subjecting them to a most deadly fire from

St. Angelo, he determined on the adoption of a novel expedient. From the upper extremity of the Marsa Muscetto* to that of the grand harbour the distance across the isthmus of Mount Sceberras is not great. Mustapha, therefore, caused a number of galleys to be transported across the land and re-launched under Mount Corradin. This service was performed by the Christian slaves, of whom a considerable number were retained in the Turkish camp for duties of this nature, and in a few days La Valette beheld no less than eighty vessels of various sizes floating in the upper portion of those waters whose entrance he had so sedulously guarded.

About this time a very important acquisition was made by the garrison in the form of a deserter of high position from the Turkish army. This man, whose name was Lascaris, was a Greek of good family, who in early youth had been captured by the Turks, and being brought up in the Mahometan faith, had attained to high rank in the army. A sense of the shame which overshadows the career of even the most brilliant renegade had long haunted Lascaris, and now, when he beheld the votaries of that religion in which he himself had been born so nobly fighting for their faith, he determined upon sacrificing all he had gained, and joining his fortunes to theirs. One evening, therefore, he descended Mount Sceberras opposite St. Angelo, and made signals, by waving his turban, to show his desire to be taken into the fort. Before this could be done he was discovered by the Turkish sentries, and a body of men were sent down to the water's edge to seize him. In this juncture, Lascaris, though a very poor swimmer, plunged into the water, and contrived to keep himself afloat until he was picked up by the boat which the Grand Master had sent to his aid.

* Now called the Pieta Creek.

## Strengthening of the Defences of St. Michaels.

On his arrival at St. Angelo he informed La Valette of the motives which had prompted him to desert his colours. He also gave information of the attack which was impending upon the spur of St. Michael's. La Valette was so struck with the noble sacrifice that Lascaris had made that he appointed him a pension from the public treasury. He had no cause to regret his confidence, for throughout the remainder of the siege Lascaris proved himself not only a valiant captain in the field, but also a most able adviser in the council.

Following out the suggestions made to him by Lascaris, La Valette took every precaution to avert the impending storm. The seaward ramparts of St. Michael's were all strengthened, additional guns were planted at every point where they could be brought to bear upon the approaching foe, and as a last step a huge stockade was constructed, running from the spur of St. Michael parallel to the line of works which faced the Corradin hill at a distance of about six yards from the shore, and only terminating at the neck of the peninsula.* This stockade was formed of huge piles driven into the bed of the harbour, and connected together by chains passing through iron rings fixed into the head of each pile. Large spars were also fastened from pile

---

* In all former histories of the siege, this stockade is described as stretching from the point of Sengles to the foot of the Corradin Hill. It always seemed to the author an almost impossible undertaking to construct such a work, passing through deep water for so great a length, and terminating at a point so close to the enemy's lines. He has lately discovered in a work published shortly after the siege, an illustration in which this stockade is shown, as now described—there can be no doubt that this position is the correct one—it answers every purpose for which the stockade was intended; is in shallow water throughout, and is in close proximity to the defenders' works.

to pile, and a barrier was thus constructed which would materially impede any boat attack on Senglea from the side of the Corradin. Similar barriers were erected in front of the posts of England, Germany, and Castile.

As the Maltese have been from a very early period celebrated as divers, they completed this work in an incredibly short space of time, and Mustapha was dismayed at perceiving so novel and formidable an obstacle rapidly rising to impede his projected attack. Anxious, if possible, to prevent its completion, he selected a body of the most expert swimmers in his army, whom he provided with axes and despatched against the barrier. The Admiral del Monte, who commanded at St. Michael's, met this attempt by a similar sally. His Maltese divers, with swords between their teeth, dashed into the water, and their superior activity in that element yielding them a great advantage over their opponents, they speedily overcame them, and but few succeeded in regaining the shore.

Whilst the assault was still impending, the Viceroy of Algiers, named Hassan, son of the redoubtable Barbarossa, and son-in-law of Dragut, arrived with a reinforcement of 2,500 men, who had all served a long apprenticeship in the desperate piratical warfare of the Mediterranean. Hassan, whose great success as a leader had made him very vainglorious, sneered at the numerous failures which had hitherto overtaken the Turkish army.

A survey of the ruins of St. Elmo led him to express his amazement that Mustapha should have allowed himself to be baffled for such a length of time by so insignificant a fort, and following up the taunt, he volunteered, at the head of the troops he had just brought with him, to lead the assault against Senglea. The Turkish general was only too glad to give the young braggadocio an opportunity of making good his words, and he was appointed to head the assault on the land side, whilst his lieutenant Candêlissa led the attack upon the spur by water.

At an appointed signal early on the morning of the 15th of July, the assault commenced by the advance of the Turkish flotilla. Its progress was accompanied by the strains of martial music, and the sun on that summer's morn flashed upon many a glittering weapon, and lighted up many a gay and fluttering pennon. It was a beautiful sight, and but for the fearful stake at issue, would have struck with admiration the gazers who crowded the bastions around. The war had, however, been carried on with so bitter a venom on either side that only a feeling of rancorous hatred was elicited by the display. Men called to mind the barbarous outrages which had been perpetrated upon their brethren at St. Elmo, and each one, as he gazed upon the proudly advancing foe, registered a vow that he would avenge that fatal day. In advance of the squadron was a boat containing two priests, who recited from the Koran such texts as were most likely to arouse the ardour of their followers; but when they neared the scene of strife these men of peace cared no longer to occupy their conspicuous station, but, resigning their post to Candêlissa, wisely returned to camp, and watched the issue of the conflict from a safe distance.

Candêlissa's first attempt was on the palisade, through which he endeavoured to force a passage. He had also provided himself with a number of planks, with which he proposed to bridge over the space between the palisade and the point. Both attempts, however, proved complete failures. The barrier was too strong to permit him to push a way through it, and the planks were not long enough to form a bridge. Galled by the fire from the ramparts, Candélissa felt that he could not remain where he was without speedily inducing a panic amongst his followers. Plunging, therefore, into the water, which reached to his neck, he drew his sword, and, calling upon his men to follow him, he waded to shore, and made a dash at the breach.

At this moment, unfortunately, a store of combustibles, which had been lodged upon the ramparts for the use of the defenders during the assault, suddenly ignited and blew up with a loud explosion, killing and wounding a number of those in the neighbourhood. All was for a time in hopeless confusion, and when the smoke cleared away the Turks were found to have established themselves on the summit of the breach, where they had planted a number of small banners in token of triumph. The dismay of the defenders speedily gave away to feelings of rage and a determination to regain the lost ground. Rallying his forces, the commander, Zanoguerra, dashed into the midst of the enemy, and the conflict once more raged with doubtful success. Long and desperate was the struggle, the tide of battle fluctuating first on one side and then on the other. At last the force of numbers began to prevail, even against the indomitable determination of the defenders, and step by step they were driven backward over the rampart.

La Valette and Mustapha, who were both watching the course of events, the one from St. Angelo and the other from the summit of the Corradin hill, decided simultaneously upon sending reinforcements to the scene of action. Mustapha, who had seen with exultation the progress made by his columns, determined to complete the success and overcome all further opposition. He therefore embarked a body of a thousand janissaries in ten large boats, and despatched them to the assistance of Candèlissa. In order to avoid the stockade, this flotilla steered well round to the northward, and thus exposed itself to the fire of St. Angelo from which the first attack had been screened by the point of Senglea. Upon the rock at the foot of St. Angelo a battery had been constructed for three guns, *à fleur d'eau*, for the express purpose of protecting the spur of St. Michael. The knight who had command of the battery, when he saw the advance of the hostile force, caused his guns to be loaded to the muzzle with grape, musket shot, and other missiles, and then quietly waited till the enemy approached within easy range. At a given signal the battery, which from its absence of elevation had escaped the notice of the Turks, belched forth its fire at a distance of little more than two hundred yards, lashing the surface of the water into a foam with its iron hail. The result was awful in the extreme. The boats were all crowded together, and the discharge had taken effect in their midst. Nine out of the ten sank instantly, and such of their occupants as were not killed were seen struggling in the water. The wondrous effect of this deadly discharge has been described with great unction by contemporary annalists, and the loss sustained by the Turks variously computed at from four to eight hundred men. For days after, the bodies of the killed floated on the water, and were seized by the expert Maltese swimmers, who reaped a rich harvest from the plunder found on them.

Meanwhile La Valette had on his side despatched a powerful reinforcement from the Bourg by means of the temporary bridge which connected that point with Senglea, and this succour reached the scene of action at the moment when the Turks were paralyzed by the incident they had just witnessed. Their appearance at this critical moment decided the fortunes of the day. With a shout of anticipated triumph they dashed at the enemy, and drove them headlong over the breach. Even Candêlissa, whose reputation for courage and daring had till that moment been above suspicion, was seized with panic, and was amongst the earliest to turn his back upon the scene of strife. On first landing at the point he had directed his boats to push off from the land, that his troops might fight the more desperately from feeling that their retreat was cut off. He now found this valiant order of his highly inconvenient, and as he stood upon the edge of the rock eagerly beckoning the boats back again, he presented a spectacle but little edifying to the gazers from the Corradin hill. He hurried ignominiously into the first boat that reached the spot, and was followed by such of his troops as were able to secure the same means of escape. The remainder fell almost unresisting victims to the fury of the besieged. Their cries for quarter were met with the stern reply, " Such mercy as you showed to our brethren in St. Elmo shall be meted out to you, and none other." From this day similar scenes of vengeance became known amongst the garrison by the name of " St. Elmo's pay."

Candêlissa and his fugitive comrades having made good their escape, the Christians employed upon their work of butchery became exposed to the fire from the enemy's batteries, which now opened furiously on the point. In this cannonade the young son of the Viceroy of Sicily, Frederic de Toledo, was killed. La Valette had hitherto, out of consideration for his father, studiously kept him from the more exposed and dangerous posts, but the enthusiasm of the young soldier could not tamely brook this state of inglorious security. When, therefore, the reinforcement left the Bourg for Senglea, Toledo contrived to join their ranks unnoticed, and bore himself right gallantly in the short but decisive struggle that ensued. His untimely fate, whilst fighting for a cause in which he had no personal interest, created an universal feeling of deep regret; even the stern and impassive La Valette himself exhibiting the most poignant sorrow at his loss.

Whilst Candêlissa had been thus engaged Hassan had on his side made several desperate but futile attempts to penetrate into the defences on the land front of Senglea. Wherever the assailing columns showed themselves they were met by an impenetrable array, which no efforts could force. The young Algerine exerted every art which eloquence could inspire to urge on his followers. He was mindful of the scornful boast he had uttered whilst standing on the ruins of St. Elmo, and he strove hard to fulfil what he had then undertaken. He now, however, learnt that he was fighting with an enemy very different from those with whom he had hitherto come in contact, and at length, exhausted with his fruitless efforts, he was compelled sullenly to withdraw his troops, and acknowledge the bitterness of defeat.

Thus ended this memorable day—one that reflected as much glory on the defenders as disgrace on their assailants. Nearly 3,000 of the flower of the Ottoman army, the great bulk of whom were janissaries and Algerine corsairs, perished upon the occasion, whilst the loss of the garrison did not exceed 250. Amongst these, however, in addition to the nephew of the viceroy, was the commander Zanoguerra, who fell at the moment of victory. La Valette caused a solemn thanksgiving for this important success, to be offered up in the conventual church of San Lorenzo. Mustapha, on his side, felt that still greater exertions were necessary to atone for the failure which had hitherto attended his arms. The strength of the garrison being now much reduced, he conceived that he would be gaining the greatest advantage from the superiority of his numbers, if he carried on his attack against Senglea and the Bourg simultaneously.

He therefore retained the direction of the attack on St. Michael in his own hands, whilst he confided that against the Bourg to his admiral Piali. To Candêlissa, whose conduct during the late assault had not raised him in public estimation, was entrusted the charge of the fleet, with directions to cruise off the mouth of the harbour, and intercept any attempts at reinforcement. This division of command created great rivalry and emulation. Each one felt that if he were the fortunate man to gain the first footing within the enemy's defences the whole glory of the expedition, and consequently its reward, would fall to him. Piali therefore determined to push forward his attack on the Bourg with the utmost vigour. A battery had already been constructed on Mount Salvator, which played upon the post of Castile and on part of that of Auvergne. To this Piali added another larger battery, nearer the point of Bighi, containing guns and mortars of greater calibre, and thus enclosed the post of Castile between two fires, reducing its ramparts to a state of utter ruin. At the same time he pushed his trenches forward, until he had approached so close to the bastion that all was ready for an assault.

Meanwhile Mustapha had employed the time in increasing the number of his guns in battery, and in harassing the garrison of Senglea by a constant and galling cannonade. On the 2nd August, anxious to forestall the operations of Piali, he delivered an assault on the land front, where Hassan had previously failed. For six hours the struggle was maintained with equal obstinacy on both sides. Five times were the Turks repulsed from the breach, and as often were they rallied by the indomitable Mustapha. At length, however, he was compelled, through the sheer exhaustion of his men, to abandon the attempt, and the wearied garrison were once more permitted to enjoy a brief repose.

Piali was now ready on his side, and on the 7th August a fresh attack was made upon both points simultaneously. Piali exerted himself to the utmost to penetrate through the gaping breaches established by his batteries in the ramparts of Castile, but in vain. Retrenchments had been formed in rear of the exposed points, and so galling a fire was maintained upon the assailants that they were unable to face its intensity. Whilst thus thrown into confusion, the disorder being rendered still more complete by the various obstacles strewn upon the breach, the garrison assumed the offensive, and dashed from their cover, driving the Turks headlong backwards. No efforts on the part of Piali could succeed in rallying them, and he was compelled to relinquish the attempt.

Mustapha's attack was at first attended with better success. His columns obtained a footing on the summit of the breach, and a desperate hand to hand encounter ensued, in which his superiority of numbers gradually made itself felt. He himself was to be seen in every direction, sword in hand, cheering on his followers, with promises of reward and booty, and eventually succeeded in driving the garrison back from the contested rampart. At this moment, when all appeared lost, and when a short time longer must have decided the fate of Senglea, Mustapha, to the amazement of the combatants, sounded the signal for retreat. At the time this step on his part appeared inexplicable, but the cause which led to it was in reality very simple. The commandant of the Citta

Notabile had heard the ceaseless din which since early d
had raged around the fortress, and had rightly conject
that the Turks were delivering a fresh assault. He de
mined, therefore, on making a diversion, and mustering
his cavalry, he sent them forth, with general direction
make an attack, wherever they might find a suitable poir

The knight in command advanced cautiously to the b
of the Marsa, where the sick and wounded of the Tur.
army were encamped. The guards of the camp had all
their posts, and were on the neighbouring heights ga
intently upon the conflict raging around. The little f
seizing the advantage thus offered, rushed upon the ca
and commenced an indiscriminate massacre of the help
creatures around them. Shrieks, yells, and groans resoun
in every direction, and a general panic spread through
army. It was stated that the relieving force from Sicily l
landed, and that its advanced guard was already in their r
The news spread like wildfire; terror and dismay were
every face, and each one, without waiting to front the ener
bethought him how best he could escape from the general m
sacre. The intelligence reached Mustapha in the thick of
contest at Senglea; and at the very moment of victory he f
the prize torn from his grasp. An immediate retreat v
sounded, and his disheartened troops assembled to meet t
new enemy supposed to be at that moment on their flar
What was his astonishment and rage when he reached t
scene of action to learn the true state of the case! T
Christians having attained their object, and created a div
sion, had wisely retired in time; and Mustapha found, to l
unspeakable indignation, that he had abandoned a victo
already in his grasp on a false alarm.

From this time he resolved to carry his point rather b

the harassing frequency of his attacks than by their intensity. Each day, therefore, witnessed a repetition of the struggle at one or both of the points of attack. It would weary the reader to enter into a detail of all the incidents by which these constant assaults were marked. Their general character was always the same. At the appointed signal the assailants rushed forward with shouts and yells, the shrill notes of the atabal rang forth with inspiriting tones, and a dash was made at the gaping breach. But there they were met by an enemy who cared but little either for the notes of the atabal or the shouts of the Moslem. Then ensued that hand to hand encounter in which the chivalry of St. John, standing on the summit of the breach, invariably proved superior to the assailants struggling up its rugged sides. Less and less obstinately was the combat maintained, until the sound of retreat, rising above the din of battle, announced one more failure to the assailants and another triumph to the garrison.

After each of these victories, however, La Valette beheld his numbers gradually thinning; his thoughts, therefore, turned more and more anxiously towards the relief expected from Sicily. His ambassador at that court had not been idle. His was indeed no easy task, and it required the most skilful diplomacy to carry his instructions judiciously into effect. Whilst on the one hand it was urgently necessary that he should stimulate the dilatory viceroy to increased exertions, it was, on the other hand, equally incumbent on him to say or do nothing which could by any possibility be construed into a cause of offence. When, however, the news had reached Sicily, first of the fall of St. Elmo, then of the blockade of the Bourg, and lastly of the repeated assaults that were made at that point and at Senglea, he could no longer

K

refrain from vehement remonstrances at a delay which se‹
certain to ensure the loss of the island.

It is very difficult to account for the conduct of the vic
at this juncture. It is a well-known fact that he was war
attached to the Order, and especially to La Valette hims
he had even intrusted his son to his care through the p‹
of the siege; and it cannot be supposed that under s·
circumstances he could be indifferent to the fate of the isla.
Whether he feared by too hasty an intervention to co
promise the safety of the Spanish fleet, or whether, as is v‹
probable, he was acting under secret instructions from Phil
himself, can never now be ascertained. It is, however, ve:
clear that but for the indomitable nature of La Valette
resistance, the succour, by means of which the island wc
eventually rescued, would have arrived only in time to behol‹
the Turkish flag waving over the Castle of St. Angelo, anc
the sad scenes of St. Elmo re-enacted upon a larger scale.

The remonstrances of the ambassador induced the viceroy
to summon a council to discuss the steps to be taken. A
proposition was then actually made, and supported by several
voices, to leave the island to its fate. Fortunately, however,
for the reputation of Philip and his viceroy, other and nobler
counsels prevailed, and an assurance was forwarded to La
Valette that if he could maintain himself until the end of
August, he should most positively be relieved by that time.

Meanwhile the daily assaults continued without intermission. On the 18th of August, however, they assumed a
more important character than usual. Both points were to
be attacked; but the assault upon the Castile bastion was
deferred for some time after that upon St. Michael's had been
commenced, partly with the hope of inducing some of its
defenders to withdraw to the assistance of their friends at

St. Michael's, and partly to enable Piali to spring a mine, which had with incredible labour been successfully driven through the rock beneath the bastion. Finding that the delay did not tempt any of the garrison to quit their posts, Piali sprang his mine, and a large portion of the rampart was thrown down by the explosion. During the panic created by this unexpected event the assailants made their onset, and when the dense smoke which hung over the scene of the catastrophe cleared away, the Turkish banner was seen planted upon the new-formed breach.

The alarm spread instantly, and the great bell of the conventual church pealed forth to notify the peril. A terrified ecclesiastic, rushing into the presence of La Valette, besought him to take refuge in the Castle of St. Angelo, as the Bourg was irrevocably lost. All was confusion and panic, and but for the presence of mind displayed by La Valette at that critical moment, the town must have been lost. Instead of following the advice of his ecclesiastical friend, La Valette seized a pike, and rushed to the scene of action, calling upon his brethren to die manfully at their post. A desperate encounter ensued, in which the Grand Master was badly wounded, but he succeeded in attaining his object, and the breach was once more cleared.

The catastrophe thus averted had been so imminent, and appeared so likely to threaten them again, that La Valette determined upon taking up his quarters permanently close to the exposed bastion. In vain his knights remonstrated with him; in vain they pointed out the inestimable value of his life to the defence. He persisted in his determination, and the result proved the clearness of his foresight. That same night the Turks renewed the attack, and the spirit inspired amongst the defenders by his presence materially aided them in successfully resisting it. The 19th, 20th, 21st of August each beheld an assault upon some point; although on each occasion it failed, the reduced numbe the garrison proved clearly that they would be unabl sustain many more such attacks.

Scarce a knight remained unwounded of that little b and La Valette was each day doomed to mourn the lo some one whose gallantry had endeared him to the he of his comrades. Nor was he spared the pang of a ne loss. His own nephew, Parisot de la Valette, was st: down in a daring sortie which he had led in company 1 another knight named Polastron, and it was only after a l and fiercely-contested struggle that their comrades succes in rescuing their corpses. La Valette was himself an witness to the scene, and rejected all attempts at condol by assuring his hearers that the whole fraternity were to as kindred, and that he did not mourn the loss of his nep: more than that of any other knight who had fallen.

Whilst the defenders were being reduced to this piti condition, the position of Mustapha was becoming but li better. The incessant attacks he had persisted in mak had, it is true, harassed the garrison beyond all endurai but their constant failure had, at the same time, produ the worst possible effect upon his own troops. They had the flower of their army, partly on those deadly breac which they had in vain endeavoured to storm, and partly a pestilence, which had latterly raged with the most frigh violence throughout their camp. Their ammunition v running low, and a scarcity of provisions had long been fi It appears strange that with so large a fleet as that wh Piali commanded, they should have found any difficulty maintaining their communications with the African coa but certain it is that from some cause or other, whilst that fleet was lying in idleness in the Marsa Muscetto, Sicilian cruisers were permitted constantly to intercept their supplies.

Long and anxious consultations were held between Mustapha and Piali. The former, who felt that his reputation—nay, even most probably his life—depended upon the successful issue of the enterprise, strongly urged that the army should, if necessary, winter upon the island; but Piali declared that he would not allow his fleet to run so great a risk. That fleet had been placed under his own especial control, and he alone was responsible to the Sultan for its safety. He announced, therefore, that as soon as the summer should commence to break up, he would quit the island, and return to Constantinople, whether with or without the army. A great and constant jealousy had, indeed, from the first existed between the rival commanders of the Ottoman forces. So long as Dragut lived, this feeling had been suppressed, and the Algerine had, by mutual consent, been permitted to take the lead in conducting the attack on St. Elmo. But after his death the ill-will of the two leaders towards each other broke out with increased rancour. Each was more intent upon depriving his rival of the honour of success than upon carrying on the main object of the expedition; and each felt that if he were not himself the principal actor at the capture of the island, he would rather that the attempt were a failure than that the other should reap the fruits of success.

Mustapha felt greatly dismayed at the now openly expressed opposition of his coadjutor, still he retained the secret of his despondency within his own breast. Instructions were issued for a fresh general assault at all points on the 23rd August. Some friendly hand among the besiegers shot

into the town an arrow, to which was attached a piec[e of]
paper containing only the word *Thursday*. The hint [was]
sufficient, and La Valette guessed at once that on that da[y an]
attack of more than usual importance was to take place. [A]
general council was summoned to deliberate upon meas[ures]
of defence. It was then strongly urged that he sh[ould]
abandon both the Bourg and Senglea, and withdraw with [a]
reduced garrison into the Castle of St. Angelo. The Gr[and]
Master, however, would not listen to this proposition. [He]
pointed out that St. Angelo was too small to contain all [the]
persons who would require shelter, nor would the suppl[y of]
water suffice for their wants. Both the Bourg and Seng[lea]
must, therefore, he said, be maintained to the last; and [in]
order to show that he was determined to carry his views i[nto]
execution, he withdrew the greater portion of the garri[son]
from the castle to reinforce those of the two towns.

Early on the morning of the 23rd, the assault took pl[ace]
as anticipated. Every member of the Order whose wou[nds]
did not positively incapacitate him had, upon this occasi[on]
quitted the infirmary, and once more resumed his post [on]
the shattered ramparts. Yet even with this aid the num[ber]
of the defenders had dwindled to a mere handful, a[nd]
nothing but their indomitable spirit could have maintain[ed]
the resistance they were throughout the day called upon [to]
offer against the most overwhelming odds. Once aga[in,]
however, they were successful, and the baffled Mustapha w[as]
compelled to withdraw his troops, now utterly demoraliz[ed,]
from the scene of their failure.

For a week after this defeat the Turks attempted nothi[ng]
further, but contented themselves with maintaining a sull[en]
cannonade from their batteries. On the 1st Septemb[er]
Mustapha once more essayed his fortune at a last despera[te]

## Arrival of the Army of Succour.

assault, and every incentive by which his troops could be stimulated to the attack was freely proffered by him. It was, however, all in vain. A spirit of disorganization and despondency had spread itself through their ranks. They declared that it was evidently not the will of Allah that they should become the masters of Malta, and they loudly demanded to be carried away from the island where so many of their comrades had found a bloody grave. It was not with men imbued with such feelings as these that victory was to be snatched from the determined and desperate garrison, and Mustapha's shattered battalions recoiled almost without a blow from the firm front still maintained against their advance.

The feebleness of this last effort of the besiegers spread the greatest exultation and the most sanguine hopes of ultimate success in the hearts of the garrison. They began to hope that they should be able, alone and unaided, to drive the enemy from their shores, and they almost ceased to wish for the presence of that relieving force whose coming had previously been looked for with such earnest anticipation.

This long-expected aid was, however, at length on its way to their rescue. On the 25th of August a fleet of 28 galleys containing 8500 troops, of whom nearly 300 were members of the Order, the remainder being Italian and Spanish soldiery, set sail from Syracuse and appeared off Malta. Whilst the viceroy was reconnoitring the island with a view to deciding upon what would be the most prudent step to take for the relief of the garrison, one of those sudden and violent storms arose, so common in the Mediterranean, and dispersed his fleet, compelling him to return to Sicily to refit. His troops were so eager to be led to the rescue that this was speedily effected, and on the 6th September he again set sail, and anchored that same night between the islands of Comino and Gozo. The next morning he landed his army in Melleha bay, a small but commodious port on the north of the island; and having witnessed the commencement of their march towards Citta Notabile, he returned to Sicily for a further body of 4,000 men, who were still at Syracuse awaiting transport.

Meanwhile, Mustapha had remained in his camp after his last failure, in a state of the most abject despondency; every effort which his ingenuity could devise, had been made to overcome the obstinate resistance of the defenders. Their works had been battered by a train, far more powerful than had ever previously been used at a siege; they had been subjected to a series of the most desperate and prolonged assaults; the ground had been honey-combed with mines. A cavalier had been raised in front of the post of Castile, from the summit of which, the interior of that bastion could be overlooked, but it had been captured by the garrison and actually converted into a post of defence. Nor was this all; at his last assault, he had thrown into the town a cask filled with combustibles, with a slow match attached, trusting to spread confusion amongst the defenders by its explosion; they had, however, succeeded in hurling it back into the very midst of a column, which was at the moment advancing to the assault, and which was consequently shattered and dispersed by the effects of a missile devised by themselves. An attempt had been made against the Citta Notabile, and that had also been baffled by the determination of its commandant. He had, in fact, been thwarted at every point; and it was at this moment, (whilst he was plunged in the depths of despondency, and whilst his troops were clamorous for the abandonment of the siege,) that he received

## Preparations for Abandoning the Siege. 137

the first notification of the landing and advance of the succouring army.

Intelligence had reached Mustapha that this aid had been preparing for the garrison, but its lengthened delay had lured him into the hope that it would never really set sail. He had moreover decided in his own mind that even if it did arrive, the efforts of its leader would be directed towards forcing the entrance to the grand harbour, and against such a step he had taken ample precautions. Great was his dismay, therefore, when he learnt that an army had actually landed upon the island, and was marching rapidly upon the Bourg. Rumour had, as usual, greatly magnified the numbers of the advancing force, and Mustapha began to fear lest he should be surprised in his entrenchments, and his entire army cut to pieces. He at once gave the order for immediate embarkation. The artillery and stores were carried off, and throughout the night of the 7th of September his men laboured with far greater diligence and zeal in removing their guns than they had originally shown in landing them. The sounds of departure were not lost upon the garrison, and with gleesome hearts they listened to the constant rumbling of wheels, which throughout the night, marked the movement going on in the Turkish camp.

With the first dawn of day, the actual embarkation of the Turkish army commenced. St. Elmo was abandoned, and all those trenches and batteries which it had taken so many months and so fearful an expenditure of blood to construct, were now relinquished into the hands of the garrison. La Valette's measures on this joyful morning were as prompt and decisive as those of Mustapha's had been injudicious. The whole town poured forth into the trenches, and in a few hours the labour of months had been destroyed. The banner of St. John was once more triumphantly raised over the ruins of Elmo, and Piali was driven to hurry his galleys out of the Marsa Muscetto, which was no longer a safe refuge, now that Mount Sceberras was again in possession of the knights.

The embarkation of the Turkish army had been barely effected, when Mustapha received more accurate intelligence as to the numbers of the relieving army. His proud spirit was struck with indignation at the thought that he should thus hastily have abandoned his position upon the approach of a force so far inferior to his own. A council of war was promptly summoned, in which it was decided by a slender majority, that the troops should be again disembarked and marched into the interior of the island to encounter the new enemy. This decision caused the greatest dismay and consternation amongst the disorganized army, who had trusted that their labours and perils were at last ended. They were with the utmost difficulty torn from the ships in which they had hoped to be borne away from the scene of so many privations and hardships. Mustapha was, however, a man endowed with too much determination of purpose to allow the discontent of a mutinous soldiery to divert him from his aim. A body of about 9,000 men was therefore landed in St. Paul's Bay, whither the fleet had proceeded when they left the Marsa Muscetto, and with this force, Mustapha advanced to meet the enemy.

The Viceroy had placed his army under the command of a Spanish officer named Della Corna, second to whom was Alvarez de Sande, a knight of the Order, who had on several occasions much distinguished himself. La Valette sent timely notice to these officers, that a body of Turks had once more landed, and were probably advancing against them. Della Corna, upon receipt of this intelligence, took prompt measures to protect himself against attack. He secured a very strong position on the summit of the ridge in front of the casal of Nasciar, and prepared to await within the entrenchments which he had hastily thrown up the onset of the Turks; but he had those under his command whose fiery zeal could ill brook such a defensive policy. A body of 200 knights, each of whom was accompanied by several armed followers, had been formed into a battalion, (by far the most efficient in Della Corna's army:) these knights were burning with eagerness to cross swords at once with their hated enemy, and to avenge in the blood of the Moslem the loss of so many of their comrades who had fallen in the defence of Malta. No entreaties, no commands could restrain their impetuosity, and they openly declared that if they were not promptly led to the attack, they would rush upon the enemy single-handed.

Della Corna perceived that he could not prevail against their impetuosity, and decided upon making the best possible use of the enthusiasm that fired his troops. No sooner did Mustapha's army reach the foot of the hill than a general advance was ordered. Down rushed the Maltese battalion, the white-cross banner waving in their van, and their brandished weapons gleaming in the sun, as though eager to be bathed in infidel blood. The Turks, who had with difficulty been brought thus far, were struck with a panic at the furious onset of the knights. Scarce waiting to strike a blow they turned at once, and fled with precipitation. In vain did Mustapha strain every nerve to rally his flying troops; twice he was unhorsed, and more than once did he with his own hand cut down the foremost of the fugitives in his vain endeavours to stem the torrent of the flight. The general terror was too universal for him to withstand, and he was at length himself carried away by the stream.

On came the knights, heedless of aught but revenge. Every precaution was neglected, all order was lost; even their very armour was cast aside that they might act with the greater vigour and promptitude against their unresisting adversaries. In tumultuous disarray they reached the shore, and strove to prevent the embarkation of the Turks. Here, however, they were brought to a check. Mustapha, before advancing into the island, had left Hassan, the Algerine corsair, with 1,500 men, to protect the point of embarkation. This force was judiciously posted, so that when the knights came streaming in confusion to the spot, they were received with such a heavy fire as almost to threaten their annihilation. Surrounded by this new foe they would inevitably have been cut to pieces, had not Della Corna promptly made his appearance with the main body of his army. As it was, many fell, and a few were taken prisoners. These were, however, speedily rescued by Della Corna, the Turks driven on board their galleys, and Malta, at last, cleared of all its foes.

The siege was now over; the shattered remnants of that powerful army, which a few short months before had landed on the island with all the pomp and circumstance of war, was wending its way homeward to Constantinople, there to meet the angry frowns of a sovereign who, till this moment, had scarcely known defeat; and it only remained that the victors should advance upon the town and greet their friends in the Bourg.

A joyful meeting it was which there took place between those enfeebled, war-worn soldiers and the gallant comrades who had so opportunely come to their rescue. Of the

9,000 men who had mustered beneath La Valette's banner, prior to the commencement of the siege, little more than 600 remained capable of bearing arms, and almost every one of that chosen few bore upon his body the marks of many an honourable scar. Their wan and haggard faces, attenuated with hardships and vigils, were now lighted up with the proud consciousness of the glorious victory they had gained. Alone and unaided they had for months withstood the shock of the most powerful armament that had ever left the port of Constantinople. Their ruined and blood-stained ramparts could tell a tale of heroism and endurance such as the world had never before witnessed. As friend met friend and were clasped in each other's arms, each one felt that another triumph had to be emblazoned upon the banner of St. John, before which all previous victories seemed pale and trivial. Well might La Valette be excused the natural exultation of the moment, when he directed that the name of his town should be changed from its old appellation of the Bourg to the proud and well-earned title of the Citta Vittoriosa.

The heroic spirits who conducted the defence of Malta have long since returned to dust, and the names even, of but too many of them have been lost to the world, but the memory of their great deeds remains as fresh and green as though it were a thing of yesterday; and the name of Malta is never mentioned, even in the present age, without recalling to the mind the picture of the scenes enacted there during the summer of 1565.

English hearts and English swords now protect those ramparts which formerly glistened with the ensigns of the Order of St. John; and should occasion ever demand the sacrifice, the world will find that British blood can be poured forth like water in the defence of that rock which the common consent of Europe has entrusted to her hands. On such a day the memory of this great siege will have its due effect, and those ramparts, already bedewed with so much noble blood, will again witness deeds of heroism, such as shall rival, if they cannot excel, the glories of the great struggle of 1565.

## CHAPTER VI.

Causes of the Failure of the Turks—Enthusiasm of Europe—Commencement of the City of Valetta—Death of La Valette—His Character—Completion of the City—Arrival of the Grand Inquisitor, and consequent Troubles—Erection of the Cathedral Church of St. John.

THE army which accompanied the Pasha Mustapha to Malta had originally consisted of 30,000 men, all picked from the flower of the Turkish army. The successive reinforcements brought to the island by the corsairs Dragut and Hassan swelled that number to upwards of 40,000. Of this vast force scarce 10,000 survived to return with their leader to Constantinople.

The rage of Solyman upon learning the disgrace which had befallen his arms was such as might have been anticipated from one who, throughout a lengthened career, had hitherto been almost invariably the favoured child of victory. Tearing the despatch which contained the unpalatable intelligence into fragments, he pledged himself to lead in person a fresh expedition against Malta at the commencement of the ensuing summer, and vowed that he would not leave one stone standing on another. Preparations were instantly commenced in the arsenal of Constantinople for the construction of a fleet of sufficient magnitude to carry out the project of the Sultan, and every nerve was strained to collect such a force as should effectually wipe away the stain upon the military renown of the empire caused by the late failure.

The position of the Order of St. John was at this moment critical in the extreme. The original garrison of Malta had barely reached 9,000 men; the reinforcement received shortly after the fall of St. Elmo added only 700 to the number. Of these little more than 600 remained unwounded.* The process of exhaustion had been carried on by Mustapha almost to the point at which he aimed. It had been his

---

\* The 8th of September, the day on which the siege of Malta was raised by the Turks, was always subsequently celebrated with great rejoicings by the Order. As the day of the nativity of the Virgin Mary, it was already a high festival of the Church, but from the year 1565 it became the most important anniversary in the calendar of Malta. On that day a solemn mass was performed for the souls of those who fell during the siege, and the names of such among them as had attained to any rank in the fraternity were registered in the records of the Church. The following list of those who were killed at St. Elmo is taken from the " Codice Diplomatico :"—

**LANGUE OF PROVENCE.**

| | |
|---|---|
| Pierre le Mas, and Louis le Mas, brothers. | Jean de Chateauneuf, and Antoine de Chateauneuf, brothers. |
| Gaspar la Motte. | Emeric du Curdurier la Pierre. |
| Louis de Puget Fuveau. | Le Chevalier d'Aux. |
| Louis de Maqueriti. | Le Chevalier Jean de Colombiers. |
| Honorat de Ventemille Figheniere. | Jean de Gelon Durand. |

**LANGUE OF AUVERGNE.**

| | |
|---|---|
| Jean de Gozon Ollionac. | Louis d'Argeroles de Saint Polque. |
| Abel de Bridiers de la Gardampe. | Claude de la Roche Aymon Villedubois. |
| Laurent de Bonlieu (this knight was taken prisoner in one of the assaults, and crucified; some accounts say flayed alive). | Guillaume de Saint Bonet. |
| | Pierre de Loné. |
| | Jean de Nachel Vernatel. |
| Jean de Vernon de Beaumanoir. | |

## Names of Knights killed at St. Elmo.

design to harass the garrison by constant assaults, in order to reduce their numbers so low that they would fall an easy prey to his arms. This policy had proved successful at St. Elmo, and would undoubtedly have answered equally well at

### LANGUE OF FRANCE.

Edmond de Sanciere Terrance.
Claude de la Brigne Bulsy.
Antoino Bligny de Cressy.
François du Chilleau.
François Boüer.
Louis Rogier la Ville.
Jean de Zimbert de Lubard.

François de la Grange Montfernier.
Artus Bonet de Brouillat.
André Roubert de Lizardiere.
Jean de Choiseul.
Georges Haultoy.
Simon de Clainchant.
Antoine des Moulins.

### LANGUE OF ITALY.

Giovanni Vagnone.
Ardicino Griselli.
Vincenzo Gabrielli.
Ardicino Pescatore.
Emilii Scarampo.
Francesco Peletta.
Jacomo Martelli.
Giovanni Vitello Vitelloschi.
Decio Mastrillo.
Girolamo Galeotto.
Alessandro de Conti di St. Georgio.
Paolo Avogadro.
Pier Francesco Somaja.
Alessandro Rusca.
Antonio Loler.

Girolamo Peppe da Ruvo.
Piero Nibbia.
Nicolo Strambino.
Carlo Sassetti.
Giovanni Battista Pagano.
Mario Conti.
Stefano de Fabii.
Rosso Strozzi.
Francesco Gondi.
Lelio Tana.
Ottaviano Bozzuto.
Bartolomeo Francolini.
Giovanni Battista Montalto.
Vincenzo Bozzuto.
Vespasiano di Gilestri.
Ambrogio Pecullo.

### LANGUE OF ARAGON.

Giovanni d'Eguaras.
Melchior de Montserrat.
Felix do Queralta.
Pedro Zacosta.
Giovanni Perez Barragau.
Fortuno Escuderro.
Francesco Monpalan.
Antonio de Montserrat.
Juan do Pamplona.

Federigo Armongol.
Onorato Fernandez de Mesa.
Gaspar de Guete.
Baldassar de Aquinez.
Antonio de Morgate.
Gaspar di Aoyz.
Miguel Bueno.
Nofre Tallada.

the Bourg had the means at his command been sufficiently unlimited. His own forces, however, suffered so much from both sword and pestilence that at the critical moment he was unable to take due advantage of the feebleness of the garrison.

The defence of Malta has justly been considered one of the most brilliant feats of arms recorded in the sixteenth century, and the historian naturally seeks for the causes of so glorious a success. Foremost amongst these must be ranked the jealousy which existed between the military and naval commanders of the Turkish armament. Mustapha and Piali were each eager to prevent the other from realising too large a share of the glory to be anticipated from the capture of

LANGUE OF GERMANY.

| | |
|---|---|
| Valthaus de Heunech. | Tchnanus Eyssembach. |
| Johann de Hassembnrg. | Turc de Duelen. |
| Florian Stezela d'Olmut. | |

LANGUE OF CASTILE.

| | |
|---|---|
| Juan Velasquez d'Argotti. | Lorenzo de Gusman. |
| Cristoval de Silva. | Luis Costilla de Nocedo. |
| Bartolomeo Pessoa. | Fernando de Acugna. |
| Juan Rodriguez de Villafuerte. | Pedro de Soto. |
| Francesco de Britto. | Juan d'Espinosa. |

Besides these there were killed during the subsequent portion of the siege the following number of knights of each langue:—

| | |
|---|---|
| Provence | 17 |
| Auvergne | 4 |
| France | 16 |
| Italy | 48 |
| Aragon | 14 |
| Germany | 4 |
| Castile | 16 |

Sir Oliver Starkey was the only English knight recorded as having been present at the siege, and he survived to occupy the dignities successively of Lieutenant of the Turcopolier and Bailiff of the Eagle.

the fortress. They were therefore ill-prepared for that mutual concession and good-will so essentially necessary for the success of their arms. The engineering tactics of the Turks were, moreover, faulty in the extreme. Their oversight in permitting the garrison of St. Elmo to maintain an uninterrupted communication with that of the Bourg detained them before its walls many weeks longer than would otherwise have been the case. Untaught by the results of that siege, they subsequently neglected to complete the investment of the Bourg, until after a considerable reinforcement had succeeded in making its way into the town from Sicily. Dragut was, moreover, undoubtedly right when he pointed out to Mustapha that he should, in the first place, have made himself master of the Citta Notabile. The fortifications of that town were comparatively insignificant, and it must, after a few days' siege, have fallen into his hands; his rear would then have been secure from disturbance, and the garrison would have been cut off from that assistance which they derived from the Citta Notabile during the early part of the siege.

Thus far the successful result of the struggle may be traced to the errors of the Ottoman tactics, but it would be a wanton robbery of that meed of glory which they had so justly earned, to deny that it was mainly owing to the heroic and indomitable bravery of the garrison, led by so gallant and determined a chief as La Valette. It was fortunate for Malta that, at a moment when its inhabitants were called upon to maintain so desperate a defence, they were led by a man who, from the energy of his character and the stern determination of his purpose, was eminently qualified to guide them through the fiery ordeal. The character of La Valette was one which elicited far more respect and fear than love. There was a stern impassiveness in his temperament, a steady and cold resolution of purpose, which marked how utterly he excluded all personal feeling from the guidance of his actions. His mind was cast in a mould so rigid and unflinching that he extorted an unwavering obedience from those who, perhaps, had they loved him more, would have followed his injunctions less implicitly. His cold and uncompromising sacrifice of the garrison of St. Elmo, in order to secure the prolongation of the siege, marks the character of the man, whilst the obedience to death which he extorted from that gallant band, even after they had broken out into open mutiny, proves the extraordinary ascendency he had gained over their minds. The crisis required a man who could sacrifice all considerations of feeling for those of duty. A stern disregard, not only of self, but also of others, when the exigencies of the case demanded it, was imperatively called for, and in La Valette the Order found a man capable of such sacrifice. He had also the rare faculty of arousing in others that deep religious enthusiasm which was the chief motive power of his own life, and the meanest soldier imbibed from his chief a lofty determination to conquer or to die, which was the great secret of their stubborn and successful resistance.

The Order were, moreover, ably seconded in their efforts by the bravery and resolution of the Maltese. It must be borne in mind that the great bulk of the soldiery was composed of the native element. Had this failed, no amount of individual heroism on the part of the knights could, in the long run, have been successful. The Maltese have, however, wherever they have been tested, proved themselves steady and resolute soldiers, and on this memorable occasion they were not found wanting. No single instance is recorded throughout the siege in which they failed in their duty, and on many occasions, (notably when the Turks attempted to destroy the stockade formed at St. Michael's,) they proved themselves capable of the most devoted heroism. The history of the siege is indissolubly interwoven with that of the Maltese inhabitants, and they have just cause to remember to this hour, with pride and satisfaction, the noble deeds of their ancestors in 1565.*

Europe had looked on with bated breath whilst the struggle was going forward. From time to time, as intelligence was brought of the successful maintenance of the resistance, a loud cry of acclaim would arise, and prayers were put up in many a Christian congregation for the ultimate success of the Cross against the Crescent. When at last it became known that that success was indeed assured, the universal exultation knew no bounds. It was at the courts of Rome and Madrid that this feeling found the freest vent. The island of Malta was looked upon as an advanced post to both these powers, and had Solyman succeeded in establishing himself at that point, the kingdom of Sicily and the States of the Church would have been continually exposed to the piratical incursions of his Algerine subjects.

The King of Spain despatched a special ambassador to Malta with congratulations to La Valette upon the auspicious result of the siege. The envoy bore with him, as a present from Philip, a magnificent poniard and sword, the hilts of which were of chased gold studded with precious stones. At Rome, a salute was fired from the castle of St. Angelo, and a general illumination of the city testified to the exultation of the inhabitants. Pope Pius IV., as a special mark of

---

* It is necessary to draw attention to this fact because most of the histories of the siege, having been compiled by writers in the interests of the Order, everything has generally been sacrificed to the object of adding to the glory of the fraternity. It is only by a careful study of facts that the heroism of the Maltese appears in its true light.

favour, offered La Valette a cardinal's hat, a dignity which had on a former similar occasion been offered to, and accepted by, the Grand Master Peter D'Aubusson, after his successful defence of Rhodes. La Valette, however, considered, and justly, that his position was far more elevated than that of a cardinal. The proffer of the pontiff was therefore graciously declined, under the plea that the office of Grand Master involved functions so diametrically opposed to those of a cardinal that he did not consider they could be combined.

In the midst of this scene of general rejoicing it became necessary for La Valette to consider what steps should be taken to avert the renewed attack for which, as he was informed by his spies, active preparations were being made at Constantinople. The position of the convent was at this crisis most desperate. The fortifications were more or less in ruins, the arsenals and storehouses empty, the treasury exhausted, and the ranks of the fraternity fearfully diminished. The general opinion of the council was in favour of an immediate abandonment of the island, and the retirement of the convent into Sicily; but La Valette felt that his renown and that of the Order had become too intimately blended with the island of Malta to brook so great a sacrifice. He expressed his determination to bury himself beneath the ruins he had hitherto successfully defended rather than permit them tamely to fall into the hands of the infidel. The same strong will and inflexible determination which had so often before overruled the decisions of his council once again triumphed; and it was at length decreed to stand or fall in defence of an island where they had already achieved so brilliant a success.

The danger was, however, imminent, and La Valette

feeling how impossible it was to oppose force to force at that critical moment, determined to adopt other means to avert the blow. He had in his pay a large number of spies in Constantinople, and he employed some of these unscrupulous agents to fire the arsenal of that city. Large stores of powder had been accumulated for the use of the expedition, and its explosion utterly destroyed not only the arsenal itself, but also the greater portion of the fleet, which was being equipped within its precincts. This blow put a complete stop to the undertaking, and the death of Solyman, which occurred not long after, prevented any renewal of the attempt.

All immediate danger of an invasion being thus happily at an end, the Grand Master turned his attention to the restoration of his ruined defences. The siege had clearly demonstrated the extreme importance of the fort of St. Elmo. La Valette determined, therefore, not only to reconstruct it upon a more extended scale than before, but also to carry out the project which had been so often previously mooted, of occupying the entire peninsula with a new town, and surrounding it with fortifications of such strength as should render it safe from the attack of an enemy. Experience had shown that the Bourg, or, as it was now termed, the Citta Vittoriosa, was but ill-suited for the head-quarters of the convent. Exposed on all sides to hills, by which it was overlooked, the difficulty of maintaining it during a lengthened siege had been so clearly shown, that some change was imperative. No other spot within the island afforded so many advantages as the Mount Sceberras. The expense, however, of such a design was enormous, and the treasury of the Order being completely exhausted, it was necessary to look for foreign assistance to carry out the project. Ambassadors were therefore despatched to all the leading courts of Europe, furnished with plans of the proposed scheme, and requesting aid for its realization.

The Order at this moment stood in very high favour throughout all the Catholic countries of Europe. The good services they had rendered to Christendom by averting the dreaded inroads of the Moslem were everywhere recognised and appreciated. La Valette received in consequence the promises of such liberal contributions that he was enabled at once to commence the realization of his project. The Pope guaranteed a subsidy of 15,000 crowns; the King of France, 140,000 livres; Philip, 90,000 livres; and the King of Portugal, 30,000 crusadoes. Whilst this assistance was being rendered from without, the members of the fraternity rivalled one another in the extent of their contributions. Many of the wealthiest commanders, not content with forwarding the entire revenues of their commanderies, stripped themselves of a large portion of their personal property, which they cheerfully tendered in aid of the good work. Thus encouraged and aided in the prosecution of his design, La Valette summoned the most able engineers and architects then procurable in Italy, and no longer delayed the commencement of the new city.

The Pope, not content with the contribution he had made in money, despatched his chief engineer, Francesco Laparelli, to aid the Grand Master by his advice and professional skill. The design of most of the principal works of Valetta may be attributed to this engineer, the general idea only having been sketched out by La Valette. Matters being thus prepared to commence operations, the 28th of March, 1566, was selected as the day on which to lay the first stone of the new city. The name to be given to it was Valetta, and the Grand Master added to it, as was the common practice in those days, the epithet "*Umilissima*." The Bourg, in memory of the recent triumph enacted within its ramparts, had received the proud title of Citta Vittoriosa; and the Citta Notabile, the ancient capital of the island, was from this moment destined to yield its long-established supremacy, and to sink into comparative insignificance, under the appellation of Citta Vecchia.

The ceremony of inauguration was performed with the utmost pomp. The entire extent of Mount Sceberras was covered with pavilions, whose snowy whiteness shone clear in the bright sunlight, with their gay pennons fluttering in the breeze. From all quarters strangers had flocked to the island eager to witness the ceremonial, the brilliant scene forming a striking contrast to the sad tragedy enacted upon the same spot in the previous year. At an early hour La Valette left the Bourg in solemn procession, accompanied by all the Grand Crosses and other dignitaries of the Order then resident in Malta, and preceded by the clergy, at whose head was the Bishop of Malta, the leading ecclesiastical dignitary of the fraternity. Arrived at Mount Sceberras, the Grand Master took up his station beneath an ample pavilion erected for the purpose on the appointed site, and there performed the operation of laying the first stone at the corner of St. John's bastion. The stone was lowered into its place after the mortar had been spread beneath it by the honoured hand of La Valette, and when it had been duly tapped with the mallet and examined with the square it was pronounced correctly laid.

Loud rang the trumpets to announce the auspicious fact to the thousands who had crowded round the spot, but louder far than the shrillest notes of the clarion burst forth the shout with which that enthusiastic multitude hailed the event. The chivalric heart of La Valette must have glowed within him at this spontaneous note of acclamation. Well, indeed, might the noble veteran and those around him rejoice, for that shout was a knell to all the hopes the infidel might till then have entertained of ever witnessing their banner floating triumphantly over the captured fortress of Malta. It was the inauguration of a new era, during which the island was to rise in importance until it attained a foremost rank amongst the strongholds of Europe.

Beneath the newly laid stone had been deposited a number of coins in gold and silver, bearing on the one side a representation of the new city, with the motto, "Melita Renascens," and on the other the date of the ceremony of inauguration. It is also recorded that a Latin inscription was affixed to the stone to the effect that the Grand Master, La Valette, in memory of the late siege, and for defence against future attacks, had determined to found a new city, which he had commenced on the 28th of March, 1566. As a precisely similar tablet was found over the old Porta Reale, it is probable that it was changed to that spot when the gate was completed, as being more conspicuous to public view. Be that as it may, there are no signs now of any such tablet on St. John's bastion. When the Porta Reale was restored in 1853 this tablet was carefully replaced on the new structure, as an interesting relic of the foundation of the city, although rather a drawback to the architectural beauty of the design. The inscription is simply an extract from the records of the council, which bear the following entry:—

"Die xxii. mensis Martii MDLXVI. Fr. Joannes de Valletta Sacræ Domus Hosp. Hier. M. Magister periculorum anno superiore a suis militibus populoque. Meliteo in obsidione Turcica perpessorum memor de condenda urbe nova eaque mœniis arcibus et propugnaculis munienda inito cum proceribus consilio die Jovis, xxviii Martii, MDLXVI. Deum Omnipotentem Deiparamque Virginem numenque tutelare D. Jo. Baptistam Divosque cœleros multa precatus ut faustum fœlixque religioni Christianæ fieret ac Ordini suo quod inceptabat bene cederet prima urbis fundamenta in monte ab incolis Xeberas vocato jecit eamque de suo nomine. Vallettam dato pro insignibus in parma miniata aurato leone appellari voluit."

It may be interesting to add the names of the dignitaries of the Order who were present on the occasion when this important decree was registered. They were as follows :—

Reverendus Dominus Magnus Magister Frater JOANNES DE VALLETTA.

Admodum Reverendus Dominus Episcopus Melitensis Frater DOMINICUS CUBELLES.

Reverendus Prior Ecclesiæ Dominus Frater ANTONIUS CRESSINUS.

Reverendus Maresciallus Dominus Frater GULIELMUS COPPIER.

Reverendus Hospitalarius Dominus Frater JACOBUS DERQUEMBOURC.

Reverendus Magnus Conservator Dominus Frater PETRUS DE JUNYENT.

Reverendus Admiralius Dominus Frater LUDOVICUS BROGLIA.

Reverendus Prior Sancti Œgidii Dominus Frater LUDOVICUS DU PONT.

Reverendus Prior Alverniæ Dominus Frater LUDOVICUS DE LASTIC.

Reverendus Prior Campaniæ Dominus Frater JOANNES AUDEBERT DIT LAUBUGE.

Reverendus Baiulivus Caspis Dominus Frater LUDOVICUS DE LALZEDO.

Locumtenens Reverendi Magni Commendatorii Frater JOANNES DE MONTAGU.

Locumtenens Reverendi Turcopolerii Dominus Frater OLIVERIUS STARCHI.

Locumtenens Reverendi Magni Bauilivii Alemanie Dominus Frater CONRARD SCOULBACH.

Locumtenens Reverendi Cancellarii Dominus Frater DON FERDINANDUS D'ALASCON.

Locumtenens Reverendi Thesaurarii Dominus Frater CAROLUS DE LA RAMA.

The record of the ceremony of the 28th of March follows immediately after the above decree, and runs thus:—

"Inchoatio Civitatis ad Montem Sancti Elmi. Die xxviii. Mensis Martii MDLXVI. fuit incepta et inchoata Civitas ad Montem Sancti Elmi cuiquidem civitati Vallettæ nomen impositum fuit faxit Deus illud faustum et felix."

There is something grand and touching in the simplicity of this brief entry, far different from the pompous verbosity so often adopted in similar cases. Doubtless the pious aspiration with which it concludes was earnestly re-echoed within the hearts of all present on the occasion.

A warm controversy has long raged in Malta in connection with these and other contemporaneous entries of the council, as to whether the name of La Valette should be spelt with one or with two *l*'s. There is no doubt that these entries show the letter doubled. It is equally clear that in the few signatures of La Valette's own handwriting it is shown single. The explanation appears probably to be that in France, of which country La Valette was a native, the name is spelt with only one *l*, whereas in Latin and Italian the consonant frequently becomes doubled, as appears to have been the practice in this case.

The foundation of the new city was not effected without considerable opposition, and for some time afterwards La Valette was frequently called upon to defend the prudence of the work he had undertaken. On the 3rd April, in the same year, the Viceroy of Sicily, Don Garcia, arrived in Malta, acccompanied by several engineers and other officers whose judgment on such matters might be considered valuable. The opinion which they expressed was that the step taken had been injudicious, and that as the project stood it was far too stupendous. That it should have been restricted to the enclosure of a much smaller space, intended only to cover the fort of St. Elmo, and should have consisted of only three bastions towards the land front, instead of the four designed by Laparelli.

These objections were overruled by La Valette, who pointed out that were the space within his proposed line of works too restricted it would be impossible to construct a town large enough for his requirements, since he not only contemplated the transfer of the convent to the new city, but also that a large portion of the inhabitants, who were now crowded into the Bourg and Senglea, for the sake of protection, should establish themselves there as well. The work now went bravely on; ditches were sunk on all sides, where the natural configuration of the rock did not form an escarp of sufficient height, and with the material thus raised the ramparts were constructed. For the first year nothing was attempted beyond the fortifications, no one being desirous of building within the city until its defence had become somewhat asssured. As already stated, the Papal engineer, Francesco Laparelli, had the supreme control of the new works, assisted in all matters of detail by Jerome Cassan, the engineer attached to the Order.

La Valette watched the progress of his favourite design with the warmest interest and the keenest anxiety. He took up his abode, in a temporary wooden structure, upon Mount Sceberras, and spent his days in the midst of his workmen. The example thus set by their chief was followed by the other members of the Order, and each one strove, by precept and example, to urge forward the progress of the work. All the leading towns of Sicily and Italy were ransacked for artificers, and at one time no less than 8,000 labourers were employed to assist the masons.

The original design had contemplated that the high ridge of rock which formed the Mount Sceberras should have been cut down to a level platform, upon which the city was to have stood, surrounded by its ramparts, formed to a great extent from the natural rock, scarped down to the water's edge. Whilst, however, this work was in progress, and before it had become far advanced, rumours reached the island of a new expedition preparing at Constantinople, of which the destination was supposed to be Malta. Selim, who had succeeded Solyman on the Ottoman throne, was a man of pacific sentiments, and too much immersed in sensuality and luxury to take any pleasure in those ambitious projects which had been so constantly cherished by his father. He ruled, however, over a nation eminently warlike in character, and amongst whom enmity to the cause of Christianity, and a craving for domination in the Mediterranean, had long become ruling passions. Unable, therefore, entirely to restrain the aggressive propensities of his subjects, Selim was compelled apparently to meet their views, by fitting out expeditions without any fixed ideas as to their ultimate destination. False alarms were thus, throughout his reign, constantly being spread, and preparations were made on all sides to resist attacks which the Ottoman sultan never seriously contemplated. The only result of the expedition which he was now preparing was to destroy the symmetry of the new city of Valetta, which, instead of being on a level platform, was, owing to this alarm, built upon the sloping ridge of the original rock, the central strip only, upon which runs the present Strada Reale, having been levelled. Hence those interminable flights of steps which in the present day weary the unfortunate pedestrian whilst toiling along under the blaze of a July sun, and which have elicited the poetical malediction of Lord Byron—

> "Adieu, ye joys of La Valette,
> Adieu, sirocco, sun and sweat—
> Adieu, ye cursed streets of stairs,
> How surely he who mounts you swears!"

La Valette had not progressed far with his new city before the want of funds began to make itself seriously felt. He had received promises of large amounts, but those pledges were very tardily fulfilled, and the funds upon which he counted from his own fraternity could only be paid in annual instalments, as the revenues of the commanderies fell due. Under the pressure of these difficulties he decided upon a measure, the successful working of which proved how high the credit of the Order for prompt and faithful payment stood in the eyes of the inhabitants. He caused a large quantity of copper money to be coined, carrying a fictitious value. These coins bore on one side the symbol of two hands clasped, and on the obverse the words "Non æs sed fides." Not money, but trust. These coins were freely taken by the artificers, and passed current throughout the island for their nominal value. The Order faithfully redeemed the trust which had been reposed in them, by promptly calling in the fictitious coinage as they received remittances from Europe, until it had been entirely withdrawn from circulation.*

The aged Grand Master continued throughout the brief remainder of his life to take the same interest in the new city which was springing up under his eyes; but he was not destined to witness its completion. One day, towards the latter end of July, in 1568, he started on a hawking expedition, in the direction of St. Paul's Bay. The sun, which at this season of the year is extremely powerful in Malta, overcame the old man, and he was brought home suffering from all the symptoms of a *coup de soleil*. A virulent fever succeeded, and after an illness of a month's duration, he died on the 21st August, 1568.

* The experiment thus successfully tried by La Valette was frequently repeated by the later Grand Masters, under the pressure of temporary impecuniosity. None used this method of raising money more freely than De Rohan, who circulated large quantities of it, probably to meet the expenditure of constructing Fort Manoel. The consequence of these successive issues of base coinage was, that when the island fell under the sway of Great Britain much of it still remained in circulation. It was redeemed by the Government at a loss of upwards of £16,000; the total nominal value of the base coinage then withdrawn being nearly £17,000, and the value of the copper only £400. It has been by some supposed that this coinage was the same as that issued by La Valette, but a little consideration must show that it would be impossible for copper coins to remain in circulation for 260 years. There exists in the museum of the Public Library a collection of dies from the mint of the Order, and several of these dies, of different dates, show the same symbol and legend as that described above; and were evidently used for the same purpose.

His body was, in the first instance, placed in the chapel attached to the Castle of St. Angelo, but four days later—namely on the 25th August—his successor having in the meantime been elected, a grand funeral *cortége* was formed for the transport of the corpse to a chapel which he had built and endowed in the city of Valetta, and which was dedicated to Our Lady of Victory. The body was placed upon the great galley of the Order, which, richly decorated and denuded of its masts, was towed in solemn procession by two other galleys, draped in black cloth. They bore at their sterns the Turkish banners which had been captured during the late siege, and which they now trailed ignominiously in the water. The body having entered the Marsa Muscetto, was there landed, and the procession being re-formed by land, it was conveyed with similar solemnities to the place of burial, where it was lowered into the grave, amidst the lamentations and regrets of all who witnessed the melancholy ceremony.

The memory of La Valette has always been held in the highest veneration by the succeeding generations of the fraternity. The Order had, during the five centuries of its existence, witnessed but few who could have the slightest claim to be compared with him in all those qualities which should distinguish the leader of so powerful an institution. In his early life he had been present at the siege of Rhodes under L'Isle Adam, and had borne an honourable part throughout that long and desperate struggle. From that hour he had followed the fortunes of his Order in all their wanderings, and had raised himself step by step through all the various dignities in their gift, until at length he was called to the supreme authority at a time of the most imminent public danger. History has shown how fully qualified he proved himself to meet the crisis. In his public character he earned a reputation and position such as has fallen to the lot of few men to achieve. Stern and inflexible in character, he was rigidly just and honourable in all his actions. Throughout his long career he proved himself the terror of evil-doers, and the implacable enemy to disorder of every description. By his fraternity he was respected and feared, more perhaps than he was loved; and his character was undeniably such as to excite the former rather than the latter feeling, in the minds of those over whom he held command. The crisis during which he was placed at the head of his Order demanded a man of iron will, and in La Valette that man was found. So long, therefore, as the necessity for such qualifications continued, he was essentially the right man in the right place, and, as such, received the willing obedience and warm admiration of his fraternity. During the last two years of his life, however, when peace appeared to have been once more assured to the convent, that austerity was no longer recognised as a virtue on his part; and at the time of his death there were not a few who, having felt the rigidness of his rule most irksome, hailed the event as a relief, and though outwardly mourning for the loss of one who had proved so brilliant an ornament to his Order, were at heart not ill-pleased to look forward to the prospect of a new chief, whose governance might prove less inflexible.

La Valette was succeeded by Peter de Monte, of the *langue* of Italy, and the Grand Admiral of the Order. This knight was as strongly impressed with the necessity of the work then going forward as La Valette had been, and he no sooner assumed the reins of government than he announced his intention of pushing forward to a speedy conclusion the labours of his predecessor. Towards the end of 1570, the fortifications being then in a very advanced state, the Papal engineer Laparelli took his departure, leaving the further prosecution of the works in the hands of Jerome Cassan, the engineer of the Order, under the control of the Commander De la Fontaine, to whom that branch of superintendence had been specially delegated.

So eager was De Monte to bring his new city into a forward condition, that although it was still in a very unfinished state even as regarded the fortifications, he determined to move the head-quarters of his convent there as soon as possible, and on the 17th March, 1571, the transfer was effected. This event was celebrated with great magnificence, and may be considered as the date when the city of Valetta was first inhabited. It was, however, even at that time far from ready for occupation, and the palace in which the Grand Master resided was as yet only a wooden structure, containing a hall and two inner rooms.

In order to encourage private building as much as possible amongst the fraternity, De Monte caused a decree to pass the council, that any knight who built a house for himself within the new city should have the privilege of its disposal by will at his death, a power which he did not possess with respect to the rest of his property; all of which, excepting one-fifth portion, merged into the public coffers at his decease. This boon greatly encouraged the constructive tendencies of the fraternity, and ere long a series of magnificent mansions, as in those days they were justly considered, commenced to rise in all directions. It had been originally intended to build a palace for the Grand Master upon the site where the Auberge de Castile now stands, but the nephew of De Monte having, at this period, erected a large pile of building in front of the Piazza San Georgio, which appeared well adapted for the purpose, it was purchased from him, and appropriated as a palace. It is, indeed, most probable that when the young De Monte commenced this work, he contemplated its purchase as a residence for his uncle, since it is hardly conceivable that he should have required so extensive and palatial a pile for his own use.

The celibacy of the knights has had a great effect upon the construction and arrangement of these houses. Whilst the reception rooms are numerous, spacious, lofty, and richly decorated, the sleeping apartments are few in number, cramped in space, and generally bear an appearance of meanness but little consistent with the grandeur that marks the remainder of the buildings. Deprived of the blessings of domesticity, the knights required none of those comforts which adorn an English home, and lavished all their care upon the apartments that were destined for the reception of their friends.

When the line of fortifications had become sufficiently advanced, the usual division of posts was made for each *langue*. The land front consisted of four bastions. That of St. Peter, on the left of the line, was made the post of Italy. St. James's bastion, containing a cavalier which dominated over all the surrounding works, was the post of France. St. John's bastion, containing a second cavalier of similar construction, the post of Provence; and St. Michael's bastion, on the right of the line, the post of Auvergne. To the right of this latter bastion, overlooking the Marsa Muscetto, was St. Andrew's bastion, which was made the post of Spain. The line of ramparts from that point to St. Elmo, facing the Marsa Muscetto, was the post of Germany, and that from St. Elmo to St. Peter's bastion, facing the Grand Harbour and completing the circuit, was made the post of Castile. St. Elmo itself was garrisoned by detachments from all the *langues*, as was also St. Angelo, on the other side of the harbour, the old posts of the different *langues* in the Bourg and Senglea being still retained by them, in addition to their new lines of defence.

Each *langue* also constructed for itself an auberge; a building in which the head of the *langue*, or Conventual Bailiff, as he was termed, resided, and where all its members, when in Malta, took their meals and conducted their business. The Auberge of Provence stands in the Strada Reale, and is now the Union Club. The Auberge of Auvergne, also in the Strada Reale lower down, is a court of justice and police office. The Auberge of France is in the Strada Mezzodi, and contains the late Commissariat (now the omnivorous Control) Department. The Auberge of Germany was pulled down many years ago, and on its site the Collegiate Church of St. Paul was erected, through the munificent liberality of Adelaide, the late Queen Dowager of England, widow of William IV. The Auberge of Aragon, which stood near that of Germany, was for many years the residence of the Bishop of Gibraltar, but has now passed temporarily into private hands. The Auberge of Italy stands at the head of the Strada Mercanti, and is now occupied by the Royal Engineers. The Auberge of Castile stands by the side of that of Italy, and is appropriated for the joint mess establishment of the Royal Artillery and Royal Engineers. This building possesses far more architectural pretensions than any of the others, its elevated site aiding materially to set off the grandeur of its general appearance. Until of late it ranked indubitably as the finest structure in Malta, but within the last few years an opera-house has been built within its immediate vicinity of a very florid style of architecture, the result of which, whatever its own merits may be, has been greatly to injure the effect of the Auberge of Castile. This opera-house is constructed upon the site set apart for the Auberge of England. From the time that that *langue* had been suppressed by Henry VIII., until the latest days of the Order's existence, hopes were from time to time entertained of its revival. Care was therefore always taken that the place of the *langue* should be preserved intact. In all elections and councils members of other *langues* were nominated to act for that of England. Similarly, when the general arrangements of the new city were mapped out, a site (and that one of the best in Valetta) was set apart and preserved religiously for the use of the English *langue*. Towards the end of the eighteenth century a new *langue*, called the Anglo-Bavarian, was created, and for their use an auberge was erected facing the Marsa Muscetto, near St. Elmo. This structure, which though extensive, is far plainer than any of the others, is now an officers' barracks.

The short rule of De Monte, which ended in 1572, was succeeded by that of John L'Eveque de la Cassiere, chief of the *langue* of Auvergne, and consequently Grand Marshal of the Order. An altercation between him and the Bishop of Malta, touching the extent of the ecclesiastical jurisdiction of the latter, led to the introduction into Malta of an accredited member of the Holy Inquisition, who, under the title of Grand Inquisitor, became ever afterwards a fruitful source of discord and uneasiness to future Grand Masters. He was originally despatched to Malta in consequence of an appeal made by La Cassiere against the bishop to Pope Gregory XIII. Differences had often before this time sprung up between the Grand Masters and the bishops of Malta. The ecclesiastical functions and powers of the latter had never been very clearly defined, and were often the cause of a collision between himself and the head of the government. The intervention of the Grand Inquisitor, however, so far from alleviating this evil, added yet another most fertile source of discord to those already existing. Instead of two, there were now three heads in the island, and although both bishop and inquisitor nominally acknowledged the supremacy of the Grand Master, yet by their acts they proved that that acknowledgment was only nominal.

At the time when this new ecclesiastical authority was first despatched to Malta, the Pope, at the request of the council, had directed that he was not to act independently, but that in all matters affecting church discipline a tribunal was to be formed, in which he was to be associated with the Grand Master, the Vice-Chancellor, the Bishop, and the Prior of the Church. It was not long, however, before the ambition of the Grand Inquisitor, supported as he was by the Pope, gradually usurped for himself an independent and separate tribunal within the island. In order to extend his authority and to free it from all control on the part of the Grand Master, the Inquisitor adopted the following method:—Any Maltese who desired to free himself from his allegiance to the Grand Master, was given a patent, issued from the office of the Inquisitor, by virtue of which he became a direct subject of the Inquisition, and was no longer liable to any of the secular tribunals of the island. The Bishop of Malta, in his turn, gradually adopted a similar measure, and by a simple tonsure freed even laymen from all control but his own. These abuses did not, of course, spring into full vigour at once, but they gradually became so glaring that it appeared as though the Grand Master would eventually lose all authority in the island, over which he was the nominal sovereign.

It was during the rule of La Cassiere that the church of St. John the Baptist was built in the new city of Valetta, and became the conventual church of the Order. The expense of its construction was entirely defrayed by La Cassiere out of his magisterial revenues, and he further endowed it with an annuity of a thousand crowns. By a decree of the first Chapter General held after the erection of this church, a chapel was assigned within its precincts to each *langue*. The chapels form the aisles of the church, and are filled with monuments to the most distinguished members of the several *langues*. The pavement of the entire church is one of the most beautiful specimens of mosaic work in Europe, and is composed of a succession of monumental records to the memory of the most celebrated amongst the Bailiffs, Grand Crosses, and Commanders. This pavement glistens with an endless variety of coloured marbles, representing the emblazonment of the arms of the illustrious deceased; jasper, agate, and other similar valuable stones being plentifully intermixed.

The treasury of the church was enriched with numerous costly gifts in gold and silver, the quinquennial offerings of the Grand Master and other leading dignitaries. In addition to the magnificent reliquary enclosing the hand of St. John, there were statues in solid silver of the twelve Apostles; an exquisite gold cup presented by Henry VIII. to L'Isle Adam; the sword and poniard given to La Valette by Philip of Spain; numberless crosses and censers in gold and silver, together with several gigantic candelabra of the latter metal. The Chapel of the Virgin was lighted with a lamp of solid gold suspended by a ponderous gold chain, and several of the altars were richly decorated in the same costly manner. Beneath the church La Cassiere caused a crypt to be constructed, into which he transferred the bodies of L'Isle Adam and La Valette, and it is in that vault that their venerated remains now rest beneath two handsome monuments erected by himself to their memories. It was his intention, in constructing this crypt, that his own corpse should lie by the side of those heroes who had reflected so much glory on the title of Grand Master. His death, however, at Rome, whither he had been called by the Pope, seemed at first to render it likely that his wish would remain unfulfilled; ultimately it was decided to transport the corpse to Malta for interment in the site originally designed for it by himself. His heart, however, was first removed and embalmed, and is still preserved at Rome.

At the foot of the tomb of La Valette lies Oliver Starkey, his faithful secretary; the last Englishman who can be said to have regularly held the dignities of that *langue*, viz: the Turcopoliership and the Bailiwick of the Eagle. The Latin inscription on the tomb of La Valette is from the pen of Starkey.

> "Ille Asiæ Libiæque pavor tutelaque quondam
> Europæ, et domitis sæva per anna Getis
> Primus in hac alma quam condidit urbe sepultus
> Valetta æterno dignus honore jacet."

# CHAPTER VII.

Arrival of the Jesuits—Ecclesiastical Disputes—Commencement of the Floriana Enceinte—The Margarita Lines—Naval Victory in the Dardanelles—Visit of the English Fleet—The Cottonera Lines—Lower St. Elmo—Fort Ricasoli—Fort Manoel—Conspiracy among the Slaves—Fort Tigné.

AFTER the completion of the city of Valetta and its enceinte, nothing of much interest occurred during the remainder of the century. The death of Hugh de Verdala, the successor of La Cassiere in 1595, brought to a close an epoch in the existence of the Order which had been marked by a brilliant succession of glorious deeds. From the year 1476, when Peter d'Aubusson was first called to the supreme dignity, till the death of Verdala in the last decade of the sixteenth century, the Order had maintained itself with a reputation and prosperity such as, in spite of all its glorious achievements, it had never previously attained. Within that time it had twice successfully resisted the whole strength of the Ottoman Empire, and even on the third occasion, though driven from the Island of Rhodes, they had gained for themselves a meed of glory almost as ample as though they had remained victors in the strife. During this golden period of their career they had witnessed the rule of three chiefs whose names have descended to posterity as amongst the noblest heroes which the age has produced. History cannot, during that century, point to any who have attained greater glory than has attached itself to the illustrious triumvirate of the Hospital, Peter d'Aubusson, Villiers L'Isle Adam, and John de la Valette. That age had, however, now passed away, and though during the two centuries through which the Order yet struggled, they could boast of many a chief whose talents in the council chamber, and whose skill in administration were of no mean order, still the vigour of their former days was evidently lost, and the deeds of their latter time will bear no comparison with those that had gone before.

It was during the reign of Verdala that the Bishop of Malta, in órder to strengthen his power, and to gain additional support in the constant warfare which he maintained against the authority of the Grand Master, summoned the Jesuits to Malta, where they established themselves, and in their turn endeavoured to form a separate jurisdiction of their own. Malta was, from this time, doomed to witness the extraordinary spectacle of four distinct religious powers— the Grand Master, the Bishop, the Grand Inquisitor, and the Jesuits, a source of endless dispute and jealousy. Pope Gregory XIII. had already decreed that the offices of Bishop of Malta and of Prior of the Church were to be held exclusively by conventual chaplains. As most of these chaplains were Maltese, and as members of this nation had no means of attaining to the dignities monopolized by the Knights, this decree was received by them with great favour, as it reserved to their own body two of the leading offices in the gift of the fraternity.

The seventeenth century opened with the accession of Alof de Vignacourt to the dignity of fifty-second Grand

Master. This knight, at the age of seventeen years, had joined the ranks of the fraternity in 1564, at the time when they were preparing for the attack of the Turks, and in the following year he passed through all the dangers and fatigues of the siege of Malta. As the length of his services increased he rose in dignity until he had attained the post of Grand Hospitaller, and in 1601 he was raised to the then vacant office of Grand Master.

The rule of Vignacourt, like that of several of his predecessors, was disturbed by the pretensions of the Bishop of Malta. This dignitary, whose name was Cagliares, during one of his numerous disputes with the Grand Master and council, visited Rome to enforce his pretensions, and appointed a suffragan to maintain the interests of his see during his absence. The arrogance of this deputy far exceeded even that of his superior, and some of the more youthful and hot-headed amongst the knights were unable to restrain their indignation at the intolerable assumption of his conduct. A band of these malcontents attacked the Bishop's palace by night, threatening to throw the offending ecclesiastic into the Marsa Muscetto, and it was with no little difficulty that Vignacourt was able to rescue him out of their hands. He despatched the suffragan to Rome with a complaint of his conduct, addressed to Paul V.; but the Pope, who was bent on supporting the clergy in their pretensions against the Grand Master, took a very high tone in the matter. He acquitted the bishop's nominee from all blame, and called upon the Grand Master and council, under pain of his anathema, to make due reparation for the indignities to which he had been subjected. Resistance was totally in vain. Vignacourt was compelled to submit, and to restore the suffragan to his position and dignities. Similar scenes occurred with the Grand Inquisitor, and these incessant disputes rendered the office of Grand Master by no means a bed of roses.

The name of Vignacourt has, in Malta, become inseparably connected with the aqueduct which he caused to be constructed in the island. Destitute as the city of Valetta and those on the other side of the harbour are of all natural springs, the inhabitants were, before Vignacourt's time, compelled to depend for their water supply entirely upon tanks, and, in the event of a dry spring, were sorely distressed during the following summer. To obviate this evil, Vignacourt constructed a very fine aqueduct, connecting the city of Valetta with a spring of water in the Bengemma Hills, in the vicinity of the Citta Notabile. This aqueduct, which is upwards of nine miles in length, carries the water into every part of the city, and supplies the fountains which have been erected in different convenient situations. A worthier monument this, and a nobler memorial than the proudest trophy of war or the most costly sculptured tomb. The gratitude of posterity will recall the memory of Vignacourt so long as Valetta stands, as the founder of one of the most useful and enduring works which that city possesses.

In 1623, Antoine de Paule, Grand Prior of St. Gilles, was elected Grand Master. His rule is marked by the fact that in it was held the last Chapter General of the Order, until the close of the eighteenth century. The unpopularity of these great councils had been constantly augmenting, and the difficulty of maintaining the magisterial authority within their jurisdiction so great, that no Grand Master after De Paule ventured to summon into existence a council in which he himself had so little weight and influence. Upon this occasion the Pope had insisted that the Grand Inquisitor should take his seat as president of the Chapter. De Paule and his council remonstrated that it was diametrically opposed to the constitution of their Order that a stranger should assume the post of president in their chief assembly, and that the community at large would never tolerate the intrusion. The Pope, however, was obstinate, and insisted upon enforcing the nomination. The aged Grand Master, who had not sufficient energy to support him in a broil with the court of Rome, yielded the point without further remonstrance; and as it was highly probable that the younger knights would, by some violent action, resent the intrusion thus forced upon them, he sent the majority of them away from the island on a cruise, and held the chapter during their absence. The statutes of the Order were all revised during this session, and the laws, as thus amended, remained the code in force up to the period of its dissolution.

Much dissatisfaction was caused by the repeated interference of the Pope with the patronage of the *langue* of Italy. Vacancies were bestowed by him on his own relations and dependents, without regard to the claims of seniority or the wishes of the council. The Italian knights became so discontented at this misappropriation that they broke out into mutiny, refusing to perform any of their duties. Many abandoned Malta, and, returning to their homes, threw-off the habit of the Order in disgust.

Throughout the reign of De Paule, naval expeditions on a small scale continued to be carried on against isolated points in the Turkish dominions; more for the sake of the plunder to be obtained, than with a view to enfeebling the power of their enemies. From this low point of view they were very successful, and the influx of wealth consequent on the many rich prizes they annually seized, raised the island of Malta to a position of opulence and commercial importance which for centuries it had not known.

In the year 1632, a census was held of its population, and the numbers then recorded as present in the island amounted to 51,750 souls. When L'Isle Adam a century previously had first established his convent there, the population barely exceeded 17,000; they had consequently tripled in numbers during that time, in spite of the fearful losses entailed during the siege under La Valette.

In 1635 the Grand Master, desirous of making effectual preparations to resist a rumoured invasion of the Turks, called in an Italian engineer named Floriani, to inspect the fortifications, and to suggest such additions as he might consider necessary to place them in a state of better defence. On the 17th of October in that same year, Floriani presented to the council a project for a new enceinte to enclose a considerable space beyond the Valetta front; the proposed new line running across the peninsula of Mount Sceberras nearly at the point of its junction with the main land. This report was prefaced with a long list of the defects under which he considered the defences of Valetta laboured, concluding with the remark that although he had been engaged during his professional career in the fortification of many towns, and had consequently obtained a considerable amount of experience in the art, still he did not consider himself gifted with such high talents as would enable him to convert a bad work into a good one, and that he was compelled therefore, to suggest the enclosure of the first line within a second, whose trace should be more in accordance with his ideas of perfection.

The council were taken completely by surprise at this

unlooked-for report; they had been accustomed to regard the enceinte of Valetta, with its deep ditch and stupendous escarp, as a most powerful front; the whole of the stone for the city having been quarried there until it had attained a magnitude greater than that of any artificial ditch in Europe. They could not conceive that a work which they had always looked upon with such great favour could in reality be so defective as was reported by Floriani, and they therefore nominated a commission to investigate the matter, and to report upon the new project designed by that engineer.

The opinion of the commission was diametrically opposed to that of Floriani; they considered that the existing landfront of Valetta was excellent, and only required a few additions to render it perfect; whilst at the same time they found every possible fault with the proposed new enceinte. Amongst other objections, they urged that whilst the centre of the trace was too strongly fortified, its flanks were extremely weak, and exposed to fire from the neighbouring heights.

Rendered uncertain as to what steps he should take in this diversity of opinion, De Paule, who entertained the highest possible regard for the talent and experience of Floriani, determined on despatching an envoy to the various courts of Italy, with plans of the existing works and proposed additions, in order that he should consult the leading engineers of that country, and collect their various opinions on the matter. The Chevalier de Vertoua was selected for this office. He was expressly directed to visit the headquarters of the rival armies of France and Spain, who were at that time carrying on war in Piedmont. From this mission, De Verteua returned on the 25th February, 1636, and reported to the council that the general opinion of the engineers he had consulted was decidedly antagonistic to the new project, and that they all preferred the addition of some fresh works to the existing enceinte.

Notwithstanding all these unfavourable reports, the weight of Floriani's influence with the Grand Master was so great, that his project was sanctioned, and commenced during the course of the year 1636. It is uncertain whether De Paule was still alive at the time, as he died on the 10th of June, 1636. He was succeeded by Paul Lascaris, under whose rule the work was prosecuted with great vigour for two years, during which period a large amount of money was expended, and the new enceinte much advanced.

In 1638 an ecclesiastic named Fiorenzola, a monk of the Order of St. Augustin, visited Malta. Strange as it may seem for so holy a man to have excelled in the art of fortification, it is nevertheless the fact that the reverend father's talent in that line had gained him a high reputation, and that his engineering labours materially aided him in attaining the dignity of a cardinal, to which he was ultimately raised. The report of Father Fiorenzola upon the fortifications, compiled at the urgent request of the Grand Master, was presented on the 28th September, 1638. He highly commended the original trace of Valetta, which he considered well adapted to the site, and most judiciously arranged. The only suggestion which he made to increase the strength of this portion of the work was the addition of three ravelins to its curtains; after which, he declared that the front might be considered impregnable. On the other hand, he objected entirely to the new work then progressing in the suburb, and already known as the Floriana, in honour of its designer. He considered that this enclosure occupied a soil so rocky, that it could never have been made use of by an enemy to construct approaches to the place, whereas the new work would, if captured, be in itself a material assistance to the besiegers in providing them with cover. He also made the same objection that others had previously put forward, viz.: that the centre of the line was encumbered with a quantity of useless work, whilst the flanks were too weak, and their bastions too acute. He wound up his remarks on this head by stating that although a sum of 80,000 scudi had been already expended, it would be far better at once to destroy the work than to spend double that amount to complete it.

The locality which Fiorenzola considered the most dangerous, and consequently the most vital point to secure, was the hill of Sta. Margarita, which dominated over Vittoriosa, and rendered its defence a matter of great difficulty. The harbour itself lay completely open to fire from this point, which, when occupied by an enemy, would prevent the retention of the smallest craft by the garrison; and thus Valetta, finding itself cut off from all succour, would not hold out long, but would yield without difficulty from the simple adoption of a blockade. A project was submitted by him for the occupation of these heights by an enceinte, which should bring them within the limits of the defences of Vittoriosa. This new design met with very general approval on all sides; the Floriana was at once discontinued, and the works on the Margarita hill commenced. Three bastions, with their connecting curtains, were traced and completed, after which, from want of funds, no further progress was made till the year 1716.

The Chevalier de Verteua, who, in obedience to his instructions, had visited all the courts of Italy, had, amongst other places, presented himself at that of the Grand Duke of Tuscany, and after minutely informing him of the existing state of the fortifications and of the new project of Colonel Floriani, had requested his advice and that of his leading engineers on the subject. No answer was given to this request until the year 1639, when the Grand Duke wrote to Lascaris, sending him a plan of what he considered the most advantageous method of strengthening the Valetta front. This design was compiled from the joint suggestions of John Medici, Marquis of St. Angelo, his general of artillery; of Francis Bracelli, commander of the forces at Leghorn; and of Captain Contagallina, a man of very high reputation as a soldier. The principal feature in this design was the addition of four large counterguards to the Valetta bastions, which, by the size of their flanks, should remedy the imperfection of those in the main line. These were at once commenced in accordance with the plan forwarded, and were for many years known as the counterguards of the Marquis of St. Angelo.

In the following year, viz., 1640, that officer paid a visit to Malta, to inspect the works and suggest improvements. He urged that the lines commenced by Cardinal Fiorenzola should be at once completed, enclosing Burmola in its enceinte, and that the point of Corso should be occupied with a fort, of which he submitted a trace. The main features of his design were adopted when the fort was built in 1670.

Whilst these works were being carried on, the Order were continuing their naval operations against the Turks. In 1638, an action was fought between six of their galleys and three large Turkish men-of-war, which were engaged in convoying a fleet of merchant-ships to Tripoli. In this battle the knights were completely victorious, and captured the whole Turkish flotilla, including the men-of-war. In 1640, six Barbary pirates were seized in the harbour of

Goletta by the general of the galleys; and in 1644, three galleys, under Piancourt, overcame a large and formidable galleon, after a desperate conflict. In this affair the Turks lost 600 men, and amongst the captives was a sultana from the imperial seraglio, who was then on a pilgrimage to Mecca. This loss so incensed the sultan that he despatched a herald to Malta, threatening an immediate attack.

Lascaris upon this took prompt measures to ensure the security of the island. Knights were summoned from all quarters to assist in the defence, and volunteers in great numbers also flocked to the island, anxious to share in the glory of a second siege. Among these was the Count D'Arpajou, who brought at his own expense a reinforcement of 2,000 men. The Order were so grateful for this munificent aid that they elected the count commander-in-chief over all the forces in the island, a post hitherto always held by the Grand Marshal. D'Arpajou at once proposed the resumption and speedy completion of the Floriana, which had been for some time discontinued.

The Count de Pagan, who arrived in Malta at the same time, made a lengthened report to the Grand Master, in the course of which he suggested sundry improvements to the works. As regarded the Valetta front, he deemed that its principal defect was the smallness of the flanks and their great height, which prevented a large portion of the ditch from being seen. This evil he proposed to remedy by providing additional flanks on a lower level, and retiring them from view by means of orillons or rounded flanks, to be thrown forward in their front. The suggestion was carried into effect, and left the trace of the Valetta front very much what it now is. In order to remedy the principal defect of the Floriana, which having been traced on a straight line was very badly flanked at its extremities, and much exposed to the enemy's batteries, particularly on the side of the Marsa Muscetto, he was of opinion that the curtains on either side of the centre bastion should be retrenched, so as better to cover the ground and at the same time to gain a flank from the interior. He also suggested that the Margarita lines should be forthwith completed, and that their trace should be so far extended as to comprise the whole of Burmola within the enceinte, in order that they should completely cover the harbour from the heights, and also provide a place of shelter for the inhabitants of the surrounding country in a time of danger. The Chevalier de Clerville, one of the leading engineers of the King of France, coincided with the Count de Pagan in his opinion, but further suggested the construction of a horn-work outside the Porta Reale, which should see the ground on either side. He also proposed to add some redoubts to the interior of the Floriana. The Chevalier Palavicini urged the necessity of the occupation of the point of land at the entrance of the grand harbour, opposite Point Dragut, called the Point of Corso, a project for which had been already submitted by the Marquis of St. Angelo.

It would have been imagined that after so many reports had been made and so much trouble taken to obtain the opinion and advice of the leading engineers of Europe, the works would have been prosecuted with vigour; but such was far from being the case, for the Turks having turned their arms against the island of Candia, and Malta appearing no longer directly menaced with invasion, the convent relapsed into tranquillity, and no further steps were taken to increase their security. The naval war with Turkey was, however, by no means suspended, and assistance was promptly rendered to the Venetians to aid in their defence of Candia. Naval combats constantly occurred, in which the superiority of the knights over their opponents was usually very decided. In 1656 an engagement of greater importance than usual took place between the combined fleets of Venice and Malta, on the one side, and that of the Turks on the other. In a contemporary newspaper, published in London, called the *Mercurius Politicus*, there is the following graphic account of this action. It runs as follows:—

"London, September 1656, from Venice, August 15, *stili novo*.—The particulars of our last victory are now brought hither by the Sieur Lazaro Mocenigo, who entred here on the 1st of this month, in a Turkish galley which was taken from those infidels, and all the men in her had turbans on their heads. At his arrivall the people declared an extraordinary joy. All the shops were shut up, and the duke, accompanied by the senators, went and sang 'Te Deum,' and the ringing of bells continued till next day in all churches. On the third day a solemn mass was celebrated by the duke and senators in the church of St. Marke, where all the ambassadors of princes were present. And that the rejoycing might extend to the very prisons, the senate took order for the releasing of all persons imprisoned for debt, and some of the banditi were also set at liberty.

"In the meantime, the said Sieur Mocenigo, who had contributed so much of prudence and courage to the gaining of this victory, had first the honour of knighthood conferred upon him by the senate, with a chain of gold 2000 crownes value, and then was declared generallissimo, in the room of the late slain Lorenzo Marcello, in memory of whom it is ordered there be a publick service celebrated next week at the publick charge.

## Naval Battle in the Dardanelles. 183

"Now that so renowned a victory may in some measure be known, take the following relation :—

"*A particular relation of the manner of the late victory obtained by the Venetians against the Turks.*

"After the Venetian fleet had made a month's stay at the mouth of the Dardanelles, to wait for and fight the enemy, in the meanewhile, arived the squadron of Malta, which consisted of seven galleys. On the 23rd of June last past, the Captain Bassa appeared in sight of the castles; his fleet consisted of twenty-eight great ships, sixty galleys, nine galeasses, and other small vessels.

"The navy of the republick was composed of twenty-eight great ships, twenty-four galleys, and seven galeasses, to which joyned (as was said before) the galleys of Malta, commanded by the Lord Prior of Roccelia. The navy of the republick kept in the narrowest part of the channel, so that the Turks could not come forth without accepting the battel which was offered.

"At the beginning the Captain Bassa raised two batteries upon land on both sides the river, the one on the part of Natolia, the other on the part of Grecia; thinking thereby to oblige our ships and galeasses to forsake their station, and so facilitate their own going forth. The courage of the Venetian resisting their shot with undaunted boldness, rendered the advantage they had taken unprofitable; whereupon the Captain Bassa, who had express order to attempt going out, upon the 26th of the same month, in the morning, favoured with a pleasant north wind, made all his greatest ships to advance in good order; but (whether they durst not expose themselves, or for what other reason is not known) they withdrew behind the point of Barbiera, and thither also the Captain Bassa repaired with his galleys.

"About ten of the clock it pleased God to send a small north-west wind, which occasioned the Venetian navy to move, and the honorable Eleazer Mocenigo (who having finished the charge of a captain of a galley, would needs continue with the fleet as a volunteer, and commanded the left wing) found means to advance with the *Sultana of St. Marke*, wherein he was, and passing beyond the Turkish fleet, endeavoured to hinder its retreat, keeping the mouth of the channel, and fighting valiantly.

"The battel being thus begun, the Captain-general, Lorenzo Marcello, accompanied with the General of Malta, came up, intermingling with the rest of the Venetian commanders and vessels, fell to it *pel mel*. After the Turks had used their utmost endeavours to avoid the fight, being hemmed in by the Venetian fleet, and having no place left to escape, they were forced to fight with the more eagerness because they had lost all hope of making a retreat, and so commended their safety to the conflict; whereby they gave means to the Venetians the more to exalt their triumph and glory over their enemies, all the enemy being totally routed by the sword, by fire, and by water, the Captain Bassa only saving himself with fourteen galleys; which hath crowned the republick with one of the greatest victories that ever was heard of in former times.

"The number of the enemies dead cannot be known nor discovered among so many ships and galleys taken and consumed by fire and water. About the shore there were seen huge heaps of dead bodies, and in the bay of a certain little valley there appeared so great a quantity of carcasses that it caused horror in the beholders.

"The number of Christian slaves freed on this occasion is near upon five thousand. That of the Venetian's men killed and wounded doth not amount to three hundred, which makes the victory memorable to all ages.

"The battel lasted from ten a clock in the morning until night, but the burning of the greatest part of the enemies fleet continued for two daies and two nights; on the first whereof the Venetians were forced to maintaine the fight, to subdue some Turkish vessels which stood out upon defence.

"The Venetians having reserved some of the enemies ships of all sorts, in memory of the successe, beside eleven which those of Malta had taken, it was resolved upon by the Venetian commanders to burn the rest, to free themselves from the trouble of sailing with so numerous a fleet, and to keep their owne in readiness for all attempts.

"Three Venetian ships were burnt, two in the fight, and one by some other accident, which is not well known, and their fleet received no other damage.

"The only thing to be deplored in this successe was the losse of the Captain-generall Marcello, who was killed with a cannon shot, and four men more, who were next to him, after that, with his own galley, he had subdued a potent sultana, and (by the grace of God) seen the Turkish fleet in confusion, dispersed, defeated, and, by consequence, the great victory secured, and her upon the point of surprising another sultana. His soule hath received her reward in heaven, and his name will live with perpetuall glory in the memory of the world.

"Eleazer Mocenigo, by a new musquet shot, lost one of his eies, as he was at first attempting to prevent the Turks' passage; notwithstanding which hee never failed to doe great things the whole time of the conflict.

"The valour, courage, and magnanimity wherewith all the Venetians and Malteses did behave themselves on this occasion may better be understood by the action than by discourse."

No action of greater importance than this had occurred since the memorable day of Lepanto; and the Maltese galleys, although not numerous, appear to have done their duty nobly on the occasion, as the eleven vessels captured by them, and borne off in triumph to Malta, amply testify.*

Whilst these maritime successes were attesting the naval superiority of the Order of St. John, their convent still remained the scene of internal discord. The Inquisitor, the Bishop, and the Jesuits all sought their own advancement, at the sacrifice of the authority of the Grand Master. The embroilment with the Jesuits gradually culminated into an

* The "Lord Prior of Roccelia," alluded to as in command of the seven Maltese galleys, was Gregory Caraffa, Prior of La Rocella, a member of the Italian *langue*. He was in the year 1680 elected to the Grand Mastership, being the first Italian knight who had been raised to the supreme dignity for a period of 130 years. The fame which he had acquired in this action, doubtless, was the cause of his subsequent elevation. There still exists in the Auberge d'Italie a tablet commemorative of the action, and bearing the following inscription:—

"D. O. M.

"Divoq Joanni Sacræ Ierosolymitanæ Militiæ Patrono ob gloriosam a Venetis de Turcica classe ad Dardanorum ora reportatam victoriam consilio opera et fælici ausu fris D. Gregorii Carafæ, Roccellæ Prioris, et septem Melitentium triremium ducis. Qui primus in hostes invectus, ita eos deterruit ac profligavit ut ipsam etiam Imperatoriam nisi ejus ratis scopulo hæsisset in suam potestatem redegisset vicit tamen et captis ex adversariis præter tres maiores octo triremibus aliis minoribus innumerisq. tormentis æneis tum sexaginta, supra trecentos Turcis in servitutem redactis, et ex Christianis bismille ac sex centis libertati donatis ad suos triumphantis in morem reversus vivit vivetq.

"Serenissimæ Reipublicæ et Ierosolymitanæ Religionis benemerentissimus ac suæ familiæ, decus immortale in tantæ rei memoriam venerabilis lingua Italica uno corde multiplici nomine donat dicat consecrat Anno Domi. MDCLVI."

open breach. The quarrel originated in the frolic of some young knights, who, during the carnival of 1639, disguised themselves in the habit of Jesuits, and in that garb were guilty of many scandalous disorders in the town. The reverend fathers, irate at this profanation of their distinguishing costume, complained bitterly to the Grand Master, who caused the offending members to be thrown into prison. Public feeling had, however, become gradually so excited against the disciples of Loyola that this punishment, justly merited as it was, was very ill-received. A tumult arose, the culprits were released, and the Jesuits' college pillaged. The insurgents were so exasperated, and were so strong in numbers, that the expulsion of the Jesuits was decreed, and they were compelled to leave the island.

Malta is indebted to Lascaris for the very fine public library, which he established in 1650, and which gradually increased until it attained proportions which ranked it with the finest libraries in Europe. This augmentation was the result of a very wise decree, that at a knight's death his books should not be sold with the rest of his property, for the benefit of the treasury, but should be forwarded to the public library.

Throughout the rule of Lascaris, as also through those of his three successors, the war between the Turks and Venetians continued to rage in Candia, and the knights maintained their support, both by sea and land. The Turks, however, gradually attained the upper hand, and when, in 1663, Nicholas Cottoner assumed the dignity vacant by the death of his brother Raphael, the defence of Candia had assumed a most unfavourable aspect. The closing action of the war was the siege of the capital, which withstood for twenty-seven months the efforts of the Turks. The reputation for valour which the knights of St. John had established of old, did not suffer from their conduct during this memorable siege. The commandant, Morosini, wrote in the highest terms of them to his government, and Brussoni, in his "Guerra dei Turchi," also states, "Amongst the objects that they seemed most to admire was the Grand Master of Malta, and whenever he passed they viewed him with extraordinary veneration; and looking on St. Andrew's Gate, which his knights had defended, they wondered, and expressed to each other their high respect." The dignitary here alluded to must have been the knight in command of the contingent of the Order, as Cottoner did not appear in person in Candia. The island capitulated to the Turks on the 6th September, 1669, and has ever since remained in their hands.

Although all connection between the kingdom of England and the Order of Malta had ceased for upwards of a century, and the *langue* itself had been abolished, still a constant correspondence appears to have taken place on matters connected with the navigation of the Mediterranean between Charles II. and the Grand Master. Charles had despatched thither a squadron under the command of Sir John Narbrough, and a dispute arose upon the subject of salutes, the Order being unwilling to pay that compliment to the British flag. A most amusing narrative of this expedition was published at the time in the form of a diary, by the Rev. Henry Teonge, chaplain on board H.M.S. *Assistance*, one of Narbrough's squadron. That the matter was amicably arranged, may be gathered from the following extracts from Teonge's diary:—

"August 1st, 1675. This morn wee com near Malta. Before wee com to the cytty a boate with the Malteese flagg in it coms to us to know whence we cam. Wee told them from England. They asked if wee had a bill of health for prattick, viz., entertaynment. Our captain told them he had no bill but what was in his guns' mouths. Wee cam on and anchored in the harbour, betweene the old towne and the new, about nine of the clock; but must wait the governour's leasure to have leave to com on shoare, which was detarded because our captain would not salute the cytty except they would retaliate. At last cam the consull with his attendants to our ship (but would not come on board till our captain had been on shoare) to tell us that we had leave to com on shoare six or eight or ten at a time, and might have anything that was there to be had, with a promise to accept our salute kindly. Whereupon our captain tooke a glass of sack and drunk a health to King Charles, and fyred seven gunns; the cytty gave us five againe, which was more than they had don to all our men-of-warr that cam thither before.

"**August** 2nd, 1675. This cytty is compassed almost cleane **round with** the sea, which makes severall safe harbours for **hundreds** of shipps. The people are generally extremely courteouse, but especially to the English. A man cannot demonstrate all their excellencys and ingenuitys. Let it suffice to say thus much of this place, viz.: Had a man no other business to invite him, yet it were sufficiently worth a man's cost and paines to make a voyage out of England on purpose to see that noble cytty of Malta and their works and fortifications about it. Several of their knights and cavaliers came on board us, six at one time, men of sufficient courage and friendly carriage, wishing us good successe in our voyage, with whom I had much discourse, I being the only entertainer because I could speak Latine, for which I was highly esteemed, and much invited on shoare again.

"August 3rd. This morning a boate of ladys with their musick to our ship's syd, and bottles of wine with them.

They went severall times about our ship, and sang several songs very sweetly : very rich in habitt and very courteous in behaviour, but would not come on board, though invited ; but having taken their friscs, returned as they cam. After them cam in a boat four fryars, and cam round about our ship, puld off their hatts and capps, saluted us with congjes, and departed. After them cam a boat of musitians, played severall lessons as they rowed gently round about us, and went their way.

"August 4th. This morning our captain was invited to dine with the Grand Master, which hindered our departure. In the meantime wee have severall of the Malteese com to visit us, all extremely courteous. And now wee are preparing to sail for Trypoly. *Deus vortat bene.*

> " Thus wee, the *Assistance*, and the new Sattee,
> Doe steare our course poynt blanke for Trypoly ;
> Our ship new rigged, well stored with pigg and ghoose—a
> Henns, ducks, and turkeys, and wine called Syracoosa."

A subsequent entry dated in the following year shows that eventually the Grand Master saluted the British flag to the heart's content of the chaplain.

" February 11th, 1676. Sir John Narbrough cam in from Trypoly, and four more ships with him. The noble Maltcese salute him with forty-five guns. He answered them with so many that I could not count them; and what with our salutes and his answers there was nothing but fyre and smoake for almost two hours."

This civility on the part of the Order of St. John and the Maltese towards the fleet of Sir John Narbrough was probably due to the fact, that the expedition to Tripoli alluded to in the above quaint stanza ended in the liberation of a large body of Christian slaves, amongst whom were fifty knights.

The conclusion of the siege of Candia left the Turks at liberty to pursue their aggressions in other quarters; and as the Order of St. John had during the war rendered the most valuable assistance to the Venetians, Cottoner commenced to fear that his island would now be called upon to bear the brunt of the Sultan's indignation. With a view, therefore, to adding further security to the convent, and also, probably, in the hope of immortalizing his name by a stupendous work, he proposed the construction of a line of great extent, which should secure the harbours, strengthen the forts of Vittoriosa and Isola, and give an extensive place of shelter for the inhabitants of the country districts in the event of a descent. He called in Count Valperga, then the chief engineer to the Duke of Savoy, to consult with him upon his new design, and also to superintend the completion of the other unfinished works, more especially the Floriana front, which was still in a very imperfect state.

Valperga arrived in Malta on the 9th of February, 1670, and having carefully examined the site of the two towns, the heights of Sta. Margarita, and the surrounding country, formed the opinion that the security of the harbour imperatively demanded the entire occupation of those heights. He produced, therefore, a plan not very different from that of Cardinal Fiorenzola, but more extended, in which, having made use of that part already commenced, he added such portions as should connect the fronts of Isola and Vittoriosa. This project was, however, by no means sufficiently stupendous to satisfy the magnificent ideas of the Grand Master, who was not to be contented merely with the completion of a work that had been designed by his predecessors. He insisted upon the production of some new design on a far more extended scale. Thus urged, Valperga ere long presented his eminence with a second which, enclosing the whole of the Margarita lines within its circuit, rested on the extremities of the ditches of Isola and Vittoriosa. This trace was to consist of eight large bastions and two demi-bastions, forming together an enceinte not far short of five thousand yards in length.

This project was precisely suited to the taste of the Grand Master. The other members of the convent were, however, by no means so cordial in the matter, and a very strong feeling of dissent speedily manifested itself. Cottoner was possessed of sufficient influence in the council to carry his point in spite of opposition; and the construction of the new lines being decided on to the exclusion of all other work, the Grand Master laid the first stone in the bastion of St. Nicholas on the 28th of August, 1670, with much pomp and ceremony.

Cottoner had no sooner inaugurated the new fortification than he found himself opposed by almost the entire engineering talent of Europe. Criticisms of all kinds were showered without mercy on the design. It was stated that the site was not sufficiently level for the construction of a regular fortification of so great an extent; that in endeavouring to carry out this extreme regularity of design some portions became much weaker than others; that the lines of defence were too short, consequently the bastions too numerous, and that the ditches, being traced parallel to the ramparts, prevented their being properly seen; also that the space included within the lines was very small compared to the great length of the work, and that the Coradin hill should have been included. This latter criticism appears so self-evident that it seems strange it should have been overlooked, when a slight extension of the trace would have easily brought it within the circuit. There exists in the palace at Valetta a picture of Cottoner, painted during his lifetime, in which he is represented holding in his hand a plan of his new lines; and in this plan the works are made to embrace the Coradin hill. This evidence, although not conclusive, seems to render it probable that at one time it had been intended to include that dominant point.

Notwithstanding the violent opposition which his favourite design had encountered, Cottoner was not to be deterred from its prosecution, and an enormous outlay was made on the rising works. Four commissaries were appointed, who were charged with the responsibility of providing everything requisite for carrying on the work with vigour. For their accommodation houses were built in the gorges of the bastions, so that they should be enabled to remain continually on the works. All the artificers in the island were assembled on the spot, and others brought over from the neighbouring seaports; bakeries and cisterns were established for their convenience, and every effort was made to secure the utmost promptitude in the prosecution of the undertaking. For ten years the works were carried forward under the eye of the Grand Master, who felt his honour intimately bound up with the fortification to which he had given his name; and during this time a vast expenditure was incurred. At his death, which took place in 1680, the ramparts had throughout been raised to the height of the cordon; none of the outworks, however, had been commenced. By this time the treasury had become almost exhausted, and his successor, Gregory Carraffa, who had always been opposed to the project, gave directions that its further prosecution should be suspended.

Valperga had not contented himself with this work only. He had at the same time designed a horn-work, enclosed within a crown-work, beyond the front of Floriana; a fort to occupy the point of Corso, and another for the island in the Marsa Muscetto. The horn and crown works were constructed in 1682, and the fort on the point of Corso in 1670. The latter was erected mainly at the expense of the Chevalier Francesco Ricasoli, who contributed the sum of 30,000 scudi for that purpose. The Grand Master in consequence decreed that, in commemoration of this munificence, and to stimulate others to similar acts, the fort should take the name of its founder. It has therefore been always since known as Fort Ricasoli. Although this work was executed from the plans of Valperga, yet, as that engineer followed closely the trace originally proposed by the Marquis of St. Angelo, the merits and defects of the design must be attributed to the latter officer, although they have undoubtedly been endorsed by Valperga.

The new Grand Master, Carraffa, although he had suspended the further construction of the Cottonera lines, was still desirous of carrying out new works on his own account; and for this purpose called in Don Carlos de Grunemberg, engineer to the Spanish Government in Sicily. That officer paid two visits to Malta, one in 1681, and the other in 1686. The consequence of these two visits was the construction of several works of magnitude. In the castle of St. Angelo he erected the four batteries which, rising tier above tier, protect the entrance of the harbour. He then turned his attention towards St. Elmo. Hitherto it had remained very much in the state in which it had been left at the death of La Valette, consisting merely of the star fort, now called Upper St. Elmo, with its cavalier. Grunemberg, however, commenced in

1687 the construction of the surrounding works, by means of which that fort is completely isolated and raised to the position of a keep. He enclosed the entire point with a bastioned line which adds materially to the defence of the entrance to the Grand Harbour. Two of these bastions have become the last resting-places, one of Rear-Admiral Sir John Alexander Ball, who first administered the government as Civil Commissioner after the occupation of the island by the British, and the other of General Sir Ralph Abercrombie, whose body was brought here from Egypt. They have, in consequence, been since respectively designated as Ball's and Abercrombie's bastions.* It was originally intended to construct casemates in all the curtains, but these were never carried out, although they would have added materially to the strength of the works. Grunemberg further proposed the erection of a fort in the island of the Marsa Muscetto, upon a more extended scale than that designed by Valperga, but this, like the former project, was never executed.

Such, then, was the state of the fortress of Malta at the close of the seventeenth century. Valetta had been completed, and St. Elmo surrounded with an outer *enceinte*; the

* In the course of the present year (1871) it has been found necessary to disturb the remains of both these officers, and to re-inter them at a lower level in the same bastions. The leaden coffin containing the remains of Admiral Ball was found quite perfect. The outer coffin of elm, covered with crimson velvet, was of course completely decayed, fragments only remaining to prove its existence. Sir Ralph Abercrombie's coffin, also leaden, with an elm outer coffin, was found enclosed in the puncheon in which the body was brought from Egypt. The staves had, however, all given way, the hoops only retaining their places. New oak coffins have been made, in which the remains have been deposited, and the original plates containing the names and titles of the deceased have been placed upon them.

Floriana, though not perfected, was still sufficiently advanced for purposes of defence, and its horn and crown works were constructed. The Cottonera lines had risen throughout their extent to the height of the cordon, and the remainder of the works of Vittoriosa, Isola, and St. Angelo were much in the same position as they are now. Fort Ricasoli had been built and occupied, and several towers had been constructed round the coast.

It might have been thought that sufficient had now been done to ensure the security of the convent; the more so as the Turkish empire, the sworn and natural foe of the Order, no longer menaced their existence with such constant alarms. The sixteenth century had witnessed the culminating point in the glory of that empire under the sway of Solyman the Magnificent, and after his death it commenced slowly but surely to decline. Throughout the seventeenth century the onward course of this degeneracy had been continuous, in spite of many partial warlike successes, such as the siege of Candia; and at its close the Order felt themselves relieved from any further serious dread of invasion. Still their fortifications continued to multiply. Every succeeding Grand Master determined to add his quota to the pile, and wherever an unoccupied spot could be discovered, there the indefatigable fraternity continued to labour at the erection of some new work. Engineers were always to be found ready to suggest the necessity of fresh bulwarks, so that the fortress continued gradually to extend itself long after all dread of an attack from the Ottoman empire had ceased to exist.

One of the first changes made in the commencement of the eighteenth century by Raymond Perellos, the sixty-second Grand Master, was the construction of some larger vessels of war to strengthen the maritime power of the Order, which had hitherto been entirely dependent on galleys. Three vessels of large size were launched, named respectively the St. Raymond, the St. Joseph, and the St. Vincent; and the command of the new fleet was intrusted to the Chevalier de St. Pierre, a French knight of much naval experience, who made his first cruise in 1706, when he succeeded in capturing the Tunisian flag-ship of fifty guns, which was immediately added to the Maltese navy under the title of the Santa Croce.

At this period the convent of Malta was in a most flourishing condition. The bailiff of Chambray, who has left a manuscript record of these times, says that "in 1715, at the moment of the declaration of war by the Turks against the Venetians, the court of the Grand Master Perellos presented a most brilliant aspect. No less than fifteen hundred knights, many of them general officers in every army in Christendom, formed the main ornament of the residence of the Order." The preparations making by the Sublime Porte had alarmed the fraternity; and, fearing lest Malta was to be the point of attack, numbers flocked in from every quarter, anxious to reap the harvest of glory which a second successful defence of their island stronghold would present. Fortifications were repaired; magazines and storehouses replenished, and troops were taken into pay. In order to carry out the works with the greater skill, Perellos made an application to Louis XIV. of France, in the close of the year 1714, for the loan of some of his most celebrated engineers; and in compliance with that request, the French monarch despatched the Chevaliers De Tigné and De Mondion to Malta, who, after a minute inspection of the works, drew up a project for their completion, and returned to France. At the urgent entreaty of the Grand Master, however, Tigné returned once more to Malta and personally superintended the principal portion of the work then in progress and being executed in accordance with his plans, which had received the warm approval of most of the eminent engineers of Europe.

Manoel de Vilhence, the successor of Perellos, in his turn determined to add some new work to the general mass, and decided upon carrying out the project so often brought forward of a fort upon the island in the Marsa Muscetto. The necessity of a work of this description had been constantly urged by all the engineers who had visited Malta, and by none more strongly than Tigné. He has left behind him a voluminous report upon this subject, in which he handles the question with much judgment. He points out that it is useless to continue strengthening the land defences of Valetta and Floriana as long as there remains so vital a point as the whole length of the Marsa Muscetto almost unprotected. As the fortress stood in Tigné's time, it certainly was in a very insecure position. The absence of a ditch with counterscarp and glacis left the ramparts exposed to breaching, even to their very foot. In close proximity there stood the point of Tasbieg, the island, and the Point Dragut, where batteries might with every facility have been constructed, the fire from which would speedily ruin the walls. Nothing would then remain but to cross the harbour in boats, as had been done in the first assault on the Spur bastion at St. Michael's in 1565. By thus forcing their way into the very heart of Valetta, all the elaborate defences constructed at such vast expenditure would be turned and lost.

In order to prevent such a consummation, Tigné proposed the establishment of a considerable fort upon the island, which would not only secure it from occupation by the besiegers, but also see in reverse the point of Tasbieg, and prevent the establishment of either trenches or batteries there. He at the same time suggested the erection of a casemated redoubt in the form of a lunette upon Point Dragut, which, in connection with the larger work, would, in his opinion, render the Marsa Muscetto quite secure.

Owing to the peculiar nature of the ground on the island, Tigné found himself compelled to restrict his trace to a square, but he proposed several outworks which have never been carried out. Some idea of the cheapness of labour and materials may be gathered from the fact, that the estimate for this work was only £2,500, including the outworks. Whether, as is so often the case in estimates, this sum was exceeded in actual execution, it is impossible to say; still, the fact that so small an amount was put forward, proves what facilities the Order enjoyed for the erection of their bulwarks. The fort, when completed, received the name of the Grand Master under whose auspices it had been raised, and was called Fort Manoel.

The Turkish invasion proved a myth, and the island once more relapsed into calm and security, from which, however, it was somewhat rudely awakened by a domestic incident which occurred during the Grand Mastership of Emanuel Pinto. This was a conspiracy amongst the Turkish slaves in Malta, which very nearly deluged the island with blood. The plot originated in the following manner. The Christian slaves who manned a Turkish galley had risen upon their officers, captured the vessel, and brought it in triumph into the harbour of Malta, with the Pasha of Rhodes a prisoner on board. This dignitary was a man in high repute at the court of the Sultan, and the Order, fearful of drawing down upon themselves the animosity of the Porte, and anxious to conciliate the court of France, instead of subjecting him to the lot of slavery, placed him under the protection of the Bailiff du Boccage, the French envoy in Malta. The pasha was treated with every attention and respect; a house was appropriated for his use in the Floriana, and a pension of £125 a month allotted to him. He was permitted to receive the visits of the Turkish slaves, and his position was in every respect rendered as little irksome as possible.

At the head of the conspiracy which had ended in the capture of the Turkish galley, was a negro who had planned the whole affair, and who had consequently anticipated a magnificent reward from the Order for the success of his enterprise. He was, however, much disappointed at the sum awarded to him, and his active brain speedily began to hatch a fresh plot, in which, by way of a counter-conspiracy, the island of Malta should be delivered into the hands of the Turks. The number of slaves in Malta was at this time very large. Independently of those who were employed on the public works or as crews to the galleys, and who, when on shore, were lodged in the bagnio or slaves' prison, there were large numbers filling various domestic offices about the persons of the knights and also of the Maltese gentry. In fact, the greater number of the servants in the island were Turks. They were almost uniformly treated with the greatest kindness; their situation, indeed, was in many cases so far superior to what it would have been in their own country, that it was quite a common practice amongst them to refuse their liberty, even when it was tendered to them. Many filled situations of the highest trust in the household of the Grand Master, and two, who acted as his confidential valets, slept in an adjoining room to himself, and had free access to his apartment both by day and night.

The plot which the negro first devised, and which he submitted for the approval of the Pasha Mustapha, was to organize a rising amongst this large body, massacre all the Christians in the island, and then transfer its government to the Porte. Mustapha, with the blackest ingratitude, entered warmly into the design; the Pasha of Tripoli was communicated with, and promised assistance, and the slaves generally were enlisted as confederates in the plot. The festival of St. Peter and St. Paul was selected as the most appropriate day for carrying out this imitation of the Sicilian Vespers. On that day the great bulk of the native population were in the habit of flocking to the Città Notabile, where the ceremonies of the day were carried out with great magnificence. It was thought that an opportunity would thus be the more readily afforded of seizing the city of Valetta whilst denuded of so many of its inhabitants. One of the two confidential valets of the Grand Master was appointed to give the signal for the commencement of the insurrection by murdering his master and exposing his head upon the balcony of the palace. An indiscriminate massacre was then to have ensued, the armoury was to be forced to supply arms, and the gate of the city and other commanding posts to be promptly occupied by them. The forces of the Pasha of Tripoli were to join with them as soon as the successful issue of the enterprise was known, and with their assistance the island was to be held until the arrival of succours from Constantinople. Such were the principal details of the plot to which the Pasha Mustapha lent the sanction of his name and support.

It was strange that the slaves in Malta should have been

permitted such ample liberty of action. Considering their great numbers, and the natural discontent which a condition of slavery, even in its most modified form, must have generated within the minds of many, it is wonderful that greater precautions were not habitually taken to prevent the possibility of treachery. Certain it is that on the present occasion, had it not been for an accidental quarrel amongst themselves, the conspirators would most undoubtedly have succeeded in murdering every member of the Order of St. John within the convent. The discovery of the plot was made thus:—A certain public-house, kept by a Jew, was the principal resort of the chief actors in the drama. One day, shortly before the time selected for its execution, a violent quarrel sprang up between two of them, and after a fierce altercation, from words they proceeded to blows, and at length one of them drew a dagger and endeavoured to stab the other. He, however, succeeded in making his escape unhurt, but vowing vengeance. In the blindness of his rage he proceeded instantly to the commandant of the guard and revealed the entire plot. That officer lost not a moment in communicating with the Grand Master, and took with him the faithless conspirator.

Meanwhile the Jew, who was also a member of the plot, having heard the vows of vengeance which had been uttered, became alarmed, and fearing lest the discontented man might reveal the whole tale, determined to forestall him, and ensure his own safety and a reward, by himself betraying the whole affair to the Grand Master. When, therefore, the commandant of the guard with his conspirator sought an audience of Pinto, they found him engaged in listening to the tale of the Jew. The matter being thus corroborated, energetic steps were at once taken to crush the affair. Numbers of the conspirators were arrested, and subjected to torture, and by degrees all the particulars were elicited.

A similar plot had been formed on board the galleys of the Order, which were cruising near the island, and which was to have been carried into execution on the same day as the rising on shore; but a swift boat was at once sent after them, and the warning arrived in time to prevent any attempt being made. The criminality of the Pasha was clearly proved. As, however, he had been placed under the protection of the French ambassador, the Order did not deem it prudent to proceed to extremities against him, but confined him in Fort St. Elmo until a French frigate arrived from Toulon, which conveyed him to Constantinople. It was with extreme difficulty, however, that he was saved from the just indignation of the Maltese, and had he not been very securely guarded they would have torn him in pieces. Nearly sixty of the leading conspirators suffered the last penalty of the law; and in order to prevent the recurrence of such a design, it was decreed that for the future all slaves employed in a domestic capacity in the houses of knights or citizens should be compelled to retire to the bagnio every evening at sunset, and remain in confinement there till the following morning. The Jew, by whose treachery the discovery was made, received a handsome pension, and from that time the anniversary of the day was regularly celebrated so long as the Order remained in Malta.

The naval superiority of the Order had of late years dwindled gradually, and their fleet was now becoming more an appanage for show than for real service. The Ottoman navy no longer spread terror along the coasts of the Mediterranean, and so the cruises of the Maltese fleet degenerated into mere pleasure trips to the various ports in that sea.

Sonnini, in his travels in Egypt, gives the following description of the Maltese galleys at this period :—" They were armed, or rather embarrassed with an incredible number of hands; the general alone (or flag-ship of the Order) had 800 men on board. They were superbly ornamented, gold blazed on the numerous basso-relievos and sculptures on the stern. Enormous sails, striped with blue and white, carried on their middle a great cross of Malta, painted red. Their elegant flags floated majestically. In a word, everything concurred, when they were under sail, to render it a magnificent spectacle. But their construction was little adapted either for fighting or for standing foul weather. The Order kept them up rather as an image of its former splendour than for their utility. It was one of those ancient institutions which had once served to render the brotherhood illustrious, but now only attested its decay."

In the year 1782, under the Grand Mastership of Emmanuel de Rohan, a new *langue* was created in Bavaria, and joined to the dormant *langue* of England, under the title of Anglo-Bavarian. This new branch was endowed by the Elector of Bavaria with the forfeited possessions of the Jesuits, who had recently been suppressed in that country, as elsewhere. The value of this additional revenue was £15,000 a year. The dignities of Turcopolier and Grand Prior of Bavaria were attached to the new *langue*, which comprised twenty commanderies for knights of justice, and four for conventual chaplains.

The Order of Malta might at this moment have been considered in a position of the greatest prosperity. Its territories had been of late years considerably enlarged, a new *langue* had been added, its revenues were large, and its ranks were recruited from amongst the noblest families in Europe, who brought with them all the influence inseparable from high connections. Profound peace reigned between the fraternity and its ancient foes. If owing to this cause the military ardour of the knights was growing somewhat cold, still the tranquillity of the age brought with it many and substantial blessings to the island, and permitted the revenues to be devoted to other and more beneficial purposes than warlike expeditions.

The island was bristling on all sides with ramparts and guns. Rohan, tempted probably by the immortality which the construction of fortifications had bestowed upon some of his predecessors, determined upon a like measure; and a new fort arose upon the Point Dragut, which, in conjunction with Fort Ricasoli, on the opposite side, completely defended the entrance to both harbours. If Rohan designed by this construction to perpetuate his name, he failed in the attempt; since the work received the title of Fort Tigné, being named after the Grand Prior of Champagne, who designed it, and contributed largely towards the expense of its construction. It has been alleged, with some justice, that there was as much of ostentation as of precaution in many of these later works; and the Duke of Rovigo was not far wrong when he said that "all the Grand Masters since the establishment of the Order in Malta seem to have craved no other title of glory than that of having added some new defence, either to the harbour or town. Being the sole care of the government, it had ended in becoming a pure matter of ostentation, and fortifications were latterly erected in Malta very much on the same principle as palaces at Rome have been, since the chair of St. Peter has replaced on that point the throne of the Cæsars."

The quiet and apparent prosperity which at this period

shone upon the Order was but the calm usually the forerunner of a storm. There were even then gathering upon the political horizon of France clouds which foretold the commencement of that revolutionary hurricane which was to deluge Europe with blood for twenty years, and the first gust of which was to sweep the Order of St. John for ever from that island stronghold, in the ramparts of which so many successive chiefs had placed their pride and reliance.

## CHAPTER VIII.

Position and Powers of the Grand Master—His Revenues—His Election—Ceremonial of the Table—Religious Ceremonies—His Funeral—Navy of the Order—Treasury—The Property of the various *Langues*—English *Langue* in the Fourteenth Century.

BEFORE entering upon the narrative of the events which led to the expulsion of the Order of St. John from the island of Malta, and its ultimate transfer to the dominion of Great Britain, it may be interesting to give a few details with respect to the general organization of the fraternity, its social habits and observances.

The Order, though under the rule of a Grand Master, partook in its political character rather of the nature of an aristocratic republic than of a monarchy. Very little of the actual control of government was left in the hands of the Grand Master alone; all legislative powers being vested solely in the Chapter-general, and all executive functions in the Council-ordinary, over which the Grand Master presided, and in which he possessed the privilege of two votes, with an additional casting vote in any case of equal division. Whilst, however, his powers were thus jealously limited by the constitution of the Order, he practically exercised more influence in the government of the fraternity than at first sight would appear possible. No subject of debate could be introduced into the council unless by the Grand Master or his lieutenant, nor was any enactment of that body valid until it had received his sanction. He was thus enabled to exclude, even from discussion, any measure to which he was opposed; and as the council consisted of Grand Crosses whose nomination lay in his gift, he could at any time by fresh creations secure a majority to pass whatever measures he should submit for their deliberation.

The position and powers of the Grand Mastership had gradually become much changed and enlarged since the first years of the Order's existence. Peter Gerard, who is commonly recognised as the first Master of the Hospital, was nothing more than the superior of a monastic institution, of but little consideration and less wealth; and he occupied much the same post as an abbot in a second-class monastery. The position of his successor, Raymond du Puy, became somewhat changed, and the dignity of his office materially extended. Much wealth had poured into the coffers of the institution, and extensive territorial possessions in most of the countries of Europe had materially increased the consideration in which the Order was held, and had consequently tended to raise the social and political status of its head. The change which Du Puy introduced into the Order by giving it a military character, and thus creating a most important auxiliary to the feeble and tottering monarchy of Jerusalem, added much to the importance of the Master. He was no longer only a monk, and the superior of a body of monks available only for ecclesiastical and charitable duties,—he was also the leader of a chosen body of warriors, a corps which comprised within its ranks all that was knightly and noble. It was impossible that the chief of such a fra-

ternity should fail to hold in a military kingdom a very
different position from that of the cowled monk who had
preceded him; and ere Raymond du Puy brought his
lengthened sway to a close he found the Master of the
Hospital, essential as he and his brotherhood were to the
very existence of the kingdom, a personage of no mean
importance, consulted and courted by the monarch, and
treated with the most deferential respect by his subjects.

As time rolled on, and grant after grant was made to the
Order, its wealth, numbers, and political consideration increased, until in the later days of the unfortunate kingdom
the respective chiefs of the Hospital and the Temple occupied
the highest position in the state next to the monarch himself.
It was in these times that the simple appellation of Master
was exchanged for the more high-sounding title of Grand
Master. The addition was in itself of trivial importance, but
it marked the gradual advance which the office had made
towards social distinction.

The expulsion of the Order from Palestine, and its retirement to Cyprus, appeared at first likely to reduce, if it did
not utterly annihilate, its political importance, and consequently that of its head; and for some years its fate, whether
for good or ill, hung in the balance. The bold and successful
conception of Villaret determined the doubtful question in
favour of the Order; and from this time we find the Grand
Master occupying a far more important position than even
in the most palmy days of Christian domination in the East.
The acquisition of the island of Rhodes, without divesting
him of any of the prestige which, as the head of a powerful
military fraternity had fallen to his lot, had given him the
dignity and privileges of a sovereign prince. Though his
dominion was but small and his subjects few in number, the

P

military colony at Rhodes was far from unimportant. The powerful navy which they speedily organized, and with which they scoured the Levant to the great dread and hindrance of the Ottoman pirates with whom those waters swarmed, rendered most valuable assistance to the commerce and general interests of Europe. The fraternity ere long, therefore, raised themselves to a position in public estimation far more elevated than that which they had occupied in the East, and the Grand Master, sovereign prince as he was, entered into communication with the various courts of Europe very much on a position of equality.

The transfer of the convent to Malta, and the terrors generally inspired by the acquisitions of the Algerine corsairs upon the northern shores of Africa, enhanced this consideration. The island, garrisoned by the redoubtable Knights of St. John, became an advanced post and bulwark of Christianity. Sicily and Italy were protected from the aggression of the infidels by this barrier, and both the Pope and the Spanish monarch, feeling the importance of the services thus rendered, invariably tendered the right hand of friendship to its ruler, and treated him with a consideration which his position would scarcely have otherwise warranted.

Having thus assumed sovereign functions and dignities, we find that he also by degrees surrounded himself with much of the state usually accompanying royalty. The revenue attached to his office during the last century of its existence amounted to upwards of £40,000 a year. This sum was derived from the following sources:—

1st. In every grand priory one commandery was set apart for the benefit of the Grand Master. He nominated its commander without reference to seniority, and its revenues

## Election of a Grand Master.

for the first two years, after each new appointment, were appropriated to him, and a pension therefrom afterwards.

2nd. He was entitled to one nomination to a commandery in each grand priory every five years, and the first year's revenue of the newly appointed commander reverted to him.

3rd. He received customs, excise, and stamp duties to the amount of upwards of £20,000 a year.

4th. He received a table allowance from the public treasury of £600 a year.

The election of a Grand Master took place on the third day after the death of his predecessor. The reason for this prompt action was that the Pope assumed to himself the right of nomination so long as it remained vacant, but he did not possess that right after the election of a successor had been duly made by the Order. Immediately after the death of the Grand Master had been notified to the Council Ordinary of the Order, they at once nominated a lieutenant, in whose hands the government was vested temporarily. The qualifications for a voter upon the election were, that he must be eighteen years of age, and have resided in Malta for three years; that he had performed three caravans (of which more hereafter), and that he was not in debt to the treasury.

On the day of election the proceedings commenced with the celebration of mass in St. John's Church; after which, the *langue* retired into their respective chapels. Each *langue* nominated three knights of justice, into whose hands they confided the further conduct of the election. The twenty-four knights thus selected, chose from amongst themselves a president, and then proceeded to elect a triumvirate consisting of a knight, a chaplain, and a serving brother. This triumvirate nominated a fourth member; and the four, a fifth, and so on until the original three were raised to the number of sixteen. The sixteen then elected the Grand Master, and in case of an equality of votes, the knight of the original triumvirate had a casting vote.

The private household of the Grand Master was superintended by twelve knights; chief of whom was the Seneschal. This dignitary acted as the executive of the Grand Master in all cases where he did not appear in person. He was commandant of the militia of the island, and was assisted in this branch of his functions by two Grand Crosses, under the title of Lieutenants-General. In case of the serious illness of the Grand Master, the Seneschal retained his official seals until either his death or recovery. In the former case the sacrament of extreme unction was administered by him.

Next in rank to the Seneschal were the Maître' d'Hotel, the Master of the Horse, and the Treasurer. The Maître d'Hotel had the entire management of the internal economy of the palace, and regulated all its ceremonies. The Master of the Horse controlled the stable department, and was in command of all the cavalry of the Order; no horse, mule, or donkey could be exported from the island without a written permit from him. He also took possession, on behalf of the Grand Master, of all the equipages of knights dying in Malta, which became the inheritance of that dignitary, and the disposal of which was superintended by the Master of the Horse. The Treasurer had charge of the finance department; the remaining officers of the household were of inferior rank.

The Grand Master had sixteen pages, who were received into the Order as knights of justice at twelve years of age, instead of the ordinary age of sixteen. Their term of service was for three years, during which time they were entirely maintained by their friends. Although the expenses of the post were very considerable, there were numerous candidates always awaiting vacancies, owing to the advantage of being received into the Order at such an early age. Their service as pages counted towards the time of residence in Malta, which every member was obliged to complete before he could become eligible for office. Two of these pages were in daily attendance on the Grand Master, and accompanied him whenever he left the palace. Should the Grand Master return to the palace after dark, six of them lined the staircase with torches. When he dined in public they waited on him at table, and one of them performed the duties of taster. The guests were permitted to give them sweetmeats from the table. During the carnival, which was kept up with great magnificence, these youths formed one of the most attractive features in the display. They were mounted on a splendidly decorated car drawn by six richly caparisoned mules, and preceded by two trumpeters and a kettle-drummer on horseback.

The ceremonial of the table when the Grand Master dined in public was very elaborate; the grandest occasions being on the festivals of Christmas and Easter. The private invitations to these feasts were issued two days beforehand; but on the morning itself, the principal Maître d'Hotel gave a public invitation during the celebration of high mass in St. John's Church. For this purpose immediately after the offertory he rose and, staff in hand, saluted the members of the council one after the other, inviting them to partake of a repast which the Grand Master proposed to give on that day in honour of the Order. At half-past ten a.m. the guests proceeded to the palace, and were ushered into the audience chamber, where the Grand Master was in waiting to receive them. The dinner was served at eleven o'clock. At the entrance of the dining hall the cup-bearer tendered a basin for the Grand Master to wash his hands; the seneschal holding the towel. Whilst this ceremony was proceeding, the prior of the church advanced to the head of the table and said grace. He then retired into the ante-chamber where the guests were also washing their hands, in readiness to return with them as soon as the Grand Master was seated. That dignitary, after having performed his ablutions, took his seat at the head of the table upon a couch of crimson velvet beneath a daïs. The guests then entered the apartment and seated themselves according to rank upon each side of the table, and the dinner commenced. It was a point of etiquette upon these occasions that no one should presume to drink until the Grand Master had set the example.

The public *levées*, which were held very frequently at the palace, resembled in their etiquette that usually adopted at the courts of Europe. The religious ceremonials, in which the Grand Master took a part, were also very numerous. Most of these solemnities were on the ordinary church anniversaries, and were not in any way remarkable. There were, however, two which were held in particular veneration. One was on the 8th of September, the festival of the Virgin Mary, and also the anniversary of the raising the siege of Malta by the Turks; and the other was on the 24th of June, St. John the Baptist's day, who, as the patron saint of the Order, was held in peculiar veneration. The following account of the first of these is taken from a manuscript in which all the ceremonials connected with the Grand Master are detailed with the utmost minuteness.

At eight o'clock in the morning all the Grand Crosses then in Malta assembled at the palace in full costume, with their mantles "*à bec*," and accompanied the Grand Master in solemn procession to St. John's Church. The street from the palace to the church was lined by a double file of the island militia, dressed in the ancient Maltese costume, which from its gay colours added much to the effect of the scene. Arrived at the church, high mass was commenced by the Prior of St. John's; but at the close of the epistle it was interrupted by the arrival of the grand standard of the Order. It was the privilege of the *langue* of Auvergne to have charge of this banner, and the knights of that *langue* took their turn in regular order as standard-bearers during those festivals in which it made its appearance. In time of war, however, no such roster was preserved, but the Grand Marshal selected any member of the *langue* that he preferred for this high honour. Upon the festival now being described, the standard-bearer entered the church arrayed in full armour with the sopra vest of the Order and a silver helmet on his head, surmounted by a nodding plume, forming, as the manuscript remarks, "a magnificent spectacle." He was accompanied by one of the Grand Master's pages, bearing the sword and poniard presented to La Valette by the King of Spain. They were followed by the whole *langue* of Auvergne, headed by the Grand Marshal, carrying the rod of justice in his hand. The standard-bearer and page proceeded up the church until they arrived at the high altar, which they saluted three times. They then turned towards the Grand Master, who was seated on his throne, and also saluted him the same number of times, after which they mounted the daïs, and placed themselves, the standard-bearer on the right, and the page on his left. The mass was then proceeded with, and, whilst the gospel was being read, the Grand Master took the sword and dagger from the hands of the page, and, drawing them from their scabbards, held them aloft till the gospel was concluded. This ceremony was a relic of the ancient custom of the Order invariably to draw their swords during the reading of the gospel as a token of their readiness to combat in its behalf. This custom fell into disuse during later years. Whilst the host was being elevated, the standard-bearer knelt and embraced his banner. At the conclusion of the ceremony, it was borne to the church of Our Lady of Victory, after which it returned, accompanied by the Grand Master, to the palace. Upon this occasion ten young women received a dowry of forty crowns each from the public treasury. Upon the vigil of this feast a solemn mass was celebrated for the repose of the souls of those who had fallen in the siege, and visits were paid to the tomb of La Valette in the crypt of the church.

The other ceremonial to which allusion has been made, was the exposure to public adoration of the hand of St. John the Baptist. This precious relic, which was given to the Grand Master Peter d'Aubusson by the Sultan Bajazet as the price of his treachery towards that monarch's brother Zizim, or Djem, had been brought from Rhodes by L'Isle Adam, and was deposited by La Cassiere in a chapel of St. John's Church, called the Oratory. It was enclosed in a magnificent silver *custode* secured by eight locks, one of the keys of which was deposited in the charge of the Grand Master, as Turcopolier, and the other seven were held by the remaining conventual bailiffs. On the vigil of the feast of St. John these keys were all collected by the Master of the Horse, who, in presence of the Grand Master and council, opened the *custode*. The Prior of the church bore the relic in procession to the high altar, where it remained throughout the next day, except whilst being borne in procession. The hand itself was contained in a gold reliquary, richly studded with diamonds and pearls, the Grand Prior of Barletta having also presented it with a magnificent diamond ring.

It was contrary to etiquette for the Grand Master to pay any visits, and this rule was but seldom deviated from, and then only on most important occasions. He was, however, sufficiently gallant to pay a visit of congratulation to the three convents of St. Ursula, St. Catherine, and St. Magdalen, both at Christmas and Easter. He also called upon the Benedictine nuns of the Citta Vittoriosa when he took formal possession of that city upon assuming the magisterial dignity. He was bound to inspect the hospital of the fraternity periodically, and upon these occasions he tied an apron round his waist, and personally distributed their respective portions of food to each patient. He was supposed in this manner to fulfil his duties as a Hospitaller knight.

Should the Grand Master fall dangerously ill, the Prior of the church was notified of the fact, and the host was brought into the palace. During this time the great bell of St. John's Church tolled forth at intervals, and as the palace was in close proximity to the church, the expiring chief could distinctly hear his own passing bell. After his death, his body was embalmed and lay in state until his burial. The funeral procession was thus formed:—First the governor of the city, followed by the battalion of guards with drums and fifes, playing a funeral dirge; then the clergy of the island according to their respective grades; next the corpse, borne by the senior knights of justice, the Conventual Bailiffs holding the pall, and four pages with standards surrounding the coffin; then followed the officers of the household, the Grand Crosses, and other dignitaries, and the procession was closed by the other members of the Order and the public in general. The funeral service being completed, and the body lowered into its last resting-place, the Seneschal advanced, and breaking his wand of office, threw it upon the coffin, exclaiming, "Gentlemen, our master is dead." The Master of the Horse followed in the same manner, breaking the spurs of the deceased, and the Treasurer likewise, who threw a purse into the grave. The ceremony then closed, and the members returned from the mournful scene to speculate on the excitement of the coming election, which would take place on the morrow to fill the vacant dignity.

The navy of the Order was under the supreme control of the Bailiff of Auvergne as Grand Marshal, supported by the Bailiff of Italy as Grand Admiral. These two officials had charge of the land forces as well as of the navy. Indeed, the two services were so intermixed that it would be difficult to trace any line of distinction between them, except that the militia of the island did not serve on board ship, nor did the battalion of the guard. The other troops served indiscriminately ashore or afloat, as they were required. Every knight, during his residence in Malta, was bound to complete four caravans or cruises of six months each, during which time he was attached either to the battalion of the galleys or the battalion of the ships. As the two dignitaries named above, the Marshal and the Admiral, held their offices as heads of their respective *langues*, without regard to any special aptitude for the posts, it became necessary to select an officer subordinate to them, in whom the real control should be vested. This knight was called the General of the Galleys, and was elected by the council. Until the latter end of the seventeenth century the fleet of the Order had consisted exclusively of galleys, and it was with a navy thus composed that they had earned that brilliant reputation which had gained for them the supremacy of the Mediterranean, and the privilege that the flag of every nation upon those waters should salute that of

St. John. Even Louis XIV., a monarch most unyielding in affairs of ceremony and precedence, admitted the right of the Hospitaller galleys to the first salute from his vessels. We have already shown that towards the end of that century, an addition was made to the navy, of larger vessels, and these latter eventually so far increased in number as to lead to a division in the organization and duties of the marine, a second officer being appointed, called the Commandant of the Vessels. The number of the galleys varied from six to eight, although in time of war they were sometimes increased beyond the latter number. The fleet of men-of-war latterly amounted to seven, of which, three were frigates.

The Bailiff of Aragon was the Grand Conservator, and, as such, had supreme control over the treasury, assisted by the really working official, the Conventual Conservator. The revenues of the fraternity were controlled by a committee called the Chamber of the Treasury; these revenues consisted of the following items, which formed the ordinary sources of the income of the fraternity :—

1st item—*Respensions.* These payments were made from every commandery, and consisted of a certain proportion of their income as decided by a chapter general. It was usually fixed at one-third of the net income of the commandery. The annual receipts from this source during the last decade of the Order's existence was £47,520.

2nd item—*Mortuary and Vacancy.* Whenever a commander died, the entire revenue of his commandery, from the date of his decease until the 1st May following, was paid into the public treasury under the title of Mortuary. The revenue for the year following was also paid into the treasury, and was called Vacancy. When the finances of the Order required extraordinary aid, a second year's vacancy was called for, and eventually this additional tax became continuous. Its annual average was £21,470.

3rd item—*Passages.* This was a sum of money paid to the Order by members on being admitted into its ranks. It was of two kinds: the majority and the minority; the former, which was paid by knights at the age of sixteen, or by pages at the age of twelve, was £100; for chaplains it was £80; for servants-at-arms, £92; for donats or brothers of stage, £26. The minority passage was an increased payment given for the privilege of entering the Order at an earlier age than was permitted under the restrictions of the majority passage. It was originally established in the middle of the seventeenth century, as an expedient to raise an extra fund for building additional accommodation for the Order in Malta, but it was never appropriated to the intended purpose. Its amount was but small, viz: £618, whilst that of the majority passages was nearly £20,000.

4th item—*Spoils.* This consisted of the produce of the effects of a deceased knight, which fell to the public treasury, with the exception of one-fifth part, which he was permitted to dispose of by will. The annual average from this source was £25,000.

There were various other items, but most of them are insignificant. The *priory annates* consisted of a year's revenue, paid by a commander, when nominated by a grand prior, a privilege which that dignitary was permitted to exercise within his priory once in five years. The timber upon every commandery belonged by right to the treasury, and at one time realized a large revenue; this, however, gradually diminished, and at the close of the eighteenth century amounted to less than £5,000. The annual permission to eat eggs and butter during Lent, realized upwards of £1,000.

## Expenditure of the Order.

The ransom of Turkish slaves averaged £1,500. Various other sources raised the total revenue to an amount between £130,000 and £140,000.

Such being the average receipts into the treasury, it may be well to give a brief glance at its expenditure. The maintenance of ambassadors amounted to £3,800; the receivers of the Order, including travelling and law expenses, were paid nearly £7,000; the maintenance of the three conventual churches of St. John, St. Anthony, and the Conception, cost nearly £1,200; the expenses of the hospital reached £8,000, the sick costing about one shilling each per diem. Other charities were supported at an outlay of about £4,000 per annum. The navy cost £48,000; the army £17,000; the tables kept by the Order for its resident members, including £600 allowed to the Grand Master for his own table, cost £5,400; the expenses of offices about £1,000; the maintenance of slaves cost about £4,000; the establishment for stores was maintained at an expense of £18,000; the interest of loans contracted at various periods swallowed up £5,000; this interest ranged between two and three per cent. Various other small items swelled the general expenditure to a sum which nearly balanced the income.

The reader who is accustomed to study the balance-sheets of the great powers of Europe may be prompted to smile at these figures; and when it is remembered that out of this amount the army, navy, ordnance, and civil establishments of the Order were all maintained, it appears marvellously small. It must, however, be borne in mind that this public revenue comprised but a small portion of the total property and income of the Order. Their whole European property, in commanderies and priories, only contributed £40,000 to the Malta exchequer. It was, however, available for the support of the great body of the fraternity. The Grand Master's income of £40,000 also constituted a separate item. We cannot, therefore, estimate the gross annual income of the fraternity from all sources, during the eighteenth century, at less than half a million sterling.

The European property was divided in the following manner:—

The *langue* of Provence consisted of the two Grand Priories of St. Gilles and Toulouse,, and the Bailiwick of Manosque. The Grand Priory of St. Gilles was divided into fifty-three commanderies, and that of Toulouse into thirty. The revenue raised upon this property reached a total of nearly £50,000 a year.

The *langue* of Auvergne consisted of the Grand Priory of Auvergne and the Bailiwick of Lyons; the priory being divided into fifty-two commanderies, and its revenues amounting to £17,000.

The *langue* of France comprised the three Grand Priories of France, Aquitaine, and Champagne; the first of which contained fifty-eight commanderies, the second thirty-one, and the last twenty-four, the revenue of the *langue* being £75,000.

The *langue* of Italy comprised seven Grand Priories and five Bailiwicks. The priories were Lombardy, divided into thirty-six commanderies; Rome, into nineteen; Venice, into twenty-eight; Pisa, into sixteen; Capua, into twenty; Burletta, into twelve; and Messina, into eleven. The bailiwicks were St. Euphemia, St. Stephen, Holy Trinity of Venousa, St. John of Naples, and St. Sebastian. The revenue of the *langue* was £56,000.

The Spanish *langue* of Aragon comprised the Grand Priories of Aragon—commonly called the Castellany of

Emposta—Catalonia, and Navarre. The Castellany was divided into thirty commanderies, Catalonia into twenty-nine, and Navarre into eighteen. There were also the Bailiwicks of Majorca and Caspa. The Bailiwick of Negropont was divided alternately between this *langue* and that of Castile. The revenue of the *langue* was £41,000.

The *langue* of England was, during the eighteenth century, combined with that of Bavaria, under the title of Anglo-Bavarian, the former having become virtually extinct, and the latter having sprung into existence only at a late date. Although bearing the name of Anglo-Bavarian, and enjoying all the privileges of the venerable *langue* of England, it was, practically, exclusively Bavarian. Its two Grand Priories of Ebersberg and Poland were divided into twenty-nine and thirty-two commanderies respectively. Its revenues had not become fully developed when the Order was suppressed, and never reached £1,000 per annum. The Bailiwick of Neuberg was attached to this *langue*.

The three German Grand Priories, of Germany, Bohemia, and Dacia, contained between them fifty-six commanderies, and the revenue of the *langue* was about £10,000 a year.

The *langue* of Castile and Portugal was divided into the three Grand Priories of Castile, Leon, and Portugal, which contained between them seventy-five commanderies, and produced a revenue of £38,000.

Thus it will be perceived that the European property of the Order was divided into nearly seven hundred distinct estates, each of which afforded a liberal income to its commander, besides contributing to the treasury of its Grand Priory, and through that channel to the main treasury at Malta. Each commandery, in addition to its own chief, maintained two or more members of the Order, who were associated with him in its management, and who lived entirely at the expense of the commandery.

Whilst touching upon this branch of the subject, it may prove interesting to give a few details connected with the *langue* of England, as it existed prior to its suppression by Henry VIII. Fortunately, a very complete and valuable picture is presented to us in a report drawn up in 1338 by the Grand Prior of England, Philip de Thame, addressed to the Grand Master, Elyon de Villanova. This report, which exists in manuscript in the Record Office at Malta, has been printed by the Camden Society, under the title of the "Hospitallers in England." The insight which this document affords into the stewardship of landed property in England in the fourteenth century is most interesting, and a careful study of its contents will give the reader a very accurate representation of the position of agriculture in all its various branches at that period. The document is a record of income and outlay, and under one or other of these two heads is classed all the information it contains.

In each manor or commandery, the first item mentioned under the head of income is the mansion, with its kitchen-garden and orchard. These latter appear, in all cases, to have been more or less productive beyond the consumption of the houschold. A considerable source of profit was the *columbarium*, or dovecote, which in some cases produced as much as thirty shillings.*

Next on the list stands the rent received for arable and meadow land; the former of which varied from two shillings an acre in Lincoln and Kent, down as low as three halfpence

---

* In considering these accounts, it must be borne in mind that money bore a far higher value in the fourteenth century than at the present day.

in the counties of Somerset and Norfolk; whilst the meadow land seldom fell to a lower amount than two shillings, and in the counties of Warwick and Oxford it even reached three shillings. The value of pasture land was not calculated by the acre, but by the head of cattle; the average receipt on this score may be assumed at something like the following scale:—

| | |
|---|---|
| An ox or horse .. .. .. .. | 12d. |
| A cow .. .. .. .. .. | 24d. |
| A sheep .. .. .. .. .. | 1d. |
| A calf .. .. .. .. .. | 6d. |
| A goat .. .. .. .. .. | ¾d. |

Messuages, mills, and fisheries stand next on the list, their character being indicated by their name. The profit on stock afforded a considerable source of revenue. In some entries, however, we find that through the devastation of enemies, the damage done by inundations, and other causes, the stock has returned no profit.

A considerable source of income was derived from the churches and chapels appropriated to the Order, whose funds were paid into the treasury, vicars and chaplains being provided at their expense. A glance at the figures recorded under this head will show that, as is the case with many parishes at the present day, the lay impropriators gleaned the lion's share in the substance originally intended for the support of the Church. In the case of sixteen of these churches, the amount paid to the credit of the Order amounted to £241 6s. 8d., whilst the cost of providing chaplains for them was only £34 10s.

At this period the system of villainage, or the compulsory service of bond tenants, was universal throughout Europe;

we consequently find it figuring very extensively on the credit side of the balance-sheet. These services were generally rendered either by payments in kind—such as poultry, eggs, corn, &c.—or by the giving a certain amount of labour for the benefit of the lord of the manor. As these latter have all been entered as money payments, there can be no doubt that a fixed commutation had been agreed to between landlord and tenant, and from one of the entries in the manor of Shaldeford, it may be gathered that the price of commutation was twopence *per diem;* the gross amount received under this head reached the sum of £184 16s. 8d.

We next come to the rent paid by the freeholders, the entry for which comes under the heading of *redditus assisus.* The profit arising from the fees and perquisites paid to the manor court amounted to a considerable sum, and an officer named the steward of the manor was appointed to receive these dues.

There yet remains one item of income of a different character to the others. This was a voluntary contribution from the neighbourhood, and is called *confraria.* The mode of collection is not specified, but it is presumed a house-to-house visitation was made to extort the charity of the pious. The amount thus raised reached nearly £900, and that this sum was less than that which had frequently been previously obtained, may be gathered from several entries where the smallness of the contributions is accounted for by the poverty of the country, and the heavy taxes payable to the king for the support of his navy.

Having thus touched upon the various items which stood on the credit side of the balance-sheet, we come to those which constituted the adverse side of the ledger. The first and principal expense which fell upon the funds of the Order was the maintenance of the household. Over every commandery there was a commander in whose charge the entire estate was vested, and attached to him were other brethren called *confratres*. These, together with the chaplains, formed the upper class of the establishment, and took their meals together. There were, in fact, three different tables maintained. In addition to that mentioned above, there was a second for the free servants of the Order, and a third for the hinds or labourers kept in their employ. The principal portion of the provisions consumed at these tables was provided from the stock of the estate, and consequently cost nothing. There, however, frequently appears an item called *coquina*, for the supply of meat and fish over and above that drawn from the estate. The three tables were supplied with different kinds of bread, viz., white bread, ration bread, and black bread. There were also two kinds of beer, the *melior* and the *secunda*. In addition to their food, the commander and his *confratres* had a yearly allowance for their dress. This was the same in all the commanderies, and consisted of £1 for a robe, 6s. 8d. for a mantle, and 8s. for other expenses. The members of the household had each a pecuniary stipend, which amount not only varied greatly for the different classes, but also for the same class in different commanderies. The highest in rank was the "armiger," who in some instances received as much as £1 a-year; the usual stipend, however, for him, as well as for several others, such as the "claviger," the "ballivus," the "messor," and the "coquus," was a mark, or 6s. 8d. The wages of the "lotrix," or washerwoman, were the smallest, usually amounting to only one shilling.

A very heavy charge frequently appears under the title of *corrody*. This item signifies a claim to a seat at one of the tables of the establishment, and was probably originally granted either in repayment of money lent, or as a return for some favour. The table from which the corrodary drew his commons depended on his rank. In some instances these corrodaries were in receipt of very luxurious rations, as for instance, at Clerkenwell, William de Langford was entitled to dine at the commander's table whenever he chose, together with commons for one chamberlain at the second table, and for three inferior servants at the third. But on occasions when he did not dine there in person, he received a fixed allowance of four white loaves, two of ration bread, and two of black bread, three flagons of *melior* beer, and two of *secunda*, one whole dish from each of the three tables, in addition to which he drew each night for his bedchamber one flagon of best beer, and during the winter four candles and a faggot of wood, also for his stable half a bushel of oats, hay, straw, a shoe, and nails; all these allowances being granted for the term of his natural life.

In addition to the expenses incurred in the maintenance of the household, there was always a heavy item under the head of hospitality. The rules of the Order distinctly laid down the obligation of exercising this virtue freely, and it is clear from these accounts that those rules were liberally complied with; in fact, every commandery partook very much of the character of an inn, where both rich and poor felt certain of a hospitable reception and liberal entertainment for man and beast. No charge was made for this service; still it is probable that the item of *confraria* already alluded to was much swelled by the donations of such amongst the upper classes as had experienced the hospitality of the fraternity. How far this claim to reception and maintenance on the part of the wayfarer may have extended it is difficult to determine.

There must have been a limit, or the system would have entailed the support of all the idle vagabonds in the country. The Anglo-Saxon law appears to have limited the claim in the case of monasteries to three days, and the same margin was probably allowed at the commanderies. It may also be assumed that a day's work on the farm was extorted in return for the day's keep, thus deterring the hardened idler from seeking a shelter, the comfort of which could only be earned by the sweat of his brow.

There were, moreover, many sagacious reasons of policy which materially encouraged the practice of this hospitality. It must be borne in mind that in those days men travelled but little, and information was slow in spreading from one point to another. One can readily imagine, therefore, what an engine for the collection and distribution of important intelligence the table of the commandery must have become. The Grand Prior, in his head-quarters at Clerkenwell, might be regarded somewhat in the light of the editor of a metropolitan newspaper, receiving constant despatches from his correspondents at their various commanderies, containing a digest of all the gossip, both local and general, which may have enlivened the meals of the previous week. This information would of course be collated and compared with that arriving from other quarters, so that a system of the earliest and most correct intelligence was always at the service of the prior, which he might, when necessary, turn to the most valuable account. How often may we conceive him in a position to afford the most timely notice, even to the king in council, of some projected political movement hatched amid the solitary fastnesses of the North, or the secluded glens of the West; notice for which it may be safely assumed that a *quid pro quo* was demanded, in the shape either of a direct donation or an equally valuable exemption from some of the numerous burdens with which the less fortunate laity were oppressed.

Rank has its duties as well as its privileges, and so it was frequently necessary for the commander, whose position gave him considerable standing in the county where he resided, to receive at his table those of the surrounding gentry whom he looked upon as equals. This has in more than one case been quoted as an excuse for the large amount of the housekeeping expenses. Thus, we find at Hampton that the Duke of Cornwall is made to bear the blame of the heavy bread and beer bill. In the Welsh counties the tramps became the scapegoat, who, to quote the expressive language of the accountant of Slebech, in Pembrokeshire, "Multum confluunt de die in diem; et sunt magni devastatores, et sunt imponderosi." The accounts of Clerkenwell, the head-quarter station of the Order in England, show that its proximity to London rendered it peculiarly liable to this expense. The king had the right not only of dining at the Grand Prior's table whenever he wished, but also of sending such members of his household and court as he might find it inconvenient to provide for elsewhere, to enjoy the hospitality of the fraternity. It was, indeed, a long price the community had to pay for the presence and countenance of the monarch, and it sometimes weighed very heavily on their finances.

There is, however, one entry on the expense side of the ledger which reflects much discredit upon our ancestors, and that is the outlay for law charges. Many of these, of course, were simple and innocent enough, as for instance the salaries of their own law officers, and the fees of counsel, which appear to have been usually forty shillings a-year, with robes; but in addition to these, we find numerous others which prove the barefaced venality of our courts of justice—in those days almost all the leading judges being in the pay of the Order.

Thus in the Exchequer we find the Chief Baron, Sir Robert de Sadyngton, Baron William de Everden, and Robert de Scarburgh, William de Stoneve, the engrosser, and the two remembrancers, Gervase de Willesford and William de Broklesby, each in the receipt of £2 a-year, whilst the appointer, Roger de Gildesburgh, is down for an annual salary of £5. In the Court of Common Bench the Chief Justice, Sir William de Herle, receives £10 a-year. Judge William de Shareshall £5, Judges Richard de Aldeburgh and John de Shardelowe £2 each. In the King's Bench, the Chief Justice, Geoffrey de Scrope, was in receipt of £2, not to mention a couple of estates at Huntingdon and Penhull, which it is much to be feared were gained by him in a most unrighteous manner. His brother Justice, Richard de Willoughby, figures on the list for £3 6s. 8d., whilst in the Court of Chancery four of the clerks seem to have pocketed the annual fee of forty shillings each. All these entries are expressly stated to be payments made to the legal authorities for the quiet possession of the lands which had been transferred to the Hospitallers from the recently defunct Order of the Temple.

Such are the principal items both of income and expenditure, which appear in all the various commanderies as shown by this valuable document. From it we also learn that there were 119 brethren of the Order at that time residing in England, in addition to three donats, and eighty corrodaries; of these, thirty-four were knights of justice, one of that number being the Grand Prior, and thirteen of them commanders; thirty-four were chaplains, of whom seven were commanders, and forty-eight were serving brothers, of whom sixteen were commanders. Thus it will be seen that there were thirty-six commanderies which were situated as follows:—

| County. | Commandery. | Income. |
|---|---|---|
| | | £ s. d. |
| Berkshire | Grenham, including Shaldeford | 76 13 6 |
| Wiltshire | Anesty | 93 0 0 |
| Dorsetshire | Mayne, including Kyngeston and Waye | 96 2 10 |
| Devonshire | Bothemescomb, including Coue | 50 11 0 |
| Cornwall | Trebyghen | 75 11 4 |
| Somerset | Bucklands, including Halse | 124 10 4 |
| Hampshire | Godesfield, including Badeslee and Runham | 66 13 11 |
| Sussex | Palyng | 78 11 3 |
| Oxford | Clanefeld | 60 13 4 |
| Gloucestershire | Quenyngton | 179 8 4 |
| Herefordshire | Dynemoor, including Sutton, Rolston, and Wormbrigge | 182 7 3 |
| Pembrokeshire | Slebech | 307 1 10 |
| North Wales | Halstan, including Dongewal | 157 5 10 |
| Warwickshire | Grafton | 78 15 2 |
| Derbyshire | Yeveley | 95 6 0 |
| Yorkshire | Newland | 56 5 4 |
| Ditto | Mount St. John | 58 8 4 |
| Ditto | Beverley | 83 17 6 |
| Northumberland | Chibourn | 23 18 8 |
| Nottinghamshire | Oscington | 95 0 8 |
| Lincolnshire | Maltby | 116 6 8 |
| Ditto | Skirbeck | 84 11 8 |
| Leicestershire | Dalby, including Beaumont | 128 15 8 |
| Northamptonshire | Dyngley | 79 4 0 |
| Buckinghamshire | Hoggeshawe | 74 14 10 |
| Bedfordshire | Melcheburn | 106 2 4 |
| Ditto | Hardwyck, including Clifton and Pelyng | 69 3 5 |
| Cambridgeshire | Shenegeye, including Wendeye, Arnyngton and Cranden | 187 12 8 |
| Ditto | Chippenham | 110 16 9 |
| Norfolk | Kerbrok | 192 2 4 |
| Suffolk | Batesford, including Codenham and Melles | 93 10 8 |

| County. | Commandery. | Income. |
|---|---|---|
| | | £ s. d. |
| Essex | Mapletrestede | 77 16 8 |
| Ditto | Staundon | 34 15 4 |
| Kent | Swenefeld | 82 4 4 |
| Ditto | Sutton-atte-Hone | 40 0 0 |
| Middlesex | Clerkenwell | 400 0 0 |

It will be seen from this list that the income derived from these thirty-six commanderies amounted to 3,917*l*. 19*s*. 9*d*.

The Order possessed in addition, a number of small estates called *cameræ*; these were not of sufficient importance for the appointment of commanders, and were either administered by bailiffs, or farmed out; their proceeds went directly to the support of the *chef lieu* of the Order, and did not maintain any of the fraternity with their own limits; they were twenty-seven in number, and their gross income amounted to £750 8*s*. 6*d*.

The property which the Order possessed in Scotland appears to have realized nothing in the year of the report, viz., 1338, owing to the constant wars which were devastating the country.

"Terre et tenementa redditus et servicia ecclesie appropriate et omnes possessiones hospitalis in Scocia sunt destructa combusta per fortem guerram ibidem per multos annos continuatam unde nil hiis diebus potest levari." In happier and more peaceful days the revenue had been estimated at 200 marks, or £133 6*s*. 8*d*.

In addition to the property enumerated above, the fraternity stood also possessed of sundry manors, formerly in the possession of the Templars. The income from this source amounted to £1,002 1*s*. 9*d*. It will be seen by this statement that the Hospitallers were in the enjoyment of a very extensive addition to their income in England, owing to the destruction of the Templars. Besides the revenue actually receivable in 1338, there were a large number of estates held for life by different individuals, rent free; the property was therefore of an improving character. It must not, however, be assumed that the Order were equally fortunate with their Templar estates in other countries. Nowhere did the Templars hold so much landed estate as in England, nor was the transfer of their property to the Hospitallers by any means so honestly carried out in any other land. Even in England, many valuable Templar estates fell into secular hands; and although the report of Brother de Thame is dated twenty years after the extinction of that Order, he appears still to have been unable to obtain their restoration.

The property of the Order in Ireland consisted of twenty-one commanderies, viz.: in the county of Dublin, Kilmainham, and Clontarf; in the county of Kildare, Kilbegs, Kilheel, and Tully; in the county of Carlow, Killergy; in that of Meath, Kilmainham-beg and Kilmainham-wood; in that of Louth, Kilsaran; and in Down, Ardes; in Waterford, the four commanderies of Kilbarry, Killara, Crook, and Nincrioch; in Cork, Morne or Mora; in Tipperary, Clonmel; in Galway, Kinalkin; in Sligo, Teaque Temple; and in Wexford, Kilclogan, Bally-Hewk, and Wexford. This latter commandery had been the seat of the Grand Priory of the Hospitallers until the suppression of the Templars threw that of Kilmainham into their hands, when they removed the local seat of government to that spot. There are no records left of the value of this property, the greater portion of which had been originally in the hands of the Templars.

The dignitaries of the English *langue* were the Grand Prior of England, the Grand Prior of Ireland, the Bailiff of the Eagle or of Aquila, and the Preceptor of Torphichen in Scotland. At the time of the Reformation, this latter dignity was held by James Sandilands. He became the intimate friend of John Knox, and by the persuasion of that reformer, he renounced the Catholic religion in 1553. After this, feeling himself no longer authorized to retain his office, he resigned the entire property of the Order in Scotland into the hands of the Crown, when on condition of an immediate payment of ten thousand crowns, and an annual duty of five hundred marks, the Queen, by a deed dated 14th January, 1563-4, was pleased in consideration of " his faithful, noble and gratuitous services to herself and her royal parents," to erect them into the temporal lordship of Torphichen, creating him Lord of St. John, and giving him the lands and baronies of Torphichen, &c. The present holder of the title is the seventh in descent from this knight, and is also a James Sandilands.

The total revenues credited to the general treasury of the English *langue* in the year of Thame's report, after deducting local expenditure, was £3,826 4s. 6d. The expenditure of the general treasury in pensions, bribes, &c., was £1,389 2s. 4d., leaving a balance for the payment of responsions of £2,304 15s. 2d. The amount for which the English *langue* was liable was £2,280; that sum having been fixed as approximating to the third part of the gross receipts of the *langue*. It will thus be seen that the annual income fell a trifle above that sum. The balance came into the hands of the Grand Prior.

The income of this dignitary was £1 per diem. He also received an allowance of £93 6s. 8d. for robes for himself and household, and he lived free of charge at the priory at Clerkenwell.

Such was the mode of life carried on in the commanderies of the English *langue* during the fourteenth century, and it will not be too much to assume that in other countries a similar system was pursued. Certain differences must of course have been made to suit the habits and character of the people amongst whom they chanced to be located. Although the liberty of the English peasant in those days was hardly worthy of the name when compared with what he enjoys at the present day, still it placed him in a position far superior to that of his continental brother, and doubtless the commander in a French or Spanish manor ruled over the population who fell within the limits of his sway with an autocratic despotism which was denied to him in England. We may also assume that in no other *langue* would the accounts have shown so large an expenditure in the item of beer, either *melior* or *secunda*, nor did they probably return so large a revenue as the superior wealth of England enabled the Hospitallers to extract from its shires. Still, allowing for these and other differences, it must be admitted that this report from Brother Philip de Thame affords an excellent clue to the general mode of governance adopted by the Hospital in the management of its foreign property in the fourteenth century.

## CHAPTER IX.

Admission into the Order—The Auberges—The Hospital—The Chapter-General—Councils of the Order—Punishments—Duelling—Slaves—The Maltese—Their Connection with the Order—Festivals of the Inhabitants.

FROM the period when the Order of St. John was first divided into *langues*, and the various dignities in the gift of the fraternity apportioned to those *langues*, no confusion or intermixture was ever permitted between them. A postulant for admission into the Order preferred his request to the head of the *langue* to which by birth he belonged, either at the convent or at one of the Grand Priories in his own country. If he desired admission into the class of knights of justice, the necessary proofs of nobility were required from him, those proofs varying in the different *langues*. When it had been satisfactorily ascertained that he was of sufficiently gentle blood to entitle him to admission as a knight, he was received as a novice, if he had attained a sufficient age, and after the expiration of a probationary twelvemonth, he was duly professed as a knight of justice.

The age at which a postulant was received as a novice was sixteen, thus enabling him to become professed at seventeen; but he was not required to commence his residence at Malta till he had attained the age of twenty, and in many cases he received a dispensation postponing that residence still further. The pages of the Grand Master were entitled to admission at twelve years of age, and their services in that capacity counted towards the term of residence at the convent every knight was bound to complete to entitle him to nomination to a commandery. In later years knights were sometimes received "in minority," even as babies, a larger entrance fee, termed "passage," being in such cases paid; but this was an innovation on the established rule, introduced merely for the purpose of raising additional funds for the treasury.

A knight having thus become professed, was bound to proceed to Malta as soon as he had reached the age of twenty years, and to reside there for a certain length of time. During this time he performed such military and naval service as was required of him. Each complete year of such service constituted a caravan, and the number of these required for qualification as a commander was, until a late period, fixed at three; latterly, however, four were exacted. The residence in the convent, for the same qualifications, was fixed at five years. Before a knight could be elected a bailiff he must have been fifteen years in the Order, ten of which must have have in residence at the convent. During this period he was attached to the auberge of his *langue*, where he lived at the table furnished by the Conventual Bailiff, as will be more fully detailed presently. In due course of seniority he received promotion to a commandery, which removed him from Malta to his own country, where he resided upon the estate entrusted to his charge, and was under the direct supervision of the Grand Prior within whose district his commandery was situated. In many cases, however, knights received appointments in Malta, either in the Grand Master's household or in some official capacity which necessitated a continued residence in the island, and which was considered as an equivalent. After having held a commandery for five years he was eligible for translation to one of higher value, provided he had administered that originally entrusted to his charge with due prudence and care. He thus continued rising in dignity and with increasing emoluments until he had attained such seniority as rendered him eligible for the post of Conventual Bailiff, upon nomination to which he once more returned to Malta.

The Conventual Bailiffs (originally eight in number, but since the secession of the English *langue*, and the consequent attachment of the office of Turcopolier to that of the Grand Master, reduced to seven) ranked next in the precedence of the Order to the supreme dignity.

These officials resided each in the auberge appropriated to his *langue*. The treasury issued an allowance of sixty gold crowns per month to every bailiff for the expenses of his office, and it also granted daily a fixed allowance in kind to support the table which he was obliged to maintain in the auberge for the use of the members of his *langue*. Every member resident in Malta, whether knight, chaplain, or serving brother, was entitled to a place at one of these tables, excepting only if he were a commander holding a benefice of the annual value of £200, as a knight; or of £100, as a chaplain or serving brother; in which case he was considered as already sufficiently provided for.

The allowance issued by the treasury was by no means sufficient to cover the expense of these messes; a great proportion fell consequently upon the private resources of the bailiff. Burdensome as this charge undoubtedly was, the post of Conventual Bailiff was nevertheless eagerly sought after. In addition to the very high position which it conferred upon its holder, second in rank and influence only to the Grand Master himself, it was invariably, and as a matter of right, the stepping-stone to the most lucrative dignities in the gift of the *langue*. If either of its Grand Priories or Bailiwicks fell vacant, the Conventual Bailiff had the option of assuming the dignity; and if he preferred waiting for one of still greater value, he might retain his post and allow the vacant nomination to pass to those junior to himself, until one occurred of sufficient value to meet his expectations. Not unfrequently the selection of a Grand Master was made from amongst the Conventual Bailiffs, who, being present at the convent at the time of the election, had many opportunities of canvassing and making themselves popular with the electors.

The allowance which the bailiff was bound to provide for each person attending the table of the auberge was one rotolo\* of fresh meat, either beef, mutton, or kid, or two-thirds of that amount of salt meat; and on fast days, in lieu of the above, a due portion of fish, or four fresh eggs, together with six loaves of bread and a quartuccio of wine.\* Members were permitted to draw this allowance, and to dine away from the auberge, three times a week; but on such occasions no breakfast was allowed them. When, however, they dined at the auberge they were allowed both breakfast and supper. The above ration constituted what the bailiff was compelled to provide for his guests; but it rarely happened that he restricted himself to those limits only.

---

\* A rotolo weighs one pound and three-quarters; a quartuccio is about three pints.

The prodigality of the table actually maintained depended much on his private means and disposition. If he were generously disposed, a wealthy man, and anxious to court popularity, the surest way to attain this end was by the liberal entertainment of those who were dependent on him for their sustenance. A spirit of rivalry was thus engendered between the *langues*, and he who obtained the reputation of maintaining his auberge upon the most liberal scale generally found his account in the popularity which he thus gained.

The title of "Pilier" was given to the conventual bailiffs, and it was by this name that they were designated in all official records. They were bound to reside permanently at the convent, and were compelled to make their appearance there within a period of two years from the date of their election to the dignity. Three of the seven were permitted to be absent on leave at the same time, and they nominated lieutenants to act for them, and to supply their place at the council whilst they were away.

The nominations to commanderies were made by the Grand Master in council, with the following exceptions. In every grand priory the Grand Master had one commandery the revenue of which belonged to himself, and the nomination to this rested exclusively with him. He had also the privilege of nominating to one vacancy in every priory once in each five years; and a similar privilege was also enjoyed by the Grand Priors. The appointment of this patronage was fixed in the following manner. The first commandery which fell vacant during the quinquennial period was filled by the nomination of the Grand Master, the second by the council, the third by the Grand Prior, and all succeeding vacancies by the council, until the termination of the period. Should

R

there not be three vacancies during the time specified, the Grand Prior lost his privilege; but this rarely occurred, as translations and promotions were very frequent. A commander appointed to a bailiwick or priory resigned his commandery to take possession of his new dignity, unless he were the holder of a magisterial commandery; in that case he was permitted to hold it in connection with his new appointment.

The chaplains were received without any of the restrictions placed on the admission of the knights of justice. It sufficed that they were of respectable origin, and that they were born in wedlock. They were admitted at the age of sixteen as clerks, and were ordained as sub-deacons two years afterwards. They could not attain to the office of deacon till they were two-and-twenty, nor to that of chaplain earlier than twenty-five. They then became available for all the religious offices of the convent; they performed divine service in the church of St. John; or were attached either to the household of the Grand Master, the auberge of their *langue*, or the hospital; or they performed their caravans on board the galleys, and accompanied them during their cruise. It was from this class that the prior of the church and the bishop of Malta were selected — the former by the Grand Master in council, and the latter by the Pope. The ranks of the conventual chaplains were, during the residence of the Order in Malta, mainly recruited from amongst the Maltese, and the posts of bishop and of prior of the church, both of which ranked with the conventual bailiffs, were constantly held by natives of the island. In addition to the conventual chaplains thus created, the Order received into this division of their fraternity another class, termed priests of obedience, who were not called upon to reside in Malta, but who performed the duties of their office in the various continental priories and commanderies. These priests received the emoluments of their various benefices like the other clergy, and where such revenues were too small for their due and honourable maintenance, they drew a further provision from the local funds of the Order. They were, however, ineligible for either of the great offices appropriated to the conventual chaplains, nor were they ever appointed to the charge of commanderies, as the latter were.

As the Order of St. John had originally owed its establishment to the charitable efforts of the Amalfi merchants in the practice of hospitality, whence they also derived their name, it was but reasonable to anticipate that it should hold a high place amongst the duties incumbent on them. Accordingly we find that no pains and no expense were spared to render the fraternity entitled to the name they had assumed. Even in the midst of the bloody wars in which the Order had been so constantly involved, and at times when their reverses had threatened their utter annhilation, the doors of their convent were ever open for the reception of the worn and weary wanderer. The pilgrim, whether in health or sickness, found there a ready welcome, and he received within the walls of this charitable institution every care and attention that Christian benevolence could suggest. The knight returning from his brilliant career on the battle-field, and regardless of the renown which he and his brotherhood had gained for themselves, doffed his harness, laid aside his trusty falchion, and assuming the black mantle of his Order, proceeded to aid in those peaceful acts of charity which were ever being carried on within his convent walls.

So long as the Order remained in Palestine did this state

of things continue. During that period they had amassed from the donations and bequests of the pious an enormous and ever increasing wealth. This wealth had brought in its train many evils and much degeneracy. It had made them many bitter enemies, and had rendered lukewarm many of their most enthusiastic friends; still we never hear amongst the many crimes laid to their charge, even by the most rancorous of their opponents, any accusations of negligence in this fundamental obligation of their profession. But after their expulsion from Palestine a change speedily took place. Established in the island of Rhodes, the great demand which had once existed for their charity and hospitality was annihilated. There were no longer sick and weary pilgrims to cheer upon their way. The requirements of the hospital in the island home of their adoption soon became only those of the slender population in the midst of whom they were placed—and thus we find that noble establishment which in previous ages had called forth the enthusiastic admiration of Christendom, dwarfed down to a very limited affair. Members of the fraternity, and indeed strangers of every description could still, when sick, procure needful assistance from the hospital of the Order, and every care was taken to render that hospital as perfect and convenient as possible; but at its best it was not to be compared with the comprehensive and noble establishment which they had originally reared within the precincts of the sacred city.

Their translation to Malta produced no change in this respect. Mindful of their old traditions, one of their earliest measures when establishing their convent upon the rocky inlets of their new home was to found a hospital; and when they removed that convent to the new city built by their great chief, this institution naturally followed in the general move. The hospital of Valetta was, and still is, a capacious building, and bears evidence of having been extensively used for the purposes to which it was devoted; still it was but a hospital, and as such differed but little from other modern institutions of the same class. Supreme in its governance was the conventual bailiff of the *langue* of France, the Grand Hospitaller, who nominated an overseer of the infirmary from amongst the knights of his *langue*. Under the immediate charge of this official the whole institution was placed. The religious functions of the establishment were performed by a prior and sub-prior, who were also appointed by the Grand Hospitaller. As a committee of inspection over these officials, the Grand Master in council appointed two "*prud'hommes*," or controllers, who were held responsible for the proper management of the hospital. Physicians and surgeons were retained in the pay of the Order for the performance of the medical duties. All the utensils in the hospital, even those devoted to the humblest purposes, were of silver. As, however, they were perfectly devoid of ornament, it may be assumed that this was rather a matter of cleanliness than ostentation.

The burial of such as died within the hospital was decently and carefully ordered. Four men dressed in mourning robes carried the corpse to the grave, and with a laudable economy the statutes provided that these robes "should be preserved for another time." No mourning was permitted to be worn at the funeral of any member of the Order, either by the fraternity, or by any stranger present. The corpse was buried in the mantle of his Order.

The hospital of St. John had from its earliest foundation been ranked as a sanctuary within which fugitives from justice might escape from the fangs of the law. The exceptions to this right of sanctuary became, however, by successive decrees so numerous that it is difficult to conceive what crimes remained for which it continued to afford shelter. The statutes say, "No assassins shall find protection there, nor those who pillage and ravage the country by night, nor incendiaries, nor thieves, nor conspirators, nor those guilty of unnatural offences, nor those who have caused the death of anyone, either by secret treachery, or in cold blood, or by poison. No servant of any of the brethren shall find sanctuary there, nor those who have offered any violence, either to them, or to our judges and other ministers of justice, nor debtors, nor such malicious persons as may have committed crimes within the infirmary, under an idea that it was a sanctuary, nor, lastly, lawyers or witnesses convicted of perjury, nor murderers who infest the roads to rob and kill the passers-by."

Reduced though the hospital of St. John undoubtedly was during the later years of the Order's existence, it was, nevertheless, freely open to all who sought its hospitable shelter and the kindly ministrations of its officials. Patients flocked to Malta from Sicily, Italy, and other countries whose shores were washed by the Mediterranean, and none who sought admittance were ever turned away. As many as a thousand patients were at times assembled within the infirmary at Malta, and the charges for so large an establishment formed a very considerable item in the annual expenditure of the treasury.

It has already been mentioned that the legislative powers of the Order were exclusively vested in the Chapter General, whilst its executive functions were entrusted to the Grand Master in council. It will be well now to enter into some detail as to the composition both of the chapter and councils.

The Chapter General, which was the original assembly of the fraternity, was, during the earlier years of its existence, held regularly every five years, and in cases of emergency was often convened even between those periods. Gradually, however, a longer interval was allowed to elapse, and eventually they were almost entirely discontinued, only one having been convened during the eighteenth century. Many reasons may be alleged for the abandonment of this ancient council. The immense expense which attended its convocation, the extreme inconvenience and detriment to the interests of the community in calling away so many of its provincial chiefs from the seats of their respective governments, the turbulence which so often characterised their meetings, and the difficulty which the Grand Masters experienced in carrying out their views in an assembly where their interests had but a very slender predominance, were all so many causes to check their frequent convocation. In the absence of the Chapter General the Grand Master carried on the government, with the aid and intervention of a council only, and in these latter assemblies he was able to obtain a far greater influence and a more complete subservience than he could ever expect from the former body. The summoning of a Chapter General lay entirely with the Grand Master or the Pope. It has been shown why the former should as far as possible neglect to summon them; similar views also actuated the pontiff, as in the absence of the chapter all legislative powers were vested in him, powers which the court of Rome were never backward in exercising. The dignitaries who had seats in the Chapter General were the Bishop of Malta, the Prior of the church, the eight conventual bailiffs, the twenty-two local grand priors, and the twenty-three titular bailiffs. Such of them as were not able to attend in person were bound to send duly authorised proxies to act in their stead. On the opening of the chapter each member in token of its sovereign authority tendered as a tribute a purse containing five pieces of silver. The marshal brought into the hall the grand standard, and the other high officials surrendered the ensigns of their respective posts, which were not returned to them until the chapter had passed a fresh grant for the purpose. The business of each day closed with Divine service, in the course of which the following prayers were offered :—For peace, for plenty, for the Pope, for the cardinals and other prelates, for the emperor and other Christian princes, for the Grand Master, for the bailiffs and priors, for the brethren of the hospital, for the sick and captives, for sinners, for benefactors to the hospital, and lastly for the confraria, and all others connected with the hospital.

The duration of a Chapter General had been very wisely limited to sixteen days, in order to check any spirit of opposition and factious debate by which it might otherwise have been indefinitely prolonged. If, at the conclusion of that time, any business remained unsettled, it was disposed of by a council of reservation, elected by the chapter prior to its dissolution. The chapter was the ultimate court of appeal from the decisions of the various councils, and in its absence that appeal lay to the Court of Rome. The code of laws called the Statutes of the Order was the result of the decrees of a succession of Chapters General, no alterations, additions, or omissions to this code being introduced by any authority short of that which originally called it into existence.

Provincial chapters were held annually in every grand priory, presided over by the Grand Prior, or his lieutenant, at which every commander within the district was bound to attend, either in person or by proxy. The local interests of the fraternity were discussed at these assemblies, and all matters disposed of which did not affect the Order at large. The appeal from this court lay with the council of the Order at Malta.

The duty of the Grand Master, as head of the Order, consisted merely in enforcing obedience to the laws laid down by the chapters; and even in this comparatively subordinate office he was not permitted to act alone, but was associated with a council, without whose sanction none of his decrees were legal. The councils of the Order were of four kinds: the complete, the ordinary, the secret, and the criminal. The complete council consisted of the Grand Master or his lieutenant, as president; the Bishop of Malta, the Prior of the Church, the eight Conventual Bailiffs, or their lieutenants, and any grand cross who might chance to be present at Malta. To these dignitaries were added two members from each *langue*. Before this court all appeals were brought against the decisions and sentences of the ordinary and criminal councils.

The other three councils were composed of the same persons, excepting the two members from each *langue*. In these councils, therefore, every member was a grand cross. The ordinary council could not be held without the presence of the eight Conventual Bailiffs, or their lieutenants, none of the other members being bound to be present. At this council all nominations to vacant offices were made, all disputes arising therefrom decided, and the ordinary business connected with the government of the Order transacted. This was the council most usually employed by the Grand Master, who might assemble it at any time, and in any place he thought proper. No subject could be introduced except with his sanction and approval, and as all grand crosses had a vote, he was enabled, by a batch of fresh creations, to carry any measure upon which his views differed from those of his council. The secret council took cognisance of such matters of foreign policy as were not considered fit subjects for publicity, and its proceedings were always maintained strictly private. The criminal council received and adjudicated on all complaints lodged against individuals pertaining to the Order; who were arraigned before them, and sentence declared in accordance with the evidence.

The mention of this council leads, naturally, to the subject of the punishments common amongst the fraternity. They were as follows: First, "The Septaine." This penalty obliged the offender to fast for seven days successively, on the Wednesday and Friday being restricted to bread and water only. He was not permitted to leave his home except to attend Divine service. The statutes decreed that on the Wednesday and Friday he was also to receive discipline at the hands of a priest (usually the vice-prior) in the conventual church, during the recitation of the psalm, *Deus misereatur nostri, &c.* This latter portion of the punishment fell into disuse after the sixteenth century. "The Quarantaine" was precisely similar, except that it lasted for forty days. In both cases the offender was forbidden to wear arms during the period of his punishment.

If a more severe penalty were required, imprisonment was resorted to, no limit to which was fixed by the statutes. Loss of seniority was another punishment, and in extreme cases the offender was sentenced to deprivation of his habit, either for a limited period or for ever. The latter sentence was, practically, expulsion from the ranks of the fraternity.

No capital punishment was recognised, but in case of crimes requiring such a penalty, the culprit was deprived of his habit, and then, being no longer a member of the Order, he was transferred to the civil power, and sentenced to death. The records of the sixteenth and seventeenth centuries contain several instances of capital punishment inflicted in this manner upon quondam members of the Order. The ordinary method of carrying out the last sentence of the law was borrowed from the Turks, and consisted in placing the condemned criminal in a sack and throwing him into the Marsa Muscetto. The infliction of torture was not authorized by the statutes, but, at the same time, it was not expressly forbidden, and the records show that it was very commonly resorted to in order to extort confession. No rank was sufficiently elevated to save a prisoner from this test. During the second siege of Rhodes the Chancellor D'Amaral was subjected to torture, and his was by no means an isolated case.

The eighteenth division of the statutes is devoted to an enumeration of the various acts forbidden to members of the Order. No one was to make a testamentary disposition of more than one-fifth of his property, the remainder reverting to the treasury of the Order. They were never to mix themselves up in the quarrels either of princes or private individuals. They were not to wander from their commanderies so as "to make vagabonds of themselves." They were, consequently, prohibited from leaving the precincts of their commanderies without showing good cause, and obtaining written leave from their immediate superior. Any person connected with the Order, who came across an offender against this statute, "enacting the vagabond," was bound to secure him, and give notice of his imprisonment to the Grand Prior under whose jurisdiction he was.

No privateering expeditions against the infidel were permitted without the previous sanction of the Grand Master. This sanction was, however, always readily granted, and the time spent in such cruises was allowed to count as part of the necessary residence of the knight in the convent, and towards his caravans.

Any member of the Order appearing in public without the distinctive dress of his profession—that is, without the cross in white cloth sewn on his robe—was, for the first offence, to undergo the quarantaine; for the second, to be confined for three months in the tower, and for the third to be deprived of his habit. The following decree was issued against disturbances in the auberges:—"If any of the brethren behave insolently and in a turbulent manner in the auberges where they live, and if, amidst the tumult and noise, they break the doors, the windows, the chairs, or the tables, or any articles of that nature; or if they upset and disarrange them with reckless audacity, they shall be punished by the Grand Master and council in such manner as they may decree, even to the loss of seniority. If they conduct themselves still more outrageously, and beat the pages, the servants, or the slaves of the conventual bailiffs; for the first offence, if no blood be spilt, they shall be punished with the quarantaine; for the second, they shall be imprisoned in the tower, and for the third they shall lose two years' seniority. If, on the other hand, blood shall have been spilt, no matter how slight the wound may have been, they shall be imprisoned in the tower for six months for the first offence, and if the wound be serious, they shall lose seniority. If any member insult another in the palace of the

Grand Master, he shall lose three years' seniority; for an insult in an auberge, two years. If the disputants come to blows, they shall be stripped of the habit for a time; if either party be wounded, they shall lose their habit in perpetuity, and if he be killed, they shall be handed over to the secular power."

The following are the crimes for which the statutes decree the loss of habit in perpetuity :—" Those convicted of heresy, of unnatural offences, of being assassins, or thieves; those who have joined the ranks of the infidel, those who surrender our standard when unfurled in presence of the enemy, those who abandon their comrades during the fight, or who give shelter to the infidel, together with all who are parties to, or cognizant of, so great a treason." Privation of habit for one year was to be inflicted upon any one who, "when under arms, shall have left his ranks to plunder; also upon any one who brings an accusation against another which he is unable to substantiate. A knight who has committed a murder shall be deprived of his habit in perpetuity, and kept in prison, in order to prevent others from becoming so hardened as to commit a similar crime; and that the company of our brethren may be quiet and peaceable, whoever wounds any person treasonably, in secret, or by malice prepense, shall lose his habit in perpetuity."

The question of duelling was stringently dealt with by the statutes. It was strictly forbidden, and the severest penalties attached to any infringement of the law, which ran thus:—" In order to check the impiety of those who, neglecting the safety of their souls, invite others to a duel, and expose their bodies to a cruel death, we decree that if one brother provokes another, or if he defies him, either by speech or in writing, by means of a second, or in any other manner; and that the one who is called out does not accept the duel, the appellant shall be deprived of his habit in perpetuity without any remission. If his antagonist accepts the challenge, even if neither party appears upon the ground, they shall, nevertheless, both be deprived of their habits, without hope of pardon. But should they both have proceeded to the place of assignation, even though no blood should have been spilt, they shall not only be deprived of their habit, but shall afterwards be handed over to the secular power. Whoever shall have been the cause of any such duel or defiance, or who shall have given either advice, or assistance, or counsel, either by word or deed; or who, upon any pretence whatever, shall have persuaded any one to issue a challenge, if it shall be proved that he accompanied him to act as his second, he shall be condemned to lose his habit. The same penalty is likewise attached to those who shall be proved to have been present at a duel, or of having posted, or caused to be posted, a cartel of defiance in any spot whatever."

The above laws relate only to a premeditated duel. Brawls and *fracas* are punished under the following statute:—"If a brother strike another brother, he shall be placed in the quarantaine; if blood be drawn elsewhere than from the nose or mouth, he shall be stripped of his habit. If he shall have attempted to wound him with a knife, sword, or stone, and has not succeeded, he shall be placed in the quarantaine."

The laws against duelling were so severe, and the impossibility of checking the practice so evident in a fraternity which embraced in its ranks so many young and hot-headed spirits, men as keenly alive to an affront as they were ready to resent it, and who regarded personal courage as the first of all human virtues, that some modification or evasion was essentially necessary. It became gradually tacitly recognised that duels might be fought in one particular locality set apart for the purpose without incurring the above-mentioned penalties. There exists in Valetta a long street, so narrow as to be called *par excellence* "Strada Stretta," and this was the spot marked out as a kind of neutral territory, where irascible cavaliers might expend their superfluous energy. The fiction which led to this concession was, that a combat in this street might be looked upon in the light of a casual encounter, occasioned by a collision in the narrow thoroughfare. This street, consequently, became eventually the great rendezvous for affairs of honour. The seconds posted themselves one on either side, at some little distance from their principals, and with their swords drawn prevented the passers by from approaching the scene of strife. The records of the sixteenth and seventeenth centuries teem with entries of stabbing, wounding, and killing, the result either of premeditated duels or of casual encounters. When the former, the punishment greatly depended upon whether the authorised spot had been resorted to, and if so, the penalty was made comparatively trivial.

The question of duelling having been disposed of, the statutes proceed to provide against the nuisance to respectable persons of midnight revellers disturbing their households. The following statute proves that the fast young men of bygone days committed very nearly the same follies as at present:—"Whoever shall enter into the house of a citizen without being invited, and against the wish of the head of the family, or who shall disturb the social gatherings of the people during their festivals, dances, weddings, or other similar occasions, shall lose two years' seniority. And if either by day or by night they do any damage to the doors or windows of the people, then, in addition to the above-named penalty, they shall suffer a rigid imprisonment. Any member of the Order joining in masquerades or ballets shall suffer loss of seniority. If any one shall be so bold as to damage doors or windows by night, or who shall stop them up with plaster or stain them with dirt, or who shall throw stones at them, shall lose three years of seniority."

. The original profession of a knight of the Order having included the three vows of obedience, poverty, and chastity, the statutes, after having decreed such penalties as were necessary to check all transgressions of the two first of these vows, proceeded to deal with the third. The question of chastity was one not easily encountered in an Order constituted like that of the Hospital. On the one hand, as a religious fraternity, devoted to the service of God and the practice of charity and all good works, it was wrong to recognise any licence or infraction of the strictest laws of continence. The monk, in his cloistered retreat, mortifying his sensual appetites by fast and vigil, was not supposed to be more free from earthly passions than the knight of St. John. We all know, however, that even the inmates of monasteries constantly strayed from the strict paths of virtue, and it was not to be expected that the members of a military Order, surrounded as they were with such vastly increased temptations, could have maintained themselves more free from vice. Composed of the youth of high and noble families, not secluded from female society, but mingling with the gayest of both sexes, taught to look to military renown rather than ascetic piety, as the rightful adornment of their profession, it was not likely that they would act rigidly up to the letter of the vow they had taken. That vow was therefore construed to mean nothing more than celibacy, and the statutes content themselves with checking all open display of immorality. "It has been very rightly ordained that no member of our brotherhood, of whatever position or rank he may be, shall be permitted to support, maintain, or consort with women of loose character, either in their houses or abroad. If any one, abandoning his honour and reputation, shall be so barefaced as to act in opposition to this regulation, and shall render himself publicly infamous; he shall, after having been three times warned to desist from this vice, if a commander, be deprived of his commandery, and if a simple brother he shall lose his seniority. If any member of our Order shall be so barefaced as to recognise and publicly to adopt as his own, a child who may be born to him from an illegitimate connection, and attempt to bestow on him the name of his family, he shall never hold either office, benefice, or dignity in our Order. It is further decreed that all associates of loose women shall be ranked as incestuous, sacrilegious, and adulterous, and shall be declared incapable of possessing any property, or of holding any office or dignity in our Order. And it is hereby defined as an associate of loose women, not only those who are notorious evil livers and have had judgment passed on them as such, but also any one who, without any sense of shame or fear of God, and forgetting his profession, shall entertain and support a woman of doubtful character, notorious for her bad life and evil conversation, or who shall reside with her constantly."

These statutes were so ambiguously worded, and left so many loopholes for evasion, that it is not surprising they should gradually have become a dead letter. The presence of a large number of women of light character within the convent became a public scandal at a very early period, and many Grand Masters, even during the residence of the

Order at Rhodes, sought by the most rigorous measures to mitigate the evil. Their efforts were however in vain, and as the Order lost more and more of the religious enthusiasm which had stimulated its early founders, so did the dissoluteness of the knights become more and more outrageously opposed to the principles of their profession. After the successful termination of the siege of Malta had left the fraternity in undisputed sovereignty of that island, and had raised their military renown to the highest possible pitch, they appear to have become intoxicated with the admiration they had excited throughout Europe, and, throwing off all restraint, to have abandoned themselves to the most reckless debauchery.

At this period the city of Valetta was positively teeming with women of loose character. The streets were thronged with the frail beauties of Spain, Italy, Sicily, and the Levant, nor were the dark-eyed houris of Tripoli and Tunis wanting to complete an array of seduction and temptation too strong for aught but a saint to resist. Saints, however, there were but few in the convent in those days, so that the *demireps* and their supporters had it all their own way. During the governance of La Cassiere, that Grand Master's attempt to check the evil led to an open revolt and his own imprisonment—a sentence which was carried into effect amidst the derisive jeers of crowds of flaunting Cyprians, whom he had in vain endeavoured, for decency's sake, to banish into the adjoining casals.

This period may be marked as the worst and most openly immoral epoch in the history of the fraternity. The evil, to a certain extent, brought with it its own remedy, and after a while they became scandalized at the notoriety of their own debauchery. Still the morality of the fraternity remained at a very low ebb, and up to the latest date the society of Malta abounded with scandalous tales and sullied reputations.

Any description of the social organization of the Order would be incomplete without some allusion to the institution of slavery which flourished in their midst. Since the earliest ages, it had been an invariable custom in Eastern warfare that the prisoners taken in battle should be reduced to slavery, and this system was in full play before the Crusades had introduced a Christian element into the warfare of Asia. A spirit of retaliation led to the establishment of a similar system on the part of the Christians, and their Turkish captives were invariably reduced to the condition of slavery. After their establishment in the island of Rhodes the knights continued the practice, which ancient custom had legalized in their eyes; and both in that island and at Malta their galleys were manned by gangs of Turkish slaves. A prison was established within the convent where the slaves were placed when not employed on board ship, and whilst on shore they were constantly engaged either upon the fortifications or in the dockyards.

There can be no doubt that great cruelty was often practised upon these unfortunate captives, and the treatment which they received at the hands of their Christian masters was often disgracefully barbarous. Their lives were held as of little or no value, and the records of the Order teem with accounts of the thoughtless and barbarous manner in which they were sacrificed to the whims and caprices of their masters. During the first siege of Rhodes, a gang of those unfortunates were returning from their perilous labours of repairing the breaches made by the enemy's artillery in the ramparts. A party of young knights chanced to meet them, and commenced amusing themselves at their expense. A slight scuffle ensued, owing to an effort made by the slaves to shield themselves from their tormentors, when a body of the garrison, who were patrolling near the spot, imagining that the slaves were rising in revolt, fell on them, and without pausing a moment to ascertain the truth of their suspicions, killed upwards of 150 of the defenceless creatures before they discovered their error. So, also, we find it recorded during the siege of Malta, that some hesitation having shown itself on the part of the slaves in exposing themselves to a fire more than usually deadly, the Grand Master directed some to be hanged, and others to have their ears cut off, "*pour encourager les autres*," as the chronicler records it. We find, also, an English knight, named Massinberg, brought before the Council in 1534, for having unwarrantably drawn his sword and killed four galley-slaves; when he was called upon for his defence, this turbulent Briton replied, "In killing the four slaves I did well, but in not having at the same time killed our old and imbecile Grand Master, I confess I did badly." This defence not being considered satisfactory, he was sentenced to be deprived of his habit for two days.

The Order not only retained their slaves for their own use, they at the same time sold to private individuals any number that might be required. The truth is, that the convent of St. John became eventually neither more nor less than a vast slave mart. When the demand was brisk, and the supply scarce, the cruisers of the Order scoured the seas, and woe betide the unfortunate Turk who came within their range. The war which they unceasingly waged against the maritime power of the Turks was not so much from any sense of duty, or from religious conviction, as that they found that by thus gratifying their privateering propensities they were swelling, at one and the same time, their private fortunes and the public coffers. Honour there was none—religion there was none; it was a purely mercenary speculation, and the only extenuation which the fraternity could plead for this degradation of the principles which had governed their ancestors, was that they were merely acting by way of reprisal. The northern coast of Africa was one vast nest of infidel pirates, who scoured every corner of the Mediterranean, and whose detested flag was never seen without bringing with it all the horrors of bloodshed, rapine, and slavery. With a foe such as this it was but natural that there should be but scant courtesy shown, and had the Order invariably confined their efforts to the extermination of this noxious swarm, the historian should not be too severe in his criticisms on their subsequent behaviour to the captive enemy. It is, however, much to be feared that in their anxiety to keep the bagnio at Malta amply stocked, the knights of St. John were by no means careful to discriminate between the piratical corsair of Algiers and the peaceful mariner of the Levant.

There exists in the Record Office of Malta amongst a number of other letters written by the monarchs of England at various times to the Grand Masters, one from Charles II. to Nicholas Cottoner, in which it appears that the deportation of slaves from Malta for the use of the kings of France and Spain was of annual occurrence, and that the merry monarch of England craved to be admitted to the same privilege. The results of this traffic must have been most profitable not only from the proceeds of such as were sold, but also from the labour of those who were retained by the Order. No person can now contemplate the frowning mass of batteries and ramparts, or the yawning depths of the ditches which meet the eye on all sides as the traveller enters the harbour of Malta, without perceiving that such stupendous works could only have been erected in a spot were labour was a mere drug. The numerous gangs of slaves who were awaiting the requirements of the wealthy potentates of Europe were in the meantime amply earning the slender cost of their maintenance in the slaves' prison at Malta by toiling at those vast constructions which have raised Valetta to the position of one of the most powerful fortresses of Europe. The ramparts of that city have been reared amidst the anguish and toil of countless thousands torn from their homes and their country and condemned to drag out the remainder of their miserable existence as mere beasts of burden, labouring to rear those bulwarks which were to be employed against their own country. No existence can be conceived more utterly cheerless or more hopelessly miserable than that of the Moslem captive, whose only change from daily slavery on the public works was to be chained to the oar of a galley.

In conclusion, it may be well to say a few words upon the connection which existed between the Order and the native population. Before the islands of Malta and Gozo fell under the sway of the Order of St. John, through the act of donation granted by the Emperor Charles V., they had been an appanage of the Spanish monarchy, and attached to the vice-royalty of Sicily. Their local government had consisted of a governor or *hakim*, who was commandant of the military within the islands, and was entrusted with ample powers to maintain public tranquillity, four *giurati*, who acted under him as a council for all financial questions, and two *catapani*, for all matters relating to food, the great bulk of which was imported from Sicily. An officer named "*il secreto*" received the duties payable on imports, and another named "*il portolano*" was the superintendent of the harbours. Once every year an assembly or parliament was convened, which was divided into the three classes of nobles, clergy, and commons. This assembly prepared lists of candidates for the various above-mentioned offices, and the Viceroy selected from amongst those lists the persons by whom they were to be filled.

When the knights of St. John superseded the government of the Emperor, they maintained the leading features of the former administration. The assembly, it is true, soon became a dead letter, and the nomination to the various offices was made direct by the Grand Master in council; still the selection was invariably from among the Maltese, and their ancient customs and privileges were interfered with as little as possible. Their code of laws remained in force, and was recognised by the fraternity, the duty of carrying it into effect being left almost entirely in the hands of the Maltese.

There were three legal courts, each presided over by a native judge, the first for criminal causes, the second for civil causes, and the third for appeals from the other two. A knight was appointed who presided over the entire department, which was called the Castellany; but he in no way interfered with the administration of justice. He was replaced every second year by a fresh nomination. No member of the fraternity was, as such, amenable to the tribunals of the Maltese; but in cases where the crime rendered it advisable that he should be punished by the sentence of those courts, he was stripped of his habit as a preliminary measure, and then handed over to their jurisdiction as a secular person.

Throughout the residence of the Order in the island a very broad line of separation was drawn between themselves and the native population. The Maltese had always been a very aristocratic community; many of their families had been ennobled at a very early epoch, and the whole power of government had been vested in their hands. No more exclusive or oligarchal a community existed anywhere throughout Europe, and traces of this state of things may still be perceived in the island. The Order of St. John, eminently aristocratic though it was in its own constitution, and naturally jealous of all encroachments upon that privileged class from which its members were recruited, and whence all its power and wealth had been drawn, appeared in its connection with Malta to have been actuated by more liberal ideas and views, and its governors materially enlarged the basis of power by extending the area from which they elected their native *employés*. One natural result of this policy was a slight alienation and coldness on the part of that class who had hitherto monopolized the entire governance of the island, and this coldness, coupled with the natural reserve of the Maltese character, always acted to prevent any real amalgamation between the two parties.

The Maltese, as such, were not admitted into the highest class of the Order. Such of them as could bring forward the necessary proofs of nobility, and were otherwise eligible, could, it is true, become received as members of the Italian *langue*, and in a few cases even after marriage, on the condition that their wives should retire into Italy when about to become mothers; still the number who had entered the fraternity was but trifling, and even they were not ranked in the same position as the other members of the *langue*, being incapable of occupying the post either of Grand Master or of Conventual Bailiff. The Order were consequently always regarded as foreigners by the natives, and but little friendship or cordiality was to be traced in their social intercourse. It must not, however, be inferred from this that the Maltese were dissatisfied with the rule of the knights over them. That government was certainly a despotism, and one of the strongest nature, still it was well suited to the habits of the people, and usually wielded with equity and moderation. Those cravings for liberty and freedom of personal action which characterise the Anglo-Saxon temperament are not so strongly felt in southern latitudes, and the decrees of the Grand Master and his council met with a ready and cheerful obedience from those who felt no very urgent desire to undertake the responsible duty of governing themselves. The Order placed themselves on a decided eminence over those they governed, and when their interests clashed, it was but natural that the Maltese, as the weaker party, should be compelled to give way. Still, on the whole, they had not much cause for complaint, and there can be no doubt that the transfer of the island to the Order of St. John had brought many very solid advantages to its inhabitants.

Instead of a few officials and a slender garrison, they now saw Malta made the nucleus of the most powerful and wealthy fraternity in Europe. Every land contributed its quota to the stream of wealth which commenced from that day to pour into the island. The hamlet of the Bourg became a considerable city, and its suburbs extended themselves over the adjacent peninsula. Ere long a new city, exceeding in extent and magnificence anything which the wildest flight of imagination would have pictured in bygone years, sprang up, adorned with the auberges and other public buildings of a fraternity whose ample revenues enabled them thus to beautify their capital. Stores of grain accumulated in the public magazines, ramparts and forts sprang up to protect the island from the piratical descents of the Algerines; and Malta rose from the comparatively insignificant position into which she had for so many years sunk, to be ranked as the most important fortress and the most flourishing community in the Mediterranean.

These were no slight privileges; and the Order who had conferred such benefits on their subjects might well stand excused for a slight display of arrogance and despotism. After all, it was only with the highest class, the exclusive Maltese nobility, that the new government brought itself into disrepute; and with them it was not so much the despotism of the ruling power as the liberalism which had opened the way to office to a lower class than their own, which had engendered their disfavour. Below them there was a rising class containing much of the ambition and talent of the island, and it was amongst these that the council sought for candidates to fill the posts hitherto invariably monopolised by the nobility. With them, therefore, the Order stood in high favour; and whilst, on the one hand, the old nobility held themselves aloof, and, on the other, the lower class bowed in uncomplaining submission to the sway of a power sufficiently energetic to compel their obedience, this section, comprising most f the activity and talent of the country, became faithful adherents to the system by which their own emancipation from the dictation of the aristocracy had been secured.

Into this class of Maltese society the knights of St. John found a ready and welcome admission. Even here, however, there were great distinctions drawn between the various *langues*, some of which were far more popular than others. The French members did not find much favour with the fair ladies who swayed the empire of fashion within this coterie.

They were too arrogant, self-sufficient, and boastful ever to be received as chosen favourites, or to find a ready welcome into their domestic privacy. More than one case had occurred in which this bragging tendency on the part of Frenchmen, ever ready to imagine their attractions irresistible, had led to unpleasant results, and had clouded the fair fame of ladies whose only fault had perchance consisted in permitting rather too free an offering of adulation on the part of their knightly admirers. Whilst the French, however, were thus neglected, there were other *langues* whose members were more fortunate. The Germans, in particular, seem to have borne the palm for popularity. Their national reserve and phlegmatic temperament prevented them from falling into the errors of the more vivacious Frenchmen, and they were admitted on a footing of intimacy and freedom which the latter were never permitted to attain. The Spaniards were also very popular for much the same reason, and unless the tales recorded on this head are false, they were very successful in their intercourse with the fair ladies of Malta.

With the lower orders the rule of the knights was very popular. The works on which they were constantly engaged for the strengthening of their position yielded a continuous source of employment to the labouring class, and the ample stores of food retained in the magazines of Valetta secured them from the miseries of famine, which in olden times had so frequently been the scourge of the island. The Grand Master also sought popularity with this class by constantly providing them with amusements. Their privileges in this respect were very numerous, and always maintained with the utmost regularity.

The most entertaining of these festivals was the carnival, always celebrated in Malta with great splendour and variety of costume. The privilege of holding a carnival was granted by the Grand Master, not only on the three days immediately preceding the commencement of Lent, but at any other time when the Order desired to celebrate an event of unusual importance. These extra carnivals were called *Bubarro*. On Shrove Tuesday a *Cocagna* was given to the people. This was a vast structure reared in St. George's Square before the Grand Master's palace, and decorated with flowers, ribbons, and flags. The Cocagna was hung with fruits and provisions of all kinds—live poultry, hams, eggs, sausages, &c., were mixed with wreaths of flowers and clusters of fruit, the whole presenting a most tempting display to the assembled multitude. At a given signal there was a general scramble, and the provisions became the property of those sufficiently active and fortunate to carry them off. A master of the ceremonies was appointed to superintend on this occasion, and to give the signal for onslaught; he was termed *Il Gran Visconti*, and for the day the administration of the police was entrusted to his care.

The great festival of the Order, St. John's Day, was naturally observed with much rejoicing. In the afternoon races were held for prizes to be presented by the Grand Master, and the peculiarity of these races consisted in the course selected for the purpose. The main street of Valetta, the *Strada Reale*, extends in a straight line from Fort St. Elmo to the *Porta Reale*, a distance of upwards of half a mile. This was the course over which the races were run, and being in the heart of the town all traffic had to be stopped during their continuance. On the 1st of May the old custom of the greasy pole was introduced, which the Maltese were very expert in mounting; this was likewise erected in front of the Grand Master's palace.

In short, every effort appears to have been made by the government to render the population contented with their lot, so far as that could be ensured by a plentiful supply of amusement and festivity. In this they acted with a due discrimination as to the peculiar temperament of the Maltese people. Docile and tractable in the highest degree, they merely required the excitement of a little innocent recreation to quell any feeling of discontent which might have arisen against a government in which their interests were invariably compelled to yield to those of the fraternity, and where they had little or no voice in the legislation. That that government was, as a general rule, exercised beneficially the rapid progress made by the island clearly proves; still there were, doubtless, many laws enacted which pressed hardly on the Maltese. A little liberality on the score of sports and holidays prevented any ebullition of discontent at these political disadvantages, and by the adoption of such wise precautions the Order succeeded in maintaining tranquillity amongst the population throughout their residence in the island. It must not, however, be imagined that this docility on the part of the Maltese arose from any cravenness of spirit or want of courage. The events which marked the close of the eighteenth century, during the brief rule of the French, show clearly that the Maltese character is not wanting in firmness and resolution, and that, when roused by real wrongs and oppression, they are capable of the noblest exertions and the most heroic constancy in their efforts for freedom.

## CHAPTER X.

Position of the Order in France at the Outbreak of the Revolution—Arrival of the French Fleet before Malta—Instructions of Bonaparte for Effecting a Landing—State of the Town—Inefficiency of Hompesch—Surrender of the Island to Bonaparte.

EMMANUEL DE ROHAN, the sixty-eighth Grand Master of the Order of St. John, still held the bâton of office when the last decade of the eighteenth century commenced, and brought with it that fearful convulsion in France, in the midst of which the Order of St. John was doomed to destruction. The property of the fraternity within the limits of France was, at this period (as, indeed, it always had been) managed with a prudence and skill which rendered it a model to surrounding landowners. It was natural, therefore, that at a time when general spoliation had become a leading principle with the revolutionary party, these tempting acquisitions should attract their cupidity. The Order was in itself far too aristocratic in constitution to avoid the antagonism of the *sans culottes*, whose savage cry of *à bas les aristocrats* was then reverberating through France. Everything, therefore, marked the institution as one of the earliest victims to revolutionary rapacity.

Nor, indeed, had the conduct of the knights during the few years which immediately preceded the subversion of the monarchy been such as was at all likely to conciliate the animosity of the dominant faction. When Neckar, the finance minister of Louis XVI., demanded a voluntary contribution of one-third of the revenue of every proprietor, the Order were the first to come forward with their quota; and when subsequently the king, reduced to a state of extreme destitution, besought assistance from their treasury, they pledged their credit for the sum of 500,000 francs to aid him in his futile effort at flight. No diplomacy could therefore avert the fate impending over an institution which had added to the crime of being aristocratic and wealthy, that also of loyalty to the sovereign. The steps by which the act of spoliation was consummated were quickly taken, and met with no effectual resistance on the part of the destined victims. In the first constituent assembly the Order of St. John had been placed in the position of a foreign power, holding property within the limits of the French kingdom, and as such, was subjected to all the taxes imposed upon that kingdom. This step was soon followed by a decree, enacting that any Frenchman becoming a member of any order of knighthood, requiring proofs of nobility, should no longer be regarded as a French citizen.

These preliminary steps being taken, the grand blow was struck on the 19th of September, 1792, when it was enacted that the Order of Malta should cease to exist within the limits of France, and that all its property should become annexed to the national domains. At first, mention was made of an indemnification in the shape of pensions to be granted to the knights who were thus dispossessed of their property, but the benefit of such concession was at once neutralized by the condition that, in order to entitle a knight to his pension, he must reside within the French territories—

a practical impossibility to men of aristocratic birth at that period.

The enactment of this decree was followed by a general plunder of the various commanderies, and such members of the Order as were not fortunate enough to make their escape from the country, were thrown into prison. During this scene of anarchy the knights comported themselves with a dignity worthy of their institution. The ambassador of the Order at Paris, the Bailiff de la Brilhane, fulfilled his difficult and dangerous duties with unexampled determination till the very close. He was warned that his life was in the most imminent peril owing to the exertions he had made in defending the cause of his Order. "I am under no apprehensions," replied he; "for the moment has now arrived when a man of honour, who faithfully performs his duty, may die as gloriously on the scaffold as on the field of battle."

Great as had been the provocation, the Order did not break entirely with the French Directory, nor did they openly join the forces of those who sought to crush the revolution. A temporising policy seems to have been their aim, and in this they certainly acted with but little discrimination. They might have felt quite assured that no concessions and no professions of neutrality would lead those who now swayed the fortunes of France to regard them with a favourable eye. Their principles were essentially monarchical, and they had so far avowed them and revealed their sympathies with the fallen monarch of France, that on the arrival of the intelligence of his execution a funeral service was performed in the Conventual Church of St. John, at which the Grand Master, De Rohan, presided. The nave of the church was hung with black, and the fraternity, in deep mourning, offered up their prayers for the soul of the murdered king.

Had they openly and unreservedly thrown the whole weight of their influence into the scale of the alliance by which the progress of the revolution was sought to be stayed, they could not have reduced themselves to a worse position than that which their timid and temporising policy brought upon them. Their chief was indeed unsuited for the perilous crisis, and physical incapacity had latterly intervened to break down his energy and spirit. In 1791 he had been struck with apoplexy, and it was thought at the time that it must have ended fatally. Although he recovered from this attack, he never regained that energy of mind which was so necessary for the crisis through which he was called to guide the fortunes of his Order. His last days were clouded with the knowledge of the danger which threatened the very existence of the fraternity, and with the certainty that events were rapidly tending to that consummation. The numbers of homeless, destitute French knights who flocked to Malta, drained the resources of the treasury, and the utmost efforts of the Grand Master, nobly seconded though he was by all the *langues* who had escaped confiscation, were insufficient to relieve so universal a distress. The conduct of Rohan under these trying circumstances was most praiseworthy. Being remonstrated with by an officer of his household for the extent of his charities and for the expenditure on that score, which his diminished resources no longer admitted without curtailing the dignity of his court, he replied, " Reserve one crown daily for the expenses of my table, and let all the rest be distributed amongst my distressed brethren."

The worst had not, however, as yet arrived, though the day was near at hand when the fatal blow was to be struck. The Directory had for some time been turning their attention towards the island of Malta, and had conceived the desire of annexing it to the French dominions. The strength of its fortifications and its position in the centre of the Mediterranean, rendered it a most desirable acquisition to a nation anxious to obtain a naval supremacy in that sea, and steps were now taken to attain that consummation. For this purpose numerous emissaries were despatched into the island, whose object was to sow the seeds of discontent amongst the population, and, if practicable, to tamper with the fidelity of the knights themselves. The government of Rohan must certainly be blamed for the blindness which permitted this work to be carried on unchecked in their midst; and it seemed as though the supineness of the fraternity themselves was destined to aid the nefarious designs of their enemies.

In the midst of these gloomy presages, and at the worst crisis of the danger, Rohan died on the 13th July, 1797, and was succeeded by Ferdinand Joseph Antoine Herman Louis de Hompesch, to whose name is attached the melancholy distinction of having been the last Grand Master of Malta. He was the first German knight who had ever been raised to that office, and it has since been most undeservedly made a reproach against that *langue*, that the solitary chief whom they furnished to the Order, should so weakly and pusillanimously have betrayed its rights and interests. Hompesch, at the time of his election, was 53 years of age, and Grand Bailiff of Brandenburg, the chief of the Anglo-Bavarian *langue*.

Hompesch had not long assumed the reins of government before the storm burst which had been so long gathering upon the horizon of Malta. The following decree, published in the correspondence of Napoleon I., was drawn up by the French Directory, dated Paris, 23 Germinal, an VI. (12th April, 1798):—" Considering that the Order of Malta has placed itself of its own accord, and from the very commencement of the war, in a state of hostility against France; that it has actually made an express declaration of war by a manifesto of its Grand Master of the 10th October, 1794; that he has even protested by this insolent proclamation that he neither ought, nor could, nor would recognise the French republic; considering also, that the efforts which the Order have made, both before and since, to aid the coalition of the kings arrayed against liberty, have always accorded with this expression of their sentiments, and that even quite recently they have attained the culminating point of their efforts against the republic, by receiving into their midst and admitting to high office numerous Frenchmen, universally known as the most determined enemies of their country, disgraced for ever by having borne arms against her; seeing that everything announces on the part of the Order an intention of yielding its territories to one of the powers now at war with France, and by such means to paralyze the naval power of France in the Mediterranean; that in all respects, this Order is, as regards the French republic, in the same position as all the other powers with whom at the time of the establishment of the constitutional *régime* the nation has found itself in a state of war, without any declaration to that effect on her part, but by the simple fact, that they have placed themselves in that position; considering that there is therefore no necessity for any enactment on the part of the *Corps Legislatif* to enable the Directory to take such steps against the Order of Malta as the national honour and interest demand, the following decree is made:—

Article 1.—The General commanding-in-chief the Army of the East is desired to take possession of the island of Malta.

Article 2.—For this purpose he will at once direct against

the island of Malta the forces under his command both military and naval.

"This decree will not be printed."

A second decree was made on the same day, as follows:—

"Article 1.— The order given to General Bonaparte, commander-in-chief of the Army of the East by the decree of this day's date, to obtain possession of the island of Malta, shall not be carried into effect by him unless he considers it feasible, without risking the success of the other operations confided to his charge. The executive Directory leaves everything in this matter to his judgment.

"This decree will not be printed."

These two decrees mark most distinctly the determination of the French Government to obtain possession of the island of Malta, if practicable, and shows that the reasons for their attack subsequently put forward, after the island had fallen into their hands, were mendacious pretexts.

The decrees were, however, at the time, a secret between the Directory and those to whom their execution was entrusted;. and meanwhile the world was thrown into general alarm by the rumours of an extensive armament preparing in the French arsenals in the Mediterranean, the destination of which was as yet unknown. The restless spirit of aggression with which the young republic was imbued, rendered every nation suspicious and uneasy on the score of this vast armament, and preparations were on all sides set on foot for resistance.

One power alone continued careless and inactive in the midst of the general alarms. Whilst the note of preparation arose in every other country in Europe, the island of Malta remained in a state of supine and indolent security. Warnings had been despatched to the Grand Master, but they were unheeded. An ill-placed and most incomprehensible confidence on his part, joined to the most palpable treachery on that of his advisers, led to the engendering of a fatal sense of security, from which he was not aroused until the enemy was at the door. He had even received the most distinct notice of the destination of the French expeditionary force from the Bailiff de Schenau, the ambassador of the Order at the congress of Rastadt. That dignitary had written to him in the following terms:—

"I warn your Highness that the expedition now preparing at Toulon is intended against Malta and Egypt. I have my information from the private secretary of Mons. Treilhard, one of the ministers of the French republic. You will most certainly be attacked; take, therefore, all necessary measures for defence. The ministers of all the Powers in alliance with the Order who are now here, have received the same information as myself, but they know that Malta is impregnable, or, at all events, in a position to offer a resistance of three months' duration. Let your Eminent Highness, therefore, be on your guard. Your own honour and the preservation of your Order are concerned in the matter. If you yield without a defence, you will be disgraced in the eyes of all Europe. I may add that this expedition is looked upon here as likely to prove a disgrace to Bonaparte. He has two powerful enemies in the Directory, who have taken this opportunity of getting rid of him, Rewbell and Larevillière-Lepaux."

Such a letter as this, and coming from a source so worthy of credence, must, one would imagine, have placed Hompesch on his guard, but this was not the case. He conceived himself so secure in the friendly disposition of the French republic, that he scorned all preparations for resisting an invasion, which, he felt assured, was not aimed against his fraternity, and the terror of which was, he conceived, merely a bugbear existing in the agitated minds of nervous and timid politicians.

Such, then, was the comparatively unprepared position of Malta when, on the 6th June, 1798, a French fleet, consisting of eighteen sail and seventy transports, appeared off the island under the command of the Commodore Sidoux. Permission was demanded for a few of the vessels to enter the harbour and water; this was granted, two of the transports being admitted for that purpose, and one of the frigates for repair, the remainder lying at anchor outside. Every effort was made by the Order to mark their strict neutrality, and readiness to offer hospitality and assistance, as well to the French as to the other Powers whose fleets might approach their shores. On the 9th June, the main portion of the fleet appeared with the remainder of the forces, the whole under the command of General Bonaparte in person. The expedition, thus united, consisted of fourteen line-of-battle ships, thirty frigates, and three hundred transports; the commander-in-chief being on board the flag-ship *l'Orient*. The necessary arrangements for the preliminary operations of the descent on the island had been drawn up by Bonaparte in a despatch addressed to Admiral Brueys, dated on board *l'Orient* on the 6th June, which ran as follows :—

"Citizen Admiral; the General commanding-in-chief, having made his dispositions with regard to the island of Malta, has desired me to notify them to you, in order that you may give the necessary instructions to the fleet, in connection with those I am giving to the troops. The wish of the General is that the squadron and convoy should proceed with the least possible delay to the Bay of Marsa Scirocco, in order to effect the landing of the troops destined to attack the fortress; the vessels comprising the second squadron, viz., *le Franklin, le Spartiate, l'Aquilon*, and *le Guerrier*, proceeding at the same time to the entrance of the Grand Harbour, to establish a strict blockade.

"The General desires that Vice-Admiral Decrès, who commands the *Diane*, should arrange the details of the landing, and provide for its protection.

"The General has named the 4th and 7th light demi-brigades and the 6th, 19th, and 80th regiments of the line, with a train of artillery, as specified in the annexed return, for the landing force.

"The troops thus named are partly on board the men-of-war and partly on board the transports.

"The General desires that each ship should undertake the landing of her own men, but the vessels named for blockading the port of Valetta must embark their troops on board their respective launches, for the purpose of landing them, and must then proceed on their way, the launches being afterwards attached to *l'Orient, le Tonnant, le Peuple Souverain,* and *l'Heureux.*

"As the ship *l'Orient* has a large number of troops to land, you will give orders to employ for that purpose the light boats of the squadron.

"These arrangements require preparatory orders, both for army and navy, which I divide into two classes.

"The first is to issue to-morrow morning at an early hour the following orders:—

"1st.—That each man-of-war should, on the 7th inst., arm its launches with a howitzer or carronade, with forty rounds.

"2nd.—Give orders that the officers in command of the different detachments on board the ships should have an inspection, to see that the men's arms are in good order, and that each man is in possession of sixty rounds of ammunition and six flints, and is ready to land.

" 3rd.—To order that all the ships composing the Corsican convoy shall hoist some distinctive mark, and that they shall assemble round one of the men-of-war of the convoy, to be named by you, which shall hoist the same mark.

" 4th.—To notify to these ships that at the signal of three guns from the Admiral's ship, repeated by the commandant of the convoy, they shall rally round the frigate *Diane*, which ship, after the said three guns, shall fire four, to call the vessels round her. This frigate will carry an ensign, which you will specify, and you will notify the same to the various ships.

" The second part of the orders has reference to the time and place of landing, and will be issued when the fleet is before the Marsa Scirocco.

"By order of the Commander-in-Chief."

On his arrival before Malta, Bonaparte at once despatched the French Consul Caruson to the Grand Master, demanding free entrance into the Grand Harbour for the whole fleet, and that his troops might be permitted to land. Such a request proved of itself the object the French General had in view, and to have yielded the required permission would have been simply to surrender the fortress without an effort. Hompesch, by the advice of his council, returned for answer that it was contrary to the rules of his Order and to the treaty which they had made with France, Spain, and Naples, in 1768, to permit the entry of more than four ships of war at a time. This rule he was not prepared to abrogate, but any assistance which he could render to the sick would be tendered with the utmost pleasure and promptitude. The letter concluded with a hope that the Order might still trust to the loyalty and good faith of the French nation, with whom they had always lived in peace and harmony.

This refusal was taken on board the French flag-ship by Caruson, who at the same time informed Bonaparte that treason was rife within the town. Caruson did not return on shore, but forwarded the following letter to the Grand Master, on behalf of Bonaparte, who did not condescend to correspond personally with him :—

"9th June, 1798.

" Your Highness,

" Having been nominated to proceed on board the Admiral's ship, with the reply which your Eminence made to my request for permission to the squadron to water in your harbour, the commander-in-chief, Bonaparte, is highly indignant that such permission should have been restricted to four vessels at a time; for how long would it not take for 500 sail, at this rate, to procure water and such other necessaries as they are much in want of? This refusal has the more surprised General Bonaparte, since he is not ignorant of the preference which you have shown to the English, and the proclamation issued by the predecessor of your Eminence. General Bonaparte has determined to obtain by force what should have been granted to him of free will, in accordance with the principles of hospitality which form the basis of your Order. I have seen the stupendous armament which is under the command of General Bonaparte, and I foresee the impossibility of the Order making any resistance. It was to have been wished, therefore, that under such adverse circumstances, your Eminence, for the love of your Order, your knights, and the whole population of Malta, had proposed some measures of accommodation. The General has not permitted me to return to a town which he considers himself obliged to regard as hostile, and which has no hope save in his mercy. He has, however, given strict orders that the religion, the property, and the customs of the people shall not be interfered with."

Prior, however, to having thus openly declared war, Bonaparte had given the most detailed orders to the various generals who were to take part in the attack, as to their respective proceedings. General Baraguay d'Hilliers was to land at Melleha Bay; General Vaubois at St. Julian's; General Dessaix at Marsa Scirocco; and General Regnier at Gozo. Annexed are the various orders issued on the occasion. They are all dated on board *l'Orient*, on the 9th June. The first is to General Baraguay d'Hilliers :—

"Citizen General,—You will hold yourself in readiness to land your forces either in Melleha Bay, or in St. Paul's Bay, on the north side of the island. The General's wish is that until the moment that you receive orders to land you should be careful to do nothing to alarm or in any way cause disquietude to the inhabitants. When you receive orders to land you will endeavour to effect it by surprise, sending several of your convoy towards the shore asking permission to water, and landing several boat-loads of troops upon the most convenient point; the instant they have landed they must commence the operation of watering. You must only land as many troops as will ensure your being able to obtain possession of the batteries, towers, and posts which protect your anchorage. You will hold your convoy ready to leave at a moment's notice, and to re-embark your troops, as they will not be required to remain in Malta. The General expects that you will have three or four days in which to complete your watering. You will inform the General as soon as you have effected your landing, which must not take place until you have received fresh orders. He will then send you fresh instructions either by sea or land."

From these instructions, it is evident that the force to be landed by Baraguay d'Hilliers was not intended for the attack of the fortress. That duty was confided to Generals Dessaix and Vaubois, as the following order will show :—

"The Commander-in-chief desires General Dessaix to start at once in one of the ship's boats, to reconnoitre this evening the whole of the coast from St. Thomas's Bay to that of Vie de Sciaat. He is informed that the Admiral has directed his convoy to proceed to the entrance of the harbour of Marsa Scirocco. The General wishes that you should select the most favourable spot for landing at Marsa Scirocco. He desires that to-morrow morning, before daybreak, 300 or 400 men should land in boats at one of the spots you may have selected, out of range of any battery; at the same time that three or four of the ships of your convoy which draw the least water shall approach the harbour of Marsa Scirocco under pretext of watering. By this means you will secure your landing. The marine General du Chayla, with four men-of-war, will anchor at the distance of a mile from Marsa Scirocco to support the landing. The General desires that directly you are master of all the batteries and towers, so as to be able to anchor in security in the bay of Marsa Scirocco, you should advance on the town, and endeavour to take a gate by surprise, or to escalade at some point in the Cottonera lines which has no ditch. But if the enemy is vigilant, the General desires that you should content yourself with investing Fort Ricasoli and the Cottonera lines, communicating on your left with General Vaubois, who will land in

St. Julian's Bay and invest the other side of the town. You will only land the troops that are required for this operation, and no cavalry. You will give orders that the instant the convoy enters the Marsa Scirocco bay, they shall commence to water, and secure forage for the horses. You must be ready to leave again in three days. You will make bread, and feed your troops in the villages of Zabbar, Zeitun, Gudia, and Tarschien. You must prepare everything for your landing to-night; but you must do nothing hostile until you receive fresh orders. You will tell the inhabitants that the French do not come to change either their customs or their religion, that the strictest discipline will be maintained, and that the priests and monks shall be specially protected. The General commanding-in-chief will issue a proclamation for the whole island."

The next order is addressed to General Vaubois:—

"By order of the General commanding-in-chief, General Vaubois is desired to start to-morrow (10th June), at two o'clock in the morning, to effect a landing upon some point between St. Julian's Point and Madalena Bay. That portion of the troops which is commanded by Brigadier-General Marmont will be two or three hundred yards in advance of that commanded by General Lannes. Citizen Marmont will effect his landing on the most favourable spot, and will seize any batteries which might oppose the landing of the division. The moment that is accomplished he will take up a position in the Spinola Garden. General Lannes will send out other detachments to capture whatever batteries command Madalena Bay, such as the tower of St. Mark. As soon as the 19th regiment of the line and the 4th light have landed, Citizen Marmont will proceed to invest the city of Valetta; starting from the Cité Pinto (Casal Curmi), he will extend his posts as far as Casal Novo, in order to connect himself with the left of General Dessaix's force. General Vaubois will invest the fort of the Marsa Muscetto (Fort Manoel) and the fort which is believed to be unfinished upon the Point Dragut (Fort Tigné). The three companies of the 18th and those of the 32nd will form the head-quarter guard, and will be posted in Casal Gargur. A flying column will be formed of the 6th regiment to proceed to Casal Lia, Casal Attard, and as far as the Citta Vecchia, to conquer those places. General Vaubois will issue a proclamation, in which he will guarantee to the inhabitants the exercise of their religion and strict discipline, and that all the villages where the inhabitants remain tranquil shall be protected. The commissary of the division will arrange for the feeding of the troops in the villages."

Whilst these arrangements were made for the landing in Malta, the following order was issued as regards the island of Gozo:—

"The Chief of the Staff will direct General Regnier to hold himself in readiness to land in the bay of Ramla, and to take possession of the island of Gozo the moment he receives orders to that effect. He will reconnoitre the coast on the north of the island at once, especially the bay of Aain Rihanna, the bay of Ramla, and others, in order that he may select the most suitable spot for the disembarkation. Until he is actually about to land, he is to take care to do nothing to alarm the inhabitants. As soon as he has received the order to land, he will endeavour to effect it by surprise, sending several vessels of his convoy towards the shore, asking for water, and at the same time landing several boat-loads of troops on the spot that he thinks best suited for the purpose. The moment he has effected a landing, he is to commence watering, and load forage for the horses. He will land only as many men as are absolutely necessary to take possession of the island, and he will at once name an officer as commandant. He will organise a hospital of one hundred beds, and land all the sick. He must provision the whole of the division with the food he will seize on the island. He is to draw up a plain and simple proclamation, which he is to have translated into the native language, and copied by writers of the country, stating that the French have not come to change either their customs or religion; that the strictest discipline will be maintained, and that the priests will be specially protected. He will show much attention to the priests and monks, and will affix seals to all the property of the knights of Malta; he will have all arms collected on one spot. If he finds any villages ill-disposed, he is to take hostages from them, and convey them on board ship. General Regnier will report to me the moral state of the inhabitants, and I will direct him as to the form of administration he is to adopt, and the supplementary operations he will have to conduct. Not a horse is to be landed; the generals will easily find horses for themselves and their aides-de-camp in the nearest village."

Whilst Bonaparte was thus taking his measures for the attack, it will be well to glance at the state of affairs within the fortress. There were at the time present, in the convent, the following knights of the Order, viz:—200 of the three French *langues*, 90 Italians, 25 Spanish, 8 Portuguese, 4 German, and 5 Anglo-Bavarian, making a total of 332; of these, 50 were from age and other causes incapacitated from bearing arms. The garrison consisted of the Maltese regiment of 500 men; the Grand Master's guard of 200; the battalion of the men-of-war, 400; that of the galleys,

300; gunners, 100; the militia regiment of chasseurs, 1,200; and the crews of the galleys and men-of-war, 1,200; making a total of 3,700 men, to whom might be added 3,000 more of the island militia, on whom, under ordinary circumstances, the Order might count to do faithful service, but who had been rendered somewhat disaffected by the emissaries of the republic. With this addition, the garrison, including the knights, amounted to a total of upwards of 7,000 men, and this number could, if necessary, have been further increased by the enrolment of all the able-bodied Maltese, who were bound to serve, if required, for the defence of the island. Had the same feeling of loyalty been present on this occasion as that which had actuated the garrison during the siege by the Turks, it would not have been within the power of the French general so easily to wrest the fortress from the hands of the fraternity.

Within the council, no one talked openly of surrender, but no prompt measures of defence were taken. Hompesch himself was perfectly useless in the conjuncture; unprepared indeed to yield, but unable to take the most ordinary precautions for the general safety. Without the walls of the palace, treason stalked openly and undisguisedly; the emissaries of the republic were to be seen everywhere discouraging the loyal, seducing the vacillating, and pointing out to all the folly of attempting a resistance when no preparations had been made for such a course, and when the feelings of the garrison were so divided on the point.

On the evening of the 9th of June, Bonaparte gave his final orders to the generals who were to effect a landing, and on Sunday, the 10th June, at four o'clock in the morning, the disembarkation of the French army commenced. Eleven different points were selected for this operation, and the towers of St. George and St. Julian yielded without resistance. By ten o'clock in the morning, the whole outlying country was in the hands of the French, and all the detached forts, with the solitary exception of St. Lucian's Tower at the Marsa Scirocco, had yielded to them. By noon, 15,000 men had landed, and the heads of their columns had advanced close to the defences on the side of the Cottonera lines. Several knights who had been taken prisoners during this operation were brought before Bonaparte, who expressed himself highly indignant at finding Frenchmen in arms against their country. He is reported to have said, "How is it that I am destined constantly to meet with knights who have taken up arms against their country? I ought to give directions to have you all shot. How could you believe it possible that you could defend yourselves with a few wretched peasants, against troops who have conquered the whole of Europe?" Notwithstanding this outburst of anger, he gave instructions that the prisoners should be well treated; nor had they eventually anything to complain of on that score.

Meanwhile, treachery and panic had been working their way within the town. Hompesch, instead of endeavouring to restore order and confidence, remained buried in his palace, accompanied by only a single aide-de-camp. He did not even name a lieutenant to aid him in this juncture. The commanders of the various posts, unwilling to take upon themselves the responsibility of action, remained passive, and the French were permitted to take up their positions unmolested. At length, a feeble attempt was made to check the advance of the French by a sortie, but the Maltese regiment which was sent out for this purpose, having been received by the enemy's columns with a heavy fire, soon gave way, and retreated into the town in such confusion, that they suffered the loss of their standard. At the same time, the Chevalier de Soubiras made a diversion with a small fleet of galleys, with which he left the grand harbour, and on approaching the spot where the French were still continuing their disembarkation, he opened fire upon them. He was, however, speedily forced to retire, without having rendered any effectual opposition to the operation.

Before night, the French division under Desaix had invested the Cottonera lines and Fort Ricasoli, whilst Baraguay d'Hilliers was in possession of all the centre of the island. Vaubois had seized the Città Notabile, and Regnier was master of Gozo. Night only added to the general scene of confusion and dismay; shots were heard on all sides, and the garrison were called upon to fight, not only against the open enemy in their front, but also the insidious treachery in their midst. Everywhere the most complete disorganisation was apparent—the soldiers deserted their standards, the people collected together in threatening crowds, cries of treason were heard on all sides. Throughout this scene of confusion the French emissaries busied themselves exciting the people to acts of violence, and pointing out those knights who were in reality the most zealous in endeavouring to protract the defence, as the traitors by whom they were being betrayed. The infuriated multitude, stimulated to a pitch of frenzy by these foul calumnies and scandalous aspersions, soon proceeded to acts of violence, and several unfortunate knights fell victims to the blindness of their rage. Amongst the number, may be named the Chevalier de Vallin, who, after being stabbed, was thrown into the sea; the Chevalier de Montazet, who was murdered by the troops at Bennisa Point; the Chevalier d'Ormy and the Chevalier d'Andelard, who was killed in the endeavour to save a comrade from the fury of the populace. Many others were seriously wounded, and the mob, raging with the excitement of the moment, dragged their bleeding victims to the front of the Grand Master's palace.

About midnight a deputation of some of the leading Maltese proceeded to the palace, and in an audience with the Grand Master, demanded that he should capitulate and sue for a cessation of hostilities. They pointed out that there was palpable treason at work, that no orders were executed, that the plan organised for defence was not carried out, that provisions, ammunition, and despatches were all intercepted, and that the massacre of the knights, which had already taken place, proved that the body of the people were inimical to them. Unless, therefore, a speedy surrender were determined on, there was reason to fear that a wholesale butchery would ere long ensue. To this demand Hompesch returned a refusal, without, however, taking any active steps to render that refusal effectual; and before long a second deputation made their appearance, and announced to him that if he did not promptly yield to their demand they would open negotiations with Bonaparte themselves, and treat for the surrender of the town without further reference to him.

Alarmed at this threat, Hompesch summoned his council to deliberate upon the demand of the insurgents, and at that dead hour of the night the dignitaries of the Order assembled within the palace, and proceeded to debate upon the question. Whilst the discussion was going on, and different views were being propounded, a tumult without the door of the council chamber denoted a fresh interruption, and in a few moments in rushed a body of rioters, bearing in triumph on their shoulders the French knight, Boisredont Ransijat, the treasurer of the Order. This knight had, at the commencement of hostilities, written to the Grand Master, announcing that as a knight of the Order of St. John, his duty was to fight against the infidel, but that he could not take part in a struggle against his countrymen; at the same time tendering the resignation of his office. Hompesch had ordered the recreant commander to be confined in Fort St. Angelo, and now his friends of the revolutionary party had released him by force. This incident completed the panic of the council. Alarmed lest the city should be surrendered without reference to them, they instantly decided that a deputation should be selected to wait upon General Bonaparte, and demand a suspension of arms as a preliminary to capitulation. The individuals named for this duty were the Bailiff Saousa, the Knights Miari and Monferret, the Maltese Baron d'Aurel, and M. Fremeaux, the Dutch Consul. As soon as the deputation had departed on its errand, orders were sent by Hompesch to the different posts to cease firing, and ere long a complete silence reigned throughout the town, broken only by the distant booming of the cannon of Fort Rohan at the Marsa Scirocco, commanded by La Guérivière, a brave knight who maintained an active resistance in his little isolated post until the 11th June, when he was forced to surrender, his garrison having been twenty-four hours without food.

Bonaparte, who had all along been kept acquainted with the course matters were taking within the town, had awaited with impatience for the demand of an armistice from the Grand Master. He was so assured that his friends would secure the surrender of the place without any great effort on his part, that he had done little or nothing towards the actual prosecution of the siege. He had, it is true, landed a few pieces of artillery, and had commenced the construction of some batteries, but this was merely to terrify the inhabitants, and not with any view to actual use. Indeed, he had received the most positive injunctions from the French Directory not to prosecute his plans against Malta if he met with any determined resistance. They feared, and with reason, that the safety of the expedition might have been compromised had he been detained for any length of time before the walls of Malta, and that the dreaded English fleet would be upon their track. Anxiously, therefore, had he looked for the first proffers of surrender, which his emissaries within the town had assured him would not be long delayed.

Not a moment, therefore, was lost after the arrival of the deputation, in securing the object of the mission. General Junot, the aide-de-camp to the commander-in-chief, M. Poussielgue, in charge of the commissariat chest, and a knight of St. John, named Dolomière, who formed one of a party of *savants* accompanying the expedition with a view to studying the geology of Egypt, were nominated to treat for the surrender, and at once returned into the town for that purpose.

Hompesch received them in due state, surrounded by his council, and prepared to open the proceedings with all the customary formalities. When, however, the secretary demanded of the Grand Master what preamble he should draw up, Junot rudely interrupted him, exclaiming, "What preamble do you want?—four lines will settle the entire business, and those Poussielgue will dictate." It was evidently the intention of the French envoy to carry everything with a high hand, nor was there any one present to oppose him. The following armistice was therefore agreed to:—

"Art. 1. A suspension of arms for twenty-four hours (to count from six o'clock this evening, the 11th of June, till six o'clock to-morrow evening) is granted between the army of the French republic, commanded by General Bonaparte, represented by Brigadier-General Junot, Aide-de-camp to the said general, on the one side, and His Most Eminent Highness and the Order of St. John, on the other side.

"Art. 2. Within these four-and-twenty hours deputies shall be sent on board *l'Orient* to arrange a capitulation.

"Done in duplicate at Malta this 11th of June, 1798.

"(Signed) JUNOT. HOMPESCH."

On the following day General Bonaparte entered the town, and took up his residence at the house of the Baron Paulo Parisio, a noble Maltese, who lived near the Auberge de Castile; and here he established his head-quarters. As he entered within the stupendous fortifications of Valetta and witnessed their great strength, he exclaimed, "Well was it for us that we had friends within to open the gates for us, for had the place been empty we should have had far more difficulty in obtaining an entrance." Bonaparte had good reason for his self-gratulation; his proverbial good fortune had not deserted him. Had he been detained for a very short time before Valetta the fleet under Nelson would have been upon him, and the glorious victory of the Nile would have been anticipated, and have been fought beneath the ramparts of Malta. Bonaparte disgraced, with his army destroyed, and his fleet scattered, would have made a very different figure on the stage of Europe than he was destined to occupy as the conqueror of Egypt. Fate had, however, decreed it otherwise. The capture of Malta, and the expedition to Egypt, had been proposed by his enemies as a trap by which his disgrace might be ensured, but the cowardice of Hompesch had turned the scale in his favour, and when Europe learnt with amazement that the powerful fortress of Malta had surrendered in two days, a fresh laurel was twined in that chaplet of glory which already encircled his brow.

It may be well now to glance for a few moments at the events just recorded, as seen from a French point of view. The following narrative, written by Marmont, gives a graphic account of that portion of the operations in which he was engaged:—" Directed to land in St. Paul's Bay with five battalions, I was the first Frenchman who set foot on the island. Some companies of the regiment of Malta, who were posted on the shore, retreated without fighting. We followed them, and they retired into the town. I invested the place from the sea as far as the aqueduct, in order to connect myself with General Desaix, who had landed on the east of the town. I approached the town, and came across a horn-work, that of Floriana, covering the place on this side, but unarmed. I established posts as near to it as possible, so as to confine the garrison. I had no sooner completed these arrangements than I saw the drawbridge lowered, and a large and disorderly body of men marching against me. I collected my posts at once, and retired slowly and in good order, firing from time to time upon the head of the column, in order to check their advance. I sent orders to two battalions of the 19th Regiment, encamped at cannon shot's distance from the town, on the right and left of the road, to place themselves under cover, and only to show themselves when I arrived at the spot, and gave them orders. This was carried out as I wished. The Maltese seeing me retreat took courage. Arriving thus massed in column, close to the spot where the 19th were, this regiment showed itself, and received them with a deadly fire, which threw them into the utmost disorder. I at once charged them with my troops, and routed them. We followed them, charging with the bayonet, and killed a considerable number. I carried off with my own hands the standard of the Order, which was displayed at the head of the column. These poor Maltese soldiers, simple peasants as they were, and only speaking Arabic, argued thus with themselves: We are fighting against Frenchmen, we are led by Frenchmen, therefore the Frenchmen who command us are traitors. In their rage they massacred seven of the French knights who had led them in the sortie, and yet it had been the French knights alone who had counselled resistance. Such treatment was not encouraging. Consequently they sent me an emissary the next morning to say that if the negotiations then on foot did not lead to the surrender of the town, they would hand over to me St. Joseph's Gate (Porte des Bombes). The negotiations, however, were successful, and the capitulation was signed. Thus were celebrated the obsequies of the Order of St. John, fallen from its pristine glory and splendour by its want of firmness and its cowardice. The Maltese were furious. We had at first much uneasiness as to the carrying into effect of the capitulation. These peasant soldiers were in possession of two inner works, very lofty cavaliers closed at the gorge, armed, and commanding the whole town, called Forts St. John and

St. James. They refused to surrender them, even after we had entered the gates and penetrated within the *enceinte*. It was by the merest chance that they did not continue their resistance; and, if they had, it is impossible to say what effect this one obstacle would have had, in the position in which we then were. If the Government of Malta had done its duty, if the French knights, after having commenced a defence, had not been so rash, they would not have attempted a sortie with untrained troops to fight against veteran soldiers. They would have remained behind their ramparts—the strongest in Europe—and we could never have entered. The English squadron, already at our heels, would, a few days after our landing, have destroyed our fleet or put it to flight, and the army, landed and wanting in all sorts of supplies, after having endured for some days the extremities of famine, would have been obliged to lay down its arms and to surrender. There is no exaggeration in this picture—it is the simple truth; and one shudders in thinking of the risk we ran, so easily to have been foreseen, and so alarming. But the hand of Providence guided us, and saved us from the catastrophe."

General Baraguay d'Hilliers gives the following report of the operations conducted by him:—"The troops of the division have, during the day, taken possession of all the batteries, forts, and stations which surround the bays of Melleha and St. Paul. The Maltese troops defended the different posts which they occupied as well as they were able, but every thing yielded to our well-arranged plans, which the three columns of the landing force carried out with much gallantry and discrimination. We lost none, either killed or wounded. A Maltese soldier and a knight were killed. We took a hundred prisoners, three of whom were French knights. In sending them to you I warn you that they seem well informed, but speak with much caution. I think, however, that something may be elicited from their fears if they are questioned separately. It is only two days since they left the town. With regard to the other prisoners, as they are all militia of the country, I thought it best to send them home to their villages charged with peaceful messages to their friends, and evidently much impressed with French generosity. The forts and batteries we have taken are armed with nearly fifty guns, and are tolerably well furnished with warlike matériel. The troops, who are masters of all the forts situated between the stream which runs into St. Paul's Bay and the coast towards the island of Gozo, have taken up a position on the heights, in front of this stream; here I shall await further orders from you. I have landed about 9,000 men. The country contains no wood, and there is a very great scarcity of water, as the streams which are shown on the map, as running into the Bays of Melleha and St. Paul, are intercepted on the way, and discharge themselves into tanks at some distance from the coast, rendering it very difficult for me to obtain any. I shall, however, make the attempt to-morrow, and, if successful, which I doubt, I need not trouble you further on the matter; otherwise, I shall have to ask you for further instructions. The bearer of this despatch is directed to hand over to you three Maltese standards, which have been taken in the fort."

General Regnier reported as follows from Gozo:—"In compliance with your orders, I have taken possession of the island of Gozo. The island was defended by a militia corps composed of the inhabitants, and formed into a regiment of musketeers 800 strong, a coast-guard regiment of 1,200 men, and a company of 300 men, 30 of whom are mounted; in all, 2,300 men, who were scattered on different points of the coast, supported by forts and batteries along the whole south-side of the island. In order to avoid losing our men, and having to commence hostilities by landing near the forts, and also to escape exposing the ships to the fire of the batteries, I searched for an unguarded spot at some distance from the fortifications; I selected Redum Kbir, between the New Tower and the first battery in Ramla Bay. At this point the coast is very steep, and the inhabitants considered it secure from attack. I took advantage of a water-course formed in the cliffs as a means of climbing the heights; the whole morning was employed in assembling the convoy, arranging signals, and drawing near the shore. A change of wind and a subsequent calm delayed me considerably. At 1 p.m. I was with *l'Alceste* and the squadron at a distance of from 800 to 900 fathoms from the shore, the calm preventing us from approaching any nearer. Being anxious to effect a landing and to reach the place I had selected before the enemy had perceived my intentions and brought their troops to the spot, I placed my men in the boats, and we started for the shore; the gun-boats *l'Etoile* and *le Pleuvier* accompanying us. As soon as the enemy saw the direction we were taking, they hastened from all parts to the spot, and commenced to man the heights. I directed our boats to give way as rapidly as possible, hoping to arrive at the landing-place before them. The cliffs were lined with country people, who opened fire on the boats as soon as they came within range. The citizen Bertrand, serjeant-major of the grenadiers, was killed in my boat. The Ramla and New Tower batteries also opened fire on us. The first to draw near to the shore were the boats of *l'Aceste*, in one of which I was with General Fugières, your aide-de-camp, Bonaparte, the captains of engineers, Geoffrey and Salatier, and the third company of grenadiers. Two hundred men were by this time stationed on the cliffs commanding the landing-place, and this number was being rapidly augmented. As soon as we had landed, we climbed the cliff as quickly as possible without returning a shot, notwithstanding their heavy fire which ploughed the ground around us, and the blocks of stone which they hurled down upon us. Finding, however, that our grenadiers advanced steadily in spite of all obstacles, they fled as soon as the first of our men had gained the heights. This engagement only lasted for a few minutes; and before any of the other boats which were following had time to arrive we had captured the first battery at Ramla. The gun-boats, *l'Etoile* and *le Pleurier*, fired very successfully on the enemy and their batteries. As soon as all the troops were disembarked, I fell them in on the heights of Redum il Kbir, and commenced my march with a portion of the eighty-fifth demi-brigade, towards the city of Chambray, through Casal Nadur, intending to take possession of that fort, and cut off the communication between Gozo and Malta by the bay of Migiaro. At the same time, I directed that portion of the ninth demi-brigade which had landed, to march through Casal Xara, on the castle of Gozo, and another detachment to the Marsalfirno tower.

"The fort of Chambray was full of inhabitants, who, with their cattle, had taken refuge there. I sent them in a proclamation to inform them of our objects; and to prevent them from making a useless defence which might prove fatal to them. I posted three companies in front of the fort to await their reply, and proceeded myself towards the castle of Gozo. As soon as the inhabitants of Rabato and the castle of Gozo saw our troops approaching, they sent to announce their submission, and to hand me the keys of the castle. The governor and the other knights of Malta had escaped, and our troops entered the castle that evening. The proclamation which I had sent in to Fort Chambray had the desired effect; the drawbridges being broken, the inhabitants assisted our troops to enter the fort, by laying planks and throwing ropes to them, and returned to their houses with their cattle.

"We found in the island 150 pieces of artillery, 40 of which are in the castle of Gozo, and 72 in Fort Chambray, the remainder being divided amongst the various forts, batteries, and towers on the coast; a number of muskets, and three depôts of corn were also found. I made no prisoners, as the inhabitants who had taken up arms had no distinguishing marks, and ran away on our approach. I thought it wise to treat them kindly, in order to encourage them to go back to their homes and resume their work. Three of their wounded are in hospital. The Governor and the other knights of Malta concealed themselves, but some of them gave themselves up afterwards, and others have been arrested. I am leaving them free in the town of Rabato, until I know the fate of the Order. I have kept up the civil and judicial administration of the island, with a view to having these authorities to apply to for all the wants of the troops. Every syndic is subject to a central administration residing at Rabato, and composed of four jurors, presided over by the Governor. I replaced him by a member whom I selected from a list of candidates that I ordered the other jurors to furnish me with.

"The population of Gozo amounts to between 1,300 and 1,400. It is cultivated with care, but its principal crop being cotton, it offers but few resources for subsistence; it will not suffice completely to victual the convoy which carries my division. I trust to find sufficient cattle to furnish the troops with fresh meat while they are here. There will be great difficulty in obtaining sheep for taking away with us. The wine found in the island has been already consumed; the stores of corn may prove sufficient for the bread and biscuit which we require for ourselves, and still leave some for the people; but there is a total want of fuel for heating the ovens. Some wood must be sent to us from Malta, and if we are to remain in port for some days more, we might send for some to Sicily or Lampedusa.

"We have great difficulty in obtaining sufficient straw or barley to supply the ships that have horses on board. The inhabitants are beginning to take courage, and to see how beneficial our invasion will be to them in the end. Some had taken it into their heads that the lands belonging to the Order of Malta were going to be divided amongst them, and had already taken possession of the fields that suited them. I was obliged to put a stop to this. The Order having several farms on the island, I notified that these would henceforth be considered national property."

Such are the accounts given by the three principal actors in the drama, and they all show how lamentably weak and inefficient the defence was, and the total absence of authority that existed. The capitulation was agreed to on the 12th of June, in virtue of which the island of Malta passed for ever from under the dominion of the Order of St. John. It was couched in the following terms:—

"Art. 1. The knights of the Order of St. John of Jerusalem shall give up the city and forts of Malta to the French army; at the same time renouncing in favour of the French republic all right of property and sovereignty over that island, as also those of Gozo and Cornino.

"Art. 2. The French republic shall employ its influence at the congress of Rastadt to secure a principality for the Grand Master equivalent to the one he surrenders, and the said republic engages to pay him in the meantime an annual pension of 300,000 livres, besides two annats of the pension by way of indemnification for his personal prospects. He shall also continue to receive the usual military honours during the remainder of his stay in Malta.

"Art. 3. The French knights of the Order of St. John of Jerusalem, actually resident at Malta, shall, if acknowledged as such by the commander-in-chief, be permitted to return to their native country, and their residence in Malta shall be considered in the same light as if they had inhabited France. The French republic will likewise use its influence with the Cisalpine, Ligurian, Roman, and Helvetian republics, that this third article may remain in force for the knights of those several nations.

"Art. 4. The French republic shall assign an annual pension of 700 livres to those over sixty years of age. It shall also endeavour to induce the Cisalpine, Ligurian, Roman, and Helvetian republics, to grant the same pension to the knights of their respective countries.

"Art. 5. The French republic shall use its influence with the different powers that the knights of each nation may be permitted to exercise their rights over the property of the Order of Malta situated in their dominions.

"Art. 6. The knights shall not be deprived of their private property either in Malta or Gozo.

"Art. 7. The inhabitants of the islands of Malta and Gozo shall be allowed ashore before the free exercise of the Catholic, Apostolic, and Holy Roman religion. Their privileges and property shall likewise remain inviolate, nor shall they be subject to any extraordinary taxes.

"Art. 8. All civil acts passed during the government of the Order shall remain valid.

"Done and concluded on board *l'Orient*, before Malta, on the 24th Prairial, the sixth year of the French republic (12th June, 1798).

"The Commander Boisredont de Ransijat,
Baron Mario Testaferrata,
Dr. Giovanni Nicolas Muscat,
Dr. Benedetto Schembri,
The Bailiff of Torio Frisari,

(without prejudice to the right of dominion belonging to my sovereign, the king of the two Sicilies).

"The Chevalier Felipe di Amati."

Such were the terms of capitulation which transferred the island of Malta to the French. The standard of the Order was removed from its proud position, and the degenerate descendants of L'Isle Adam and La Valette were doomed to the degradation of witnessing the substitution in its place of the French tricolour, without having even the satisfaction of feeling that they had struck one good blow to prevent the catastrophe. For two centuries and a-half, successive Grand Masters had lavished their own fortunes, and the treasures of the Order, in rearing a frowning mass of ramparts and batteries in every direction. The opinion of all the leading engineers of Europe had been sought for to suggest fresh additions to render the fortress of Valetta impregnable. It had long been recognised as one of the most powerful fortresses in Europe, and yet, in less than two days, it had yielded with scarce a struggle to the armies of France. The cowardice and negligence, the incapacity and blindness of Hompesch, combined with the treachery of those under him, had done all that Bonaparte could have desired, and it must have been with feelings of no little exultation that he penned the following despatch to the French Directory :—

HEAD QUARTERS, MALTA, 25th Prairial, VI.<br>(13th June, 1798.)

"We sighted the island of Gozo at break of day on the 9th ;* the convoy of Civita Vecchia had arrived three days before. On the evening of the 9th, I sent one of my aides-de-camp to demand permission from the Grand Master to water in the various anchorages of the island. The consul of the republic at Malta brought me his reply, which was a direct refusal, saying 'that he could not permit the entry of more than two transports at a time, which, by calculation, would have taken upwards of three hundred days for the purpose.' The wants of the army being pressing, I was obliged to have recourse to force. I ordered Admiral Brueys to make preparations for landing. He sent Vice-Admiral Blanquet du Chayla with his squadron, and the convoy of Civita Vecchia to effect a landing in the bay of Marsa Scirocco ; the convoy of Genoa landed in St. Paul's Bay, and that of Marseilles in the island of Gozo. Brigadiers-General Lannes and Marmont landed at cannon-shot distance from the place. General Desaix directed General Belliard to land with the 21st Regiment. He captured all the batteries and forts which protected the roadstead and anchorage of Marsa

---

* For the reader's convenience, the dates throughout this despatch have been changed from the republican style to the ordinary mode of computation.

Scirocco. At daybreak on the 10th our troops had landed everywhere in spite of a vigorous, but badly-directed cannonade. By night on the 10th, the place was invested on all sides, and the rest of the island was ours. General Regnier had captured the island of Gozo; General Baraguay d'Hilliers the whole of the interior of the island of Malta, having taken prisoner several knights, and 200 men; General Desaix was within pistol-shot of the glacis of the Cottonera and of Fort Ricasoli; he had also taken several knights prisoners. The unfortunate inhabitants, frightened beyond conception, had taken refuge in the town of Malta, which was thus amply garrisoned.

"During the whole of the night of the 10th a vigorous cannonade was maintained. The besieged tried to make a sortie, but Brigadier Marmont, at the head of the 19th, captured from them the standard of the Order. On the 11th I commenced to land artillery. There are few places in Europe so strong and in such good order as Malta. I did not confine myself to military operations; I started several different negotiations, the results of which were most fortunate. The Grand Master sent on the morning of the 11th a demand for a suspension of hostilities; I despatched my aide-de-camp Brigadier Junot to the Grand Master with powers to sign a suspension of arms, if he consented as a preliminary to treat for the surrender of the place; I sent citizens Poussielgue and Dolomieu to sound the Grand Master and inhabitants as to their intentions. At midnight on the 11th, the envoys of the Grand Master came on board *l'Orient*, where, during the night, they concluded a convention for the surrender of the island. At the head of the Grand Master's deputation was the Commander Boisredon Ransijat, knight of the late *langue* of Auvergne, who, the

x

moment he perceived an intention of taking up arms against us, wrote to the Grand Master, stating that his duty as a knight of Malta was to fight against the Turks and not against his country; he declared in consequence that he would not side with the Order under these circumstances. He was at once cast into prison, and only released in order to conduct the negotiations. Yesterday, the 12th, we entered the town and took possession of all the forts. To-day at noon the fleet has anchored in the harbour. I am very much pleased with the conduct of Admiral Brueys, and with the harmony and good order which has prevailed throughout the fleet; I have also to praise the zeal and activity of citizen Ganteaume, divisional commander of the staff of the squadron. Citizen Motard, captain of frigate, commanded the landing boats; he is a young officer of much promise. We found in Malta two men-of-war, one frigate, four galleys, 1,200 guns, 1,500,000 lbs. of powder, 40,000 muskets, and other things. A list will be forwarded immediately. I annex the different orders which I have issued for the government of the island. I annex also a list of the French who are living in Malta, most of them knights who only a month before our arrival made contributions towards the invasion of England. I ask for promotion to be given to citizen Marmont.

"BONAPARTE."

## CHAPTER XI.

Departure of Hompesch—French Decrees of Spoliation—Insurrection of the Maltese—Blockade of the French within the Fortress—Arrival of the joint British and Portuguese Fleet—Narrative of the Blockade—Capitulation of the French.

FOR many years a feeling of dissatisfaction and insubordination had been growing up between the inhabitants of Malta and the government of the Order of St. John. The new and enticing doctrines promulgated by the revolutionary party in France had enlisted in their favour a great number of the more youthful and enthusiastic of the Maltese. They had been insensibly attracted by the hopes and aspirations which the new *régime* professed to realize, and they were too distant from the scene of action, and too ill-informed as to the fearful details of those events which had for some years deluged France with blood, to discover the futility of these professions.

The time had now arrived for which they had so earnestly craved, and they were at length called upon to enjoy the fruit of their labours. The White Cross banner of St. John had been lowered from the standard where it had for so many years waved in proud and undisturbed security, and in its place had been raised the tricolour emblem of liberty, equality, and fraternity. The despotism (for despotism it undoubtedly had been) of the Grand Masters was exchanged for the free and enlightened government of republican France, and the inhabitants were now able to look with confidence for the realization of those hopes and those aspirations which had been so sedulously nursed by the emissaries of that country.

Bonaparte did not allow much time to elapse before he secured himself in his new conquest, and developed the principles upon which the French government was to be based. The surrender of the fortress was completed as rapidly as possible. At mid-day on the 12th of June Fort Manoel, Fort Tigné, the Castle of St. Angelo, the Margarita and Cottonera lines were all transferred to the French, and on the following day Fort Ricasoli, St. Elmo, and the whole of Valetta and Floriana followed—the troops of the Order, who were permitted temporarily to retain the barracks which they occupied, doing so merely as the guests of the French republic, until they were otherwise disposed of.

General Bonaparte did not condescend to pay any personal respect to the chief whose sovereignty had been thus easily torn from his grasp, nor did he honour him with a visit. Hompesch, on the other hand, anxious to secure certain concessions and privileges for himself and his Order, determined to overlook the marked slight thus cast upon him, and to seek himself the interview which the French general did not appear disposed to demand. Accompanied by a body of his knights, with downcast air and stripped of the insignia of their rank, he presented himself before the victorious general. The interview was brief, and so far as he was concerned highly unsatisfactory. The requests which he preferred were refused, and he himself treated with very scant courtesy.

Hompesch put forward a claim to all the plate and jewellery belonging to the palace and attached to the office of Grand Master, but the demand was refused upon the plea that it was proposed to make him an allowance of 600,000 francs as an equivalent. Of this sum 300,000 were retained for the ostensible purpose of paying his creditors, who were very numerous, and who, since he had been stripped of his revenues, had become most clamorous for their dues. Of the balance 200,000 francs were paid in bills on the French treasury, and 100,000 francs only in cash. At his special request he was permitted to carry away with him the three relics which the Order had always held in such high veneration, namely, a piece of the real cross, of which they had originally become possessed in the Holy Land; the right hand and arm of St. John the Baptist, with which he had baptized our Lord; and the miraculous picture of Our Lady of Philermo. These, however, were stripped of their valuable cases and ornaments before they were handed over to him. Hompesch embarked at two o'clock on the morning of the 18th of June, 1798, on board a merchantman bound for Trieste, and escorted by a French frigate. The suite who accompanied him consisted of the two bailiffs of Lombardy, Montauroux and Suffrein de S$^t$ Tropez, the commander, De Lecondas, his grand chamberlain, and seven other knights, with two servants-at-arms.

Meanwhile Bonaparte had established a commission of government composed of the following nine persons, viz. :—The quondam knight, Boisredont Ransijat, Vincenzo Caruana, Carlo Astor, Paolo Ciantar, Jean François Dorell, Grongo, Benedetto Schembri, Don Saverio Caruana, Cristoforo Frendo. The duties of this commission were by the decree specified to be to take charge of the administration of the islands of Malta and Gozo, to superintend the collection of all taxes and contributions, to arrange for provisioning the island, and for its sanitary administration; they were also to organize tribunals of justice on the model of the new French courts. The two islands were to be divided into departments, each containing 3,000 souls, and a municipality was to be formed in each of the towns of Valetta and Vittoriosa. Each country department was to be under the direction of a body of five members nominated from the district. Another decree specified that all armorial bearings were to be removed within the space of twenty-four hours, that no liveries were to be worn, and that all titles or other marks of nobility were to be at once abolished. The consequences of this decree are still plainly visible in the wanton defacement of all the armorial tablets throughout the island.

Then followed a decree directing that all persons, subjects of any power at war with France, were to quit the island in forty-eight hours. All knights under sixty years of age were to quit within three days. To these decrees a number of exemptions were made of knights or others who, having befriended the French, were to be regarded as Maltese citizens, and were to be permitted to remain. One of the principal reasons given for the exemption was that they had made contributions towards the invasion of England. The property of all English, Russian, and Portuguese merchants was seized. Then came the grand pillaging decree, which ran as follows:—

"Citizen Berthollet, controller of the army, accompanied by a commissariat paymaster, will seize all the gold, silver, and precious stones which are to be found in the Church of St. John and other places connected with the Order of Malta, the plate belonging to the auberges, and that of the

Grand Master. They will at once melt the gold into ingots for convenience of transport, and they will make an inventory of all the precious stones, which will be deposited in the army chest. They will sell plate to the amount of from 250,000 to 300,000 francs to merchants of the country for gold and silver coin, which will be deposited in the chest. The remainder of the plate will be sent to the Maltese mint to be coined, and the money so obtained will be used for the payment of the garrison. Nothing is to be left in the various churches beyond what is actually necessary for the services of religion." *

All these decrees were published on the 13th of June, and on the 16th a further batch followed, the most important of which was one directing the formation of a company of volunteers to be composed of young men of from fifteen to thirty years of age, taken from the principal families of Malta, to be named by the general, who were to be armed and clothed at the expense of their families, and were to accompany the army to Egypt. Another body of sixty lads, from nine to fourteen years of age, also belonging to the principal families, were to be sent to Paris to be brought up in the colleges of the republic. Their parents were to pay 800 francs a year for their maintenance and 600 francs for the expenses of their journey. Six more youths, similarly selected, were to be placed with the fleet to be educated for the navy.

Numerous other decrees of a similar character followed during the few days that Bonaparte remained in the island, and marked the nature of the rule under which the Maltese were henceforth destined to remain.

* The whole of the plunder thus obtained was shipped on board *l'Orient*, and was lost with that vessel when she blew up at the battle of the Nile.

On the 21st of June the expeditionary force left Malta, taking with them the Maltese regiment, the Grand Master's guard, and a number of Maltese sailors. The garrison of Malta was placed under the command of General Vaubois, and consisted of the following troops:—

| | | | |
|---|---|---|---:|
| 7th Light Infantry | | | 900 |
| 6th Regiment of the Line | | | 518 |
| 41st | Ditto | | 285 |
| 80th | Ditto | | 650 |
| 19th | Ditto | 2nd battalion | 700 |
| | Total | | 3,053 |

with five companies of artillery.

The departure of Bonaparte caused no relaxation in the rigour and despotism of the French policy, and it gradually dawned on the unfortunate inhabitants that the liberty, the equality, and the fraternity for which they had so fervently prayed were practical nonentities, and that these high-sounding titles of philanthropy were but the cloaks to a tyranny, compared with which the rule of the Grand Masters was mild indeed. Ransijat himself, though a Frenchman, and warmly attached to the new order of things, of which, moreover, he was one of the principal agents in his capacity as President of the Commission of Government, has enumerated a list of some of the principal grievances under which the Maltese laboured during the few months immediately succeeding the expulsion of Hompesch; and this list, drawn up by one not likely to exaggerate the evil, shows the rapacious character of the French government. Chief amongst them may be enumerated the following:—

"1st. When Bonaparte carried away the Maltese regiment,

the Grand Master's guard, and a considerable number of Maltese sailors to swell the crews of his fleet, he engaged, on behalf of the French Government, that a certain sum should be paid to their families. This engagement was never fulfilled, although a stoppage was made from the payments to the men for the purpose, and the unfortunate women and children, deprived of the support to which they had been accustomed, were plunged into a state of utter destitution.

"2nd. The sum of 300,000 francs had been retained from the indemnity guaranteed to the Grand Master, for the ostensible purpose of paying his debts, but those debts never were paid by the French Directory. Many other knights who had been expelled from the island were also debtors to a considerable amount to the inhabitants. None of these liabilities were ever recovered.

"3rd. All the pensions which, during the previous administration, had been granted either for long and meritorious service or other causes, were suspended by the French, and the holders had no redress. Many charities, formerly provided by the treasury, were, in like manner, stopped.

"4th. The payment of the interest on loans made to the treasury of the Order by the Maltese was at once suspended, and the claim repudiated by their successors.

"5th. The quartering of the officers of the garrison upon the families of the Maltese, intruding upon their privacy, was looked upon with a very jealous eye, and gave rise to the utmost dissatisfaction, as also did the levying of a tax for the expenses of the soldiers' barracks, which was in direct contravention to the terms of the capitulation."

These were some of the principal grievances of which the inhabitants complained. Still, although thus rendered discontented, the French might have succeeded in maintaining their sway over the island had they not insulted the feelings of the people on a point where they were most sensitive. Had the French refrained from interference with the religion of Malta, and left their churches intact, they might possibly have carried their other acts of spoliation with a high hand; but they committed a grave error of policy when they commenced to plunder the churches of the costly offerings and decorations in which the inhabitants took so great a pride. From the moment that they commenced these sacrilegious depredations, all sympathy between them and the Maltese was at an end. These latter regarded with a sense of horror and detestation a nation who, openly regardless of all religion themselves, could be guilty of such acts of wanton desecration; and the spirit of discontent, which had hitherto found vent in idle murmurs, was now aroused to such an extent that ere long it broke out into open revolt.

The French had utterly mistaken the Maltese temperament, which is naturally bright, cheerful, and submissive. They had overlooked the undercurrent of firm and determined courage which forms the great mainstay of their character. Hardy, temperate, and, when aroused, capable of deeds of the most dauntless heroism, passionately attached to their country and their religion, the Maltese may be made, according to the manner in which they are governed, either the warmest friends and the most loyal subjects, or the bitterest and most dangerous enemies. The French committed the grave error of despising their new subjects, and they soon had bitter cause to rue their short-sighted policy.

The government had advertised the sale of some tapestry

and other decorations from a church in the Città Vecchia, and the crowd assembled on the occasion showed the first symptoms of revolt. The event took place on the 2nd of September, 1798, and brought on a riot of so serious a character that the sale was necessarily postponed, a step which temporarily quelled the disturbance.

The Commandant Masson at once despatched a message to General Vaubois in Valetta, announcing the fact, and praying for a reinforcement. This letter did not reach the General until eight o'clock in the evening, so that he was unable to send any assistance until the next morning. This delay was probably one of the main causes of the loss of Malta. In the afternoon the riot, which had been suppressed, once more broke out; the garrison, including the commandant, were all massacred, and the town fell into the hands of the insurgents.

The example thus set was speedily followed by the neighbouring casals, and before night the revolt had spread far and wide. Ignorant of this fact, early on the morning of the 3rd of September Vaubois despatched a body of 200 men to the assistance of Masson; but before they had proceeded far on their route they were assailed on all sides, and met with so obstinate a resistance that they were forced to retreat with all haste into the town, with the loss of several of their number, who were cut off by the insurgents. The revolt now spread over the whole island, and the French were closely blockaded within their lines by the people of the country, who hemmed them in on every side. Even within the limits of the fortress the same spirit manifested itself; but here the superior power of the garrison enabled them to check the outbreak, and a few summary executions of the leaders reduced the mass of the inhabitants to a state of sullen submission.

These vigorous acts on the part of the Maltese had been much encouraged, if not indeed originally prompted by the intelligence brought five days previously by the French line-of-battle ship the *Guillaume Tell* and the two frigates the *Diane* and the *Justice*, which had succeeded in effecting their escape after the battle of the Nile, where the French fleet had been utterly destroyed by Nelson. These three vessels were the sole relics of that glorious contest, and had fled to Malta for protection immediately after the issue of the conflict so disastrous to the French cause had become decisive. It was therefore with very gloomy forebodings that General Vaubois beheld himself blockaded within his lines by the Maltese at the very time when the utter annihilation of the French fleet in the Mediterranean had cut him off from all hopes of succour from France.

A strict examination was at once instituted into the resources of the fortress, and it was found that 36,000 salms of wheat were contained within the stores, a supply considered sufficient for the whole island for seven months, but for the town alone for a considerably longer time, should the country remain in a state of revolt. Every effort was nevertheless made to recall the insurgents to their allegiance, but in vain. An amnesty was even offered to the leaders, but the Maltese were not to be cajoled, and sternly rejected all offers of compromise.

One of the earliest steps taken by the Maltese after they had surrounded the French and blockaded them within their lines was to appeal to the King of Naples, as their sovereign, for protection; and a Portuguese squadron was despatched, under the command of the Marquis de Niza, the

Sicilian admiral, aided by Captain Ball, of the British ship *Alexander*. This squadron, consisting of four men-of-war and two frigates, arrived before Malta on the 18th September, and at once commenced to blockade the port. They were joined on the 24th October by the British fleet, consisting of fourteen sail in a very shattered condition, having undergone no repairs since the desperate battle in which they had been engaged in Aboukir Bay. On the day of his arrival off Malta, Nelson wrote a letter to Lady Hamilton, of which the following extracts affect our narrative:—"After a long passage we are arrived, and it is as I suspected, the ministers at Naples know nothing of the situation of the island. Not a house or bastion in the town is in the possession of the islanders, and the Marquis of Niza tells me they want arms, victuals, and support; and it is very certain, by the Marquis's account, that no supplies have been sent by the governors of Syracuse or Messina. However, I shall and will know everything as soon as the Marquis is gone, which will be to-morrow morning." On the following day Nelson sent the Marquis de Niza back to Naples to refit, and himself commenced to investigate personally the state of affairs. These he found most unsatisfactory, as far as the Neapolitan Government were concerned. The Maltese were most determined and enthusiastic, but they were almost totally destitute of the means necessary for maintaining their resistance. Nelson had been led to believe that they had been furnished from Sicily with supplies, arms, and ammunition; but so far was this from having been the case that their ships had actually been placed in quarantine by the Sicilians. The only assistance they had as yet received had been from the British. Sir James Saumarez, whilst taking home the Nile prizes, having been detained off Malta, took the opportunity of supplying them with 1,200 muskets and a quantity of ammunition. Nelson found 10,000 Maltese in arms against the French, under the command of three leaders, called Emmanuel Vitale, Xavier Caruana, then Canon, and afterwards Bishop of Malta, and Vincenzo Borg. They had already commenced the construction of batteries for the annoyance of the garrison. On the 5th October they had successfully resisted a powerful sortie made by the French in the direction of Casal Zabbar, and had driven them back with considerable loss. Since that date no further attempts had been made by the garrison to assume the offensive. Nelson at once despatched Captain Ball to summon the island of Gozo, which he did, and a capitulation was the result, which took place on the 30th October. Two hundred and thirty prisoners were taken, and sent in the *Vanguard* and *Minotaur* to Naples. Before quitting Malta, Nelson entrusted to Captain Ball the duty of aiding the inhabitants and organising their resistance; proposing that on the surrender of the fortress Ball should assume the government, either the King of England. He instructed Ball as follows:— on behalf of the King of Naples, or jointly for him and "In case of the surrender of Malta, I beg you will not do anything which can hurt the feelings of their Majesties. Unite their flag with England's, if it cannot, from the disposition of the islanders, fly alone."

Captain, afterwards Rear Admiral, Sir Alexander James Ball, whose name is so indissolubly linked with the fortunes of Malta at this time, was a younger son of Robert Ball, Esq., lord of the manor of Stonehouse in Gloucestershire. He was educated at Northampton, and entered the navy in 1768. His friendship with Nelson had been of long standing, and a very interesting incident is related of him in connection with that hero. In a violent storm off the island of Sardinia, on the 20th May, 1798, the *Alexander*, commanded by Ball, was in company with the *Vanguard*, bearing the flag of Nelson. The *Vanguard* becoming disabled was taken in tow by the *Alexander*; but such was the perilous condition of both ships, owing to the violence of the storm, that Nelson apprehended, should his endeavours be continued, that Ball's own ship might also be lost. Considering the case as desperate, he seized the speaking-trumpet, and with passionate threats ordered Ball to cast him loose. To this, however, Ball responded by saying, "I must not, and by the help of Almighty God I will not leave you." He succeeded in rescuing the *Vanguard*, and upon their arrival in harbour Nelson hailed him as the saviour of his life.

At this time it was the general opinion that the French would not hold out long in Malta, and Captain Ball wrote as follows, to Lady Hamilton, on the 19th October, five days before Nelson arrived: "I trust a very short time will put us in possession of the French ships in the harbour of Malta, viz., *Le Guillaume Tell*, of eighty guns, *La Diane* and *La Justice*, frigates of forty guns, besides two ships formerly Maltese. The French would be glad of a sufficient excuse to surrender, which they will soon have, as they are firing away their powder very fast. The Maltese have gone too far ever to recede."

Events, however, proved how fallacious this opinion was, as the blockade, which Ball anticipated would soon be brought to a close, had to be maintained for a period of two years before the constancy of the garrison was subdued by the force of sheer starvation. The narrative of this blockade presents but few points sufficiently salient and interesting to bear a detailed description. The journal of Ransijat, which contains a very full and minute account of all that took place from the commencement of the revolt until the surrender of the island, is throughout a mere repetition of the same scenes within the town. A total dearth of intelligence from France, which in those eventful times must have been most trying; a constant dread of bombardment, which was ever and again threatened by the besiegers, but never carried out with any vigour; a series of summonses from the hostile admirals, invariably rejected with contempt, and every now and then the arrival of some small vessel laden with corn, wine, oil, or brandy—these were almost the sole incidents by which the blockade was marked.

The inhabitants of the town had not openly joined the insurrection, which was entirely carried out by the country population; still, the great bulk of them were at heart eager for the success of their compatriots, and were only kept down from showing their feelings openly by the superior French force in their midst. Amongst these a plot was gradually hatched which, at one time, bid fair to curtail the tedious duration of the blockade and to achieve at one blow that triumph which they had hitherto only anticipated from the effects of starvation. It was arranged that the chief conspirators were each to lead a body of some fifty or sixty men to the attack of the principal posts within the city. It had been observed that the sentries usually performed their duties with great negligence, and it was hoped that they could be surprised and poinarded before they could raise an alarm. A Corsican named Guglielmo, who had been a colonel in the Russian service, was at the head of the plot, and he undertook to surprise the Grand Master's palace, then the head-quarters of General Vaubois. An ex-officer of chasseurs under the late *régime*, named Peralta, was to seize upon the Marina gate; Damato, a farrier in the Maltese regiment, was to lead a party against the Porta Reale, the principal gate of Valetta; and a barber, named Pulis, another against the Marsa Muscetto gate. Other detachments were to seize St. Elmo and the Auberge de Castile. The assaults were all to have been made simultaneously on the 11th January, 1799, and were to have been aided by a general attack from without on several points of the enceinte, by which means the attention of the garrison would be distracted, and the conspirators gain greater facilities for carrying their point.

The discovery of this plot was purely accidental. On the morning of that day a Genoese bark had entered the harbour, having eluded the blockading squadron, and had brought intelligence of important successes obtained by the French against the kings of Sardinia and Naples. General Vaubois had ordered a salute to be fired, in honour of the occasion, from the principal batteries throughout the enceinte. The Maltese without the lines, who were on the *qui vive* for the signal of the commencement of the insurrection, at once rushed to the attack of Floriana and the Cottonera lines, but were so warmly received at both points that they were compelled to retire with considerable loss. This premature advance disarranged all the plans of the conspirators in the town, and they decided upon postponing their venture till a more favourable opportunity. Having, however, no means of communicating this alteration of their plans to their friends without, the latter remained in uncertainty as to what steps they ought to take. A number of volunteers, trusting that

Y

the outbreak might be attempted during the night, found their way, under cover of the darkness, to the rocks beneath the walls of the town, near the Marsa Muscetto gate, and there awaited the course of events.

Unfortunately for them the same ill fate which had marred the morning's project pursued them still. General Vaubois had determined to celebrate the French successes, not only by the salutes he fired, but also by an extra performance in the theatre, which, as the day chanced to be a Friday, would not under ordinary circumstances have been open. The commandant of Fort Manoel and one of his officers obtained leave to attend this representation, and at its close proceeded to the Marsa Muscetto gate to return to their post. Whilst taking boat the attention of the commandant was attracted by a light and the sound of whispered conversation under the rocks. He took no notice of these suspicious incidents at the moment, being quite helpless, but when he reached Fort Manoel he despatched a small party of men to investigate the matter. These soon discovered the unfortunate Maltese crouching amidst the rocks, awaiting the signal of onslaught and the opening of the gate. The alarm was at once given, and they were all seized. Eventually all the details of the plot leaked out, and forty-four persons were executed. The terror which this unfortunate issue of the undertaking inspired amongst the inhabitants relieved the garrison from all fears of a repetition of the event.

On the 21st May, 1799, the garrison were agreeably surprised by finding that during the night previous the entire fleet, which had been blockading the ports, had vanished. The cause of this sudden raising of the blockade was the escape of the French fleet from Brest, and its appearance in the Mediterranean, joined with the Spanish fleet from Corunna. Nelson's first determination on hearing this intelligence was to raise the blockade of Malta, and to concentrate all his fleet off Maritimo. For this purpose he wrote to Captain Ball, to rendezvous with the entire blockading force at that point. It soon, however, appeared that the French fleet, although it had entered into the Mediterranean, had no intention of fighting, but had made its way as rapidly as possible to Toulon. Under these circumstances Ball's orders were at once countermanded, and he was directed to recommence the blockade with the *Alexander*, 74; the *Audacious*, 74; the *Bonne Citoyenne*, 20; the *Strombolo*, bomb-ship, 10; and the Portuguese ship the *Benjamin*, 18. These were afterwards joined by the *Lion*, 64; the *Success*, 32; and the *El Corso*, 16, English ships; and the *Principe Real*, 92; the *Affonço*, 74; the *Rainha*, 74; and the *St. Sebastian*, 64, all Portuguese ships. The squadron reappeared before Malta on the 5th June, to the great dismay of the garrison, who had taken advantage of the suspension of the blockade to despatch several small craft out of the harbour, and harass the communications of their Maltese besiegers with Sicily. Now, however, all was once more changed, and the Maltese hailed with joy the return of the fleet, which enabled them to carry on the land attack without interruption.

Throughout the blockade the greatest unanimity prevailed between the Maltese and the English. Captain Ball, who commanded the blockading squadron during all this part of the siege, had endeared himself to the Maltese, and had acted as their principal leader, organising their forces, directing the erection of their batteries, and supplying them, as far as his means permitted, with food and munitions of war.

But beyond this personal aid the land attack was maintained almost exclusively by the Maltese, who may claim the proud right of asserting that they, and they alone, confined the French garrison within their lines, and kept them there for a period of two years. This is clearly proved by the fact that during the fifteen days that the fleet was absent no attempt at a sortie was made by Vaubois.

Whilst such was the determined spirit shown by the Maltese against the French there were not wanting many amongst them who desired the return of the Order of St. John, and fears were entertained lest a counter-revolution for that purpose might break out. The following letter was addressed to Captain Ball, by one of the lieutenants of his ship, who was stationed on shore at St. Antonio :—

"For several days the minds of the inhabitants have been worked up to a degree of alarm that foreboded something very unpleasant, and a number of reports have been in circulation of the probability of a counter-revolution, which it was hinted would most likely take place on the 29th (June), the day of the celebration of the feast of St. Paul, when all the chiefs would be assembled at Citta Vielle, assisting at the religious ceremonies. On the evening of the 28th the captain of the port of St. Paul's came up to report to me the arrival of three knights of Malta, two of them Grand Croix, in a speronare. They were from Trieste, but last from Messina. He had allowed them to land, but immediately lodged them in the Tower of St. Paul's until he had received orders how to proceed. One of them, the Bailly Nevens, was almost the only knight who had been popular with the Maltese; he had commanded the regiment of chasseurs in the country, most of whom are now acting as soldiers with us. From the existing circumstances, and a knowledge of the late Grand Master having a strong party in the island who were ready to act in any way that could tend to restore him to his former government, I did not hesitate one moment in determining to send them out of the island without any loss of time; and in doing which I had not a doubt but I should meet your wishes. I therefore immediately sent the officer to St. Paul's bay again, with orders to take any papers the knights might have brought, and to send an armed speronare to see them some leagues from the island. In the course of a very few hours I found that the arrival of these persons had already caused a general movement and confusion in the island, and the captain of the port the next morning reported that during the few moments they were between the boat and the tower they had contrived to distribute upwards of fifty crowns among the crowd who assembled there, telling them at the same time that they had brought plenty of money, and that they would be followed in a few days by some vessels laden with corn, to relieve their distresses. Among their baggage was found 5,000 or 6,000 Maltese crowns. These we did not touch. I felt myself in a very awkward situation, being obliged to act in so decisive a manner, and have not a doubt by so doing but that I saved the island from becoming the scene of much greater confusion than already existed, and perhaps from the effusion of much blood."

This was the only attempt made on behalf of the Order, either to aid in expelling the French or to secure the possession of the island to themselves. Arrangements were meanwhile made by the governments of England, Russia, and Naples, that in case of a surrender the fortress should be occupied by the three Powers jointly, pending a decision by a general Congress as to its ultimate destination. The wishes of the Maltese themselves do not appear to have been in the least consulted in the matter, although the whole onus of the blockade in reality fell upon them, and they were suffering with the most heroic endurance hardships and privations but little inferior to those of the beleaguered garrison. They had erected no less than fifteen batteries, stretching from the coast in front of Ricasoli round to the high ground in the rear of Fort Manoel. The principal points, however, were the Coradin Hill and the hill in rear at Tarxien, from whence shot were fired into the heart of Valetta; the hill of Samra, which commanded the Porte des Bombes, where marks may still be seen—the effects of its fire; and the hill behind Fort Manoel, whence both that fort and also Fort Tigné were battered.*

As time wore on, and the scarcity of provisions became more and more felt in the town, large bodies of the inhabitants left Valetta, with the consent of General Vaubois, and sought refuge amongst their countrymen. These migrations were much encouraged, no impediment being placed against the departure of any save those who from their wealth or political influence were likely to be serviceable to the garrison. Ransijat, in his *Siege et Blocus de Malte*, gives some very interesting statistics with regard to the price of provisions within the town at different periods during the siege, and also of the mortality both of the garrison and population during the same time.

The following was the tariff at which provisions were procurable at the three following dates:—

* A plan exists in the Royal Engineer Office at Malta, originally forming one of Tigné's projects, but which had been used by the French engineers during the blockade. On this map the Maltese batteries are all roughly laid down and lettered.

|              | February, 1799. | | August, 1799. | | | July, 1800. | | |
|---|---|---|---|---|---|---|---|---|
|              | s. | d. | £ | s. | d. | £ | s. | d. |
| Fresh pork   | 2 | 10 | 0 | 6 | 0 | 0 | 7 | 2 |
| Cheese       | 2 | 6  | 0 | 7 | 4 |   |   |   |
| Fish, per lb.| 1 | 6  | 0 | 3 | 2 | 0 | 6 | 0 |
| Oil, per bottle | 2 | 6 | 0 | 10 | 0 | 1 | 3 | 4 |
| Sugar, per lb. | 5 | 0 | 0 | 17 | 6 | 2 | 0 | 0 |
| Coffee       | 4 | 0  | 1 | 0 | 10 | 2 | 8 | 4 |
| Wine, per bottle | 2 | 6 | 0 | 3 | 4 |   |   |   |
| Eggs, each   | 0 | 4  | 0 | 0 | 8 |   |   |   |

It will be seen that during the last months of the siege many articles ceased to be procurable at any cost, and the garrison and few remaining inhabitants were forced to content themselves with the reduced rations issued to them. Rats and other vermin were now recognised articles of consumption, and those that were found in the granaries and bakehouses were, from their superior size and plumpness, much sought after.

In order to eke out their scanty rations the soldiers had in the early part of the siege commenced the cultivation of gardens in the various ditches and other localities suitable for such operations, and had in this manner added greatly to their means of subsistence. So long as their oil and vinegar lasted the salads which they thus procured reconciled them to the loss of meat, which was latterly issued in very small quantities, and then only salted, all the fresh meat being from the commencement of the siege reserved for the use of the hospitals.

This source of provision was latterly cut off from them, not only owing to the want of oil and vinegar, but also from the scarcity of water. Captain Ball, in a report to Lord Nelson, on the 18th July, 1799, states, " I have the honour to acquaint your lordship that a deserter is this moment come out of La Valetta, who corroborates the distressed state of the French garrison; and, in addition, he says that there is very little water left on the Cotonaro side, and that they get their supply from La Valetta. General Vaubois has given orders to clear all the gardens of vegetables, to prevent any water being used there."

The following table shows the mortality throughout the siege. It will be perceived that the numbers were far higher during the first year than the second. This was principally owing to the fact that the population was very much larger during that period than it became afterwards, nearly 30,000 inhabitants having abandoned the town during the course of the blockade:—

|  | Garrison. | Inhabitants. |
|---|---|---|
| September, 1798 | 8 | 108 |
| October | 14 | 108 |
| November | 20 | 107 |
| December | 25 | 160 |
| January, 1799 | 35 | 213 |
| February | 20 | 200 |
| March | 37 | 230 |
| April | 40 | 319 |
| May | 98 | 338 |
| June | 131 | 311 |
| July | 79 | 233 |
| August | 48 | 131 |
| September | 33 | 102 |
| October | 30 | 100 |
| November | 19 | 99 |
| December | 11 | 60 |
| January, 1800 | 23 | 44 |
| February | 13 | 42 |
| March | 6 | 30 |
| April | 14 | 27 |
| May | 6 | 19 |
| June | 3 | 16 |
| July | 7 | 25 |
| August | 5 | 22 |
| Total | 725 | 3044 |

At one period the soldiers suffered severely from what is called moon blindness; losing thir sight during the bright moonlight nights of summer, and recovering it again in the daylight.

Up to a late period in the siege a company of Italian comedians had continued to reside in the town, and the theatre was constantly opened for the amusement of the garrison. The unfortunate actors had repeatedly besought permission to leave the town with the other inhabitants, but till near the close of the siege they were not permitted to do so, their services being considered as too valuable. At length, however, even the little food necessary for their support was too much needed to bestow upon non-combatants, and they were allowed to leave the town, their places being filled by amateurs from the garrison, who kept the theatre open till the very last.

When the Order of St. John left the island, the great bulk of them had proceeded to St. Petersburg, the Emperor of Russia having for many years past shown great sympathy with them. Here they were received in the most gracious manner by the wily monarch, whose ambition prompted him to desire the post of Grand Master, in order that he might upon that title found a claim to the island of Malta, should it be wrested from the grasp of the French republic. This desire on his part speedily became known to the knights, and on the 27th of October the farce was enacted of nominating the Emperor Grand Master of the Order, notwithstanding the fact that Hompesch, who was still at Trieste, had not as yet resigned his office. Paul, however, did not consider his appointment free from cavil so long as the election of Hompesch remained unannulled. He therefore caused such a pressure to be brought to bear upon that unfortunate knight that on the 6th of July, 1799, a formal act of abdication was forwarded to St. Petersburg, and from that date Paul was left in the undisturbed enjoyment of his new dignity. He soon disclosed the object for which he had sought the office by putting forward a claim to the island, which claim appears to have been recognized by all the powers interested, as will be seen by the following letter addressed to the Emperor by Lord Nelson, dated Palermo, October 31st, 1799:—

"Sire,—As Grand Master of the Order of Malta, I presume to detail to your Majesty what has been done to prevent the French from repossessing themselves of the island—blockading them closely in La Valetta—and what means are now pursuing to force them to surrender. On the 2nd of September, 1798, the inhabitants of Malta rose against the French robbers, who, having taken all the money in the island, levied heavy contributions, and Vaubois, as a last act of villainy, said as baptism was of no use, he had sent for all the church plate. On the 9th I received a letter from the deputies of the island praying assistance to drive the French from La Valetta. I immediately directed the Marquis de Niza, with four sail of the line, to support the islanders. At this time the crippled ships from Egypt were passing near it, and 2,000 stand of arms complete, with all the musket ball cartridges, were landed from them, and 200 barrels of powder. On the 24th of October I relieved the Marquis from that station, and having taken the island of Gozo, a measure absolutely necessary in order to form the complete blockade of LaValetta, the garrison of which at this time was composed of 7,000 French, including the seamen and some few Maltese, the Maltese in arms (volunteers) never exceeded 3,000, I entrusted the blockade to Captain Alexander John Ball, of the *Alexander*, of 74 guns, an officer not only

of the highest merit, but of the most conciliatory manners.
From that period to this time it has fallen to my lot to
arrange matters for the feeding 60,000 people (the population
of Malta and Gozo), and the arming of the peasantry. The
situation of Italy, and in particular the kingdom of Naples,
ofttimes reduced me to the greatest difficulties where to find
food. Their Sicilian Majesties at different times have given
more, I believe, than £40,000 in money and corn. The blockade has, in the expense of keeping the ships destined alone for
this service, cost full £180,000 sterling. It has pleased God
hitherto to bless our endeavours to prevent supplies getting
to the French except one frigate and two small vessels with a
small portion of salt provisions. Your Majesty will have the
goodness to observe that until it was known that you were
elected Grand Master, and that the Order was to be restored
in Malta, I never allowed an idea to go abroad that Great
Britain had any wish to keep it. I therefore directed his
Sicilian Majesty's flag to be hoisted, as I am told had the
Order not been restored he is the legitimate sovereign of the
island. Never less than 500 men have been landed from the
squadron, which, although with the volunteers not sufficient
to commence a siege, have yet kept posts and batteries not
more than 400 yards from the works. His Sicilian Majesty,
at the united request of the whole island, named Captain
Ball as their chief director, and he will hold it until your
Majesty, as Grand Master, appoints a person to the office.
Now the French are nearly expelled from Italy by the valour
and skill of your generals and army, all my thoughts are
turned towards placing the Grand Master and the Order of
Malta in security in La Valetta, for which purpose I have
just been at Minorca, and arranged with the English general
a force of 2,500 British troops, cannons, bombs, &c., for

the siege. I have written to your Majesty's admiral, and his Sicilian Majesty joins cordially in the good work of endeavouring to drive the French from Malta. The laborious task of keeping the Maltese quiet in Malta, through difficulties which your Majesty will perfectly understand, has been principally brought about by the goodness of her Majesty the Queen of Naples, who at one moment of distress sent £7,000 belonging absolutely to herself and children, by the exertion of Lady Hamilton, the wife of Sir William Hamilton, my gracious sovereign's Minister to the Court of the Two Sicilies, whom your Majesty knows personally, and by the bravery and conciliating manners of Captain Ball. If your Majesty honours these two persons with the decoration of the Order, I can answer none ever more deserved the Cross, and it will be grateful to the feelings of your Majesty's most faithful and devoted servant, Bronté Nelson."

On the 21st of December the Emperor replied to Nelson by the following letter:—" Monsieur L'Amiral Duc d'Abronté Lord Nelson,—J'ai reçu votre lettre du 31 Octobre. Je désire beaucoup que l'expedition que vous allez entreprendre contre Malthe réuscisse. Dans ce cas Le Général Major Prince de Wolconsky avec les trois bataillons de grenadiers, sous ses ordres y restera en garnisson en qualité de Commandant de Malthe, que sera gardi jusqu'au l'arrangement définitif par les troupes Russes, Anglaises, et Napolitaines.\* C'est avec plaisir que j'accorde à votre demande la croix de Commandeur au Capitaine Ball, et celle de Chevalier à Lady Hamilton, que vous leur remettrez accompagnes du lettres de ma part. La prise de Malthe ajouterais encore

---

\* These troops never arrived at Malta, their destination having been changed to Corfu.

une feston à la couronne de lauriers du vainqueur d'Aboukir, sur cela je prie Dieu, Monsieur le Duc d'Abronté Lord Nelson, qu'il vous ait en sa sainte et digne garde. Paul."

That Captain Ball was much gratified with his decoration is evident by the following extracts from a letter he wrote to Lady Hamilton :—" I most sincerely congratulate your ladyship on the distinguished mark of favour which his Imperial Majesty the Emperor of Russia has been pleased to confer upon you, in creating you Chanoinesse of the Order of St. John of Jerusalem. He has been graciously pleased to confer upon me the honour of Commander of the same Order, from which I derive a double satisfaction. The first in the honour of being your brother and defender, and secondly from the consideration of its being a token of regard of my invaluable friend and patron Lord Nelson. Adieu, my dear lady and sister, may you live a thousand years; but at all events may you be supremely happy while you live, prays your obliged brother and friend, Alexander John Ball. To her Excellency Lady Hamilton, C. S. J. J. Is that right? Pray tell me how to address your letter."

It is quite evident from all the contemporary despatches and correspondence that the English government at this time had no intention whatever of possessing themselves of Malta. They had undertaken to aid the insurgent Maltese by maintaining a blockade, with the sole view of driving the French from the island; and it appeared to them a matter of but little moment whether it afterwards fell into the hands of Russia, Naples, or its quondam masters. Nelson's views about Malta are so singular, that they are worthy of record. He writes to Earl Spencer: "To say the truth, the possession of Malta by England would be an useless and enormous expense; yet any expense should be incurred rather than let it remain in the hands of the French. Therefore as I did not trouble myself about the establishing again the Order of St. John at Malta, Sir William Hamilton has the assurance from his Sicilian Majesty that he will never cede the sovereignty of the island to any Power without the consent of his Britannic Majesty. The poor islanders have been so grievously oppressed by the Order that many times have we been pressed to accept of the island for Great Britain, and I know, if we had, his Sicilian Majesty would have been contented; but, as I said before, I attach no value to it for us, but it is a place of such consequence to the French that any expense ought to be incurred to drive them out."

It has been suggested that in thus depreciating the importance of Malta to England, Nelson was unconsciously reflecting the views of Lady Hamilton, whose intimacy with the Queen of Naples would lead her to use her influence to secure the restoration of the island to the Sicilian monarchy. That Lady Hamilton's influence over Lord Nelson was frequently exercised for political purposes is most true, but his peculiar views about Malta can scarcely be attributed to this cause, since, as his letter to the Emperor of Russia shows, he was quite ready to co-operate in the transfer of the island to that Power. It seems indeed, as if he utterly failed to realise the vast importance of Malta to England

In the month of December, 1799, a small body of British troops, consisting of the thirtieth and eighty-ninth regiments, in all, 1,300 men, under General Sir Thomas Graham (afterwards Lord Lynedoch), and two Neapolitan battalions, together 900 strong, landed in the island, and assumed the direction of the siege. Captain Ball, having been meanwhile elected by the people as president of the national council, had landed from the *Alexander*, and assumed the office of Governor of the Maltese, fixing his head-quarters at the palace of St. Antonio. This appointment was sanctioned by the allied powers of England, Russia, and Naples. From that time, the command of the blockading fleet devolved upon Commodore Martin, who was sent to Malta for the purpose. Shortly afterwards, General Pigot also arrived, and took over the command of the allied forces from Sir Thomas Graham, who remained under him in command of the British forces only.

On the 18th January, 1800, Nelson had fallen in, off Cape Passaro in Sicily, with a French squadron consisting of a line of battle ship and four frigates conveying troops from Toulon for the relief of Malta. The line-of-battle ship was *Le Généreux*, 74 guns, bearing the flag of Rear-Admiral Perrée, one of the vessels that had escaped from the battle of the Nile. She was now captured by Nelson's flag-ship, the *Foudroyant*; the French Admiral dying on the following day, of wounds received in the action. One of the frigates was also captured by the *Alexander*.

The failure of this effort on the part of the French fleet to relieve the beleaguered garrison of Valetta made it clear that before long a surrender must be effected. Still the gallant Vaubois determined to hold out until the very last. Whatever the faults which the French had committed on their first seizure of the island, no one can deny them a tribute of admiration for the constancy and cheerfulness with which they underwent the hardships and privations of the blockade. Not a murmur of discontent was heard amongst their ranks: on the contrary, they aided their superiors in every possible way, and to the very last moment the cry of "No surrender" was the popular watchword. Equal, if not still greater praise is due to the gallant Maltese who underwent privations nearly as great as those of the French, and who, without the training or discipline of soldiers, bore the heat and burden of the struggle for two long years without flinching, or ever once yielding to the blandishments and tempting promises of the garrison. They had from the first determined to expel the hated French from the island, and from this resolve nothing could turn them. Even when, after a year's blockade, the English fleet abandoned the enterprise and left the island for a fortnight, not a symptom of yielding up the conflict seems to have shown itself. Let it, therefore, never be forgotten that the Maltese owe their deliverance from the yoke of France to their own resolution and dogged determination.

Month after month of the year 1800 passed, and at last it became evident to all within the town that the time for surrender had arrived. Prior, however, to taking this step, General Vaubois made one last effort to save the ships of war, the sole relics of the battle of the Nile, which had found refuge in the port of Malta. Great precautions had been taken throughout the siege to protect them from the fire of the Maltese batteries, and although they had been repeatedly struck, they still remained in serviceable condition. The *Guillaume Tell* had already made a futile attempt at escape, and had been captured. She had been fitted out most completely, and took her departure on the 28th March; the night being extremely dark, and the wind favourable for her escape. There were, however, keen eyes watching for such a step on all the neighbouring heights, and the vessel was soon discovered, the signal given, and the British fleet placed on the alert. The result was, that she was pursued, and after a most desperate and heroic defence, in which the French lost 207 men killed and a vast number wounded, amongst whom were Admiral Decres and Captain Saunier, sho was captured off Cape Passaro and brought back to Malta in triumph.

· Now, a last experiment was to be made to save the two frigates, the *Diane* and the *Justice*, and on the 23rd August they both left the harbour. The result, however, was precisely similar to that in the case of the *Guillaume Tell*, as they were both captured by the British cruisers, without, however, so severe a conflict as in the former case.

Nothing now remained but to capitulate, and a council of war was assembled to deliberate on the measure. It was then found that their provisions could not extend beyond the 8th September, and it was determined that terms of surrender should be offered five days before that date. On the morning of the 3rd September, 1800, General Vaubois wrote to General Pigot (who commanded the allied forces of British and Neapolitan troops that had been stationed in the island during the last few months of the siege), and offered to capitulate. Two British officers, Major-General Graham and Commodore Martin, were nominated to arrange terms of surrender. These were at once agreed to, and on the 5th September the capitulation was duly signed, and the fortress transferred to the possession of the allied forces.

## CHAPTER XII.

*Terms of the Capitulation—Malta under the British—Subsequent History of the Order—Mutiny of Count Froberg's Levy at Ricasoli—The Plague in 1813—Additions to the Fortifications—Conclusion.*

THE terms of the capitulation under which the French were expelled from Malta ran as follows:—

"Art. 1. The garrison of Malta and the forts dependent thereon shall march out, to be embarked for Marseilles, on the day and hour appointed, with all the honours of war, such as drums beating, colours flying, matches lighted, having at their head two four-pounders, with their carriages, artillerymen to serve them, and a waggon for the infantry. The civil and military officers of the navy, together with everything belonging to that department, shall be conducted to the port of Toulon. (This was granted, so far as feasible.)

"Art. 2. The General of Brigade Chanez, commandant of the city and forts; the General of Brigade d'Hannedel, commandant of the artillery and engineers, the officers, non-commissioned officers and soldiers, the officers, troops, crews, and all others employed in the navy; Citizen Pierre Alphonse Guys, general commissary of trade for the French Republic in Syria and Palestine; those employed in civil

*Terms of the Capitulation.*

and military capacities, the commissioners of the army and navy, the civil administrators and members of whatsoever description of the constituent authority, shall take with them their arms, their personals, and all their property. (Granted, except that the soldiers must ground their arms.)

"Art. 3. All those who bore arms in the service of the Republic during the siege, of whatsoever nation they may happen to be, shall be regarded as making part of the garrison. (Granted.)

"Art. 4. The division shall be embarked at the expense of his Britannic Majesty, each person receiving during his passage the pay of his rank. according to the French regulation. The officers and members of the civil administration, with their families, shall also receive a salary, in proportion to the pay of the military, and according to the dignity of their office. (Granted.)

"Art. 5. A proper number of waggons and shallops shall be provided for transporting and shipping the personal baggage of the generals, their aides-de-camp, commissaries, chiefs of different corps, officers, Citizen Guys, civil and military administrators of the army and navy, together with the papers belonging to the councils of the civil and military administrators of the different corps, the commissaries of both army and navy, the paymaster of the division, and all others employed in the civil and military administration. These effects and papers to be subject to no kind of inspection, being guaranteed by the generals as containing neither public nor private property. (Granted.)

"Art. 6. All vessels belonging to the Republic, in sailing condition, shall depart at the same time as the division for a French port, after being properly victualled for the voyage. (Refused.)

"Art. 7. The sick capable of being removed shall be embarked with the division; those whose health obliges them to remain in Malta shall be properly treated, and the commander-in-chief shall leave a French physician and surgeon to attend on them. The commander-in-chief, on evacuating Malta, will entrust them to the honour and humanity of the English general. (Granted.)

"Art. 8. All individuals, of whatsoever nation, inhabitants or not of Malta, shall not be molested for their political opinions, nor for any acts committed whilst Malta was in the power of the French Government. (This article does not appear to come under the terms of a military capitulation; but all the inhabitants who wish to remain or are permitted to remain, may depend upon being treated with justice and humanity.)

"Art. 9. All the French inhabiting Malta and those of the Maltese who are desirous of following the French army, and retiring to France with their property, shall have the liberty to do so. Those who possess movables and estates impossible to be disposed of immediately, and who intend settling in France, shall be allowed six months from the signature of the present capitulation for the sale of their estates and other effects. (Granted, with reference to the answer given to the preceding article.)

"Art. 10. As soon as the capitulation shall be signed, the English general shall permit the commander-in-chief of the French forces to despatch a felucca, properly manned, with an officer to carry the capitulation to the French Government, who shall be provided with the necessary safe-guard. (Granted.)

"Art. 11. The articles of capitulation being signed, the gate called 'Des Bombes' shall be given up to the English general, and occupied by a guard, consisting of an equal number of French and English, with orders to permit neither the soldiers of the besieging army nor any inhabitant of the island whatsoever to enter the city until the French troops shall be embarked and out of sight of the port. As soon as the embarkation shall have taken place, the English troops shall occupy the gates, and free entrance be allowed into the city. The English general must perceive that this precaution is absolutely necessary, to prevent all disputes, and in order that the articles of the capitulation may be religiously observed. (Granted conformably to what has been already provided against by the answer to the first article; and all precaution shall be taken to prevent the armed Maltese from approaching the gates occupied by the French troops.)

"Art. 12. All alienation of property and sale of estates and effects by the French Government whilst it was in possession of Malta, together with all exchange of property between individuals, shall be maintained inviolate. (Granted as far as justice and law will permit.)

"Art. 13. The agents of the allied powers residing in the city of Valetta at the time of its surrender, shall not be molested, and their persons and property shall be guaranteed by the present capitulation. (Granted.)

"Art. 14. All ships of war and merchant vessels coming from France with the colours of the Republic, and appearing before the port, shall not be esteemed prizes, nor the crews made prisoners, during the first twenty days after the date of the present capitulation, but shall be sent back to France with a proper safeguard. (Refused.)

"Art. 15. The commander-in-chief, the other generals, their aides-de-camp, the subaltern officers, shall be embarked all together with the commissioners and their suites. (Granted.)

"Art. 16. The prisoners made during the siege, including the crew of the *Guillaume Tell* and *La Diane*, shall be restored and treated like the garrison. The crew of *La Justice* to be used in the same manner, should she be taken in returning to one of the ports of the Republic. (The crew of the *Guillaume Tell* is already exchanged, and that of *La Diane* is to be sent to Majorca to be exchanged immediately.)

"Art. 17. No one in the service of the Republic shall be subject to a reprisal of any kind whatsoever. (Granted.)

"Art. 18. If any difficulties shall arise respecting the terms and conditions of the capitulation, they shall be interpreted in the most favourable sense for the garrison. (Granted, according to justice.)

"Done and concluded at Malta, the 18th of Fructidor, in the eighth year of the French Republic (4th September, 1800).

"Signed on behalf of the French by the General of Division Vaubois, and the Rear Admiral Villeneuve.

"On behalf of the English, by Major-General Pigot and Captain Martin, commander of the allied fleet before Malta."

It will be seen by the above that Captain Ball was no longer in command of the blockading squadron. He had, some time before the close of the siege, been elected by the Maltese as their chief, and this appointment had been ratified by the allied powers. He had therefore landed from the *Alexander*, and had taken up his residence in the palace of St. Antonio, from whence on the 1st September, 1800, he addressed the following letter to General Pigot, which marks the position he held himself to occupy:—

"In the conference which I had the honour of having with you on the subject of my right to sign any capitulation to which the French may be reduced, you informed me that your instructions do not admit of my interference. I therefore conceive it my duty officially to give my reasons for claiming a right, as chief of this island, to be consulted, and to sanction the terms to which the enemy may be obliged to submit. When the troops of different nations co-operate, it has been customary for the commander of each national force to sign the capitulation. A recent instance occurred last year. The combined forces besieging St. Elmo were commanded by the Duke de Salandra, a general in his Sicilian Majesty's service; but the commanders of the British, Russian, and Turkish troops joined their signatures to the capitulation, which was the result of their joint efforts. I consider the Maltese a distinct corps, who have besieged La Valetta twelve months with unexampled bravery and perseverance, without the aid of foreign troops. At present they have three thousand troops who occupy the advanced posts, and three thousand militia enrolled, ready to act. They have lately been maintained at the joint expense of the courts of England, Russia, and Naples; and if I am not allowed, as their chief, to sign the capitulation alluded to, I am apprehensive it will give much offence to the two latter courts as well as the Maltese, who conceive that both in a military and civil point of view, they are entitled to an important voice. You were pleased to inform me that in the event of the surrender of La Valetta, you have orders to hoist the British colours only in that garrison. In answer, I beg leave to acquaint you that when Rear-Admiral Lord Nelson commanded in the Mediterranean I received orders from him to hoist the colours of St. John of Jerusalem whenever I enter La Valetta, in conformity to an agreement between the ministers of the courts of England, Russia, and Naples, since which I have been lately informed by the Honourable Mr. Paget, the British minister at Palermo, that he has not received counter-orders. If there be any objection to the execution of that order, I trust there will not be to the hoisting his Sicilian Majesty's colours with those of his Britannic Majesty. I shall only trespass one observation in support of his Sicilian Majesty's *continued right* to the sovereignty of this island. In June, 1798, the French invaded this island without any previous declaration of war, and reduced the inhabitants to capitulate, three months after which, the Maltese in the country, who are three-fourths of the population of the island, revolted and besieged the French in La Valetta and the adjacent posts; they then sent a deputation to his Sicilian Majesty to *renew* their acknowledgments to him as their lawful sovereign, and to solicit his aid to expel the French, in which his Majesty was pleased to acquiesce, and from that period has contributed in troops, money, and ammunition, to their support. It will be therefore presumed that the English come here as an ally to his Sicilian Majesty, and cannot intend to dispossess him of the sovereignty of this island by assuming an exclusive right to hoist British colours in La Valetta. I beg leave to express, Sir, the satisfaction I feel in having to discuss such subjects with an officer of your rank and character, as I am confident you will avoid as much as possible giving offence to the allies of his Britannic Majesty."

That this request was not complied with is shown by the following extracts from a letter, which Ball wrote to Lord Nelson, dated Malta, 27th September, 1800:—

"I had the pleasure of writing to your Lordship the 5th instant, on the surrender of La Valetta, and sent copies of my correspondence with Major-General Pigot, on the subject of my right to sign the capitulation, and my order to hoist the colours of the Order of St. John of Jerusalem, both of which he would not allow, as his order from Sir R. Abercromby directed the contrary." ..... "I have the satisfaction to acquaint your Lordship that the Maltese give me daily additional proofs of their confidence and obedience to my orders. A large party had shown a disposition to punish the Jacobins in the manner they were treated at Naples, but there has not been the smallest irregularity committed. The people are happy and contented, and the English in general observe that La Valetta and its port are among the very few places which have exceeded their expectations. It is certainly a very interesting spot." ..... "Colonel Fardillo, who commands the Neapolitan troops here, applied to sign the capitulation, but was refused." ..... "P.S. I have just received a letter from General Graham, who conducted the business of the capitulation, saying that General Vaubois objects to my signing as Chief of the Maltese."

At four o'clock on the afternoon of the 4th September, the English troops occupied Floriana, Fort Tigné, and Ricasoli, and two British men-of-war entered the harbour. General Vaubois and Admiral Villeneuve dined that evening with General Pigot in Cazal Balzan, where he had established his head-quarters. On the 8th of September, the bulk of the French troops embarked on board the transports prepared for their reception, and set sail for Marseilles.

During the siege, which lasted two years and a day, the garrison expended fifty-two thousand shot and shell and seven hundred thousand musket cartridges. During these two years the garrison only consumed the full rations of seven months. All the horses and mules had been killed for the use of the sick in the hospitals, after the beef had failed. Those of the inhabitants who had interest enough to obtain for the invalid members of their families a small portion of liver, or other entrails, were considered very fortunate. A flight of quails, passing over Valetta on the day that the commissioners were sent to treat for a surrender, enabled General Vaubois, by the aid of a good cook, to furnish them with an excellent dinner of, what they supposed to be, a great variety of food. Some surprise having been afterwards expressed by the commissioners, at being supplied with such a variety of excellent dishes, at a time when it was thought that the resources of the garrison were thoroughly exhausted, General Vaubois confessed that the quails and a couple of tame rabbits constituted the only animal food on the table.

On assuming the occupation of the fortress, General Pigot issued an address to the inhabitants, announcing that his Britannic Majesty took the Maltese nation under his protection, and pledged himself to render them contented and happy, and to reverence their religion and its ministers. He also announced that their former chief Captain Ball could no longer remain among them, as the exigencies of the naval service called him elsewhere.

There can be no doubt that the position occupied by Captain Ball was somewhat anomalous. He had endeared himself to the Maltese population, and had acquired so great an influence over them, that he was unhesitatingly obeyed, and looked upon as their chief. This led to some jealousy between him and General Pigot, who refused to recognise his independent position. As a result of this feeling, Ball was not at first named Civil Governor of the island, but was sent back to his duty, and that post was filled by Mr. Cameron; an appointment which gave great and just offence to the Maltese, who found that, after all they had suffered and done to rid themselves of their French masters, the English appeared to neglect their just claims to consideration.

This feeling was so strongly displayed, that the British Government wisely yielded to it, and the following year replaced Mr. Cameron by Sir Alexander Ball, as he then was, he having, in the interim, been made a knight of the Bath.

By the treaty of Amiens it was proposed to restore Malta to the Order of St. John of Jerusalem, with a condition that a Maltese *langue* was to be established, to be supported by the territorial revenues and commercial duties of the island, both French and English *langues* being suppressed, no individual belonging to either nation being admissible into the fraternity. The British forces were to evacuate the island within three months of the conclusion of the treaty, and the fortress was then to be garrisoned by Neapolitan troops until the Order had organized a force of their own.

This part of the treaty of Amiens (the tenth article) gave the most grave offence to the Maltese, and they petitioned boldly against it. They had carried on the struggle for two years in the hope of obtaining the blessing of free institutions under the protection of Great Britain, and they felt that to be transferred once more to the Order of St. John was fatal to such hopes. Moreover, in the then enfeebled condition of the Order, they saw plainly that such transfer was but a preliminary to the re-occupation of the island by the French, and a renewal of all their miseries. They therefore addressed a lengthy memorial to the British nation, in which, after recapitulating the services they had rendered in blockading the French within their lines, they enumerated the following grievances:—That the British had signed a capitulation with the French without consulting the Maltese; that by this capitulation they had permitted them to carry off the plunder which they had taken from the Maltese inhabitants, although they knew well that the garrison was reduced to such extremities that in a few days it must have surrendered at discretion; and that they had disarmed the Maltese before permitting them to enter the town. The memorial went on to state that the land expenses of the war, and the pay of the Maltese battalions was found by the Maltese themselves, and that they had mortgaged much of their public property for the purpose: they therefore demanded either that the island should be yielded up to them, or that they should be indemnified for their losses. In fine, they claimed the island by right of conquest from the French, who themselves, by right of conquest, had acquired it from the Order of St. John. They then protested against the restoration of the Order, which they considered was degraded and become infamous by their recent surrender of the island. The memorial then goes on to say—" Feeling our own political weakness, and putting a boundless confidence in the sincerity of the British Government and the faith of the British nation, we rather wished to become subjects of the king, and enjoy all the advantages of a free nation under a monarch who is the father of his people, than to assert and maintain our own entire independence; but never can we believe that, abusing our confidence and violating all the laws of justice, human and divine, we are to be forcibly delivered over by our auxiliary allies as a conquered nation, or as vile slaves sold for a political consideration to new masters, and to masters whose tyranny, extortion, and sacrilege, have rendered them the execration of all virtuous people, and to whom, whatever misery may ensue, we will never submit." The memorial closes with a very pertinent criticism on the project. "We do not enter into the profound views of cabinets, but be it permitted to us to observe solely, that if France had no other intention than the re-establishment of the Order in its pristine splendour and independence, why have they not chosen a place where they could be more independent? And why have they considered the possession of Malta as necessary to the re-establishment of the Order? It is but too clear to us that Malta is not intended to be taken out of the hands of the English to leave it long in those of the Order of St. John of Jerusalem."

Most fortunately for England and for the Maltese the transfer never took place. Governor Ball, who was fully alive to the injustice and impolicy of the measure, delayed the execution of the treaty and the surrender of the island by every means in his power, and the result proved the wisdom of his tactics. War broke out, the treaty was annulled, and Malta remained in the possession of the British.\*

At the death of the Emperor Paul, the Pope named John de Tommasi as Grand Master of the Order of St. John. This nomination was, of course, in direct contravention of the statutes, but was accepted by the few fragments of the dispersed fraternity who could be assembled together. Tommasi proclaimed his appointment to a conclave who had

---

\* A pension of £600 a year, charged on the revenues of Malta, was settled upon Sir John Ball and his next immediate descendant, as a reward for the important services he had rendered to the island. His son is still in the receipt of this annuity.

met in the priory church of Messina, on the 27th of June, 1802. Nothing of any importance in the interests of the Order was proposed at this meeting; nor, indeed, were they capable of much amelioration. Tommasi resided until his death at Catania, and when that event took place, in June, 1805, the Pope, who declined any longer to take upon himself the responsibility of naming a Grand Master in violation of the statutes, contented himself with selecting the Bailiff Guevara Suardo as lieutenant, and from that day till now he has continued these appointments.

The *chef lieu* of the Order, which during Tommasi's life was established at Catania, was moved to Ferrara in 1827, and was subsequently again changed to Rome, where it is still fixed. In the year 1814, a general chapter of the French, Spanish, and Portuguese *langues* was held in Paris, under the protection of the newly-restored French king. A Capitular Commission was named by this chapter, to act as an executive council for the institution, under the presidency of Prince Camille de Rohan, Grand Prior of Aquitaine. The most important act accomplished by this commission was the revival of the dormant English *langue*. In the years 1826 and 1827 three several instruments of convention were signed for this purpose, and in 1831 a chapter of the newly-appointed knights then forming the English *langue* was held. Sir Robert Peat was elected Grand Prior of England, and since that period the chief offices of the *langue* have been filled; the Duke of Manchester being the present Grand Prior.

The seventh article of the Treaty of Paris, signed on the 30th of May, 1814, determined the ultimate destiny of Malta in the following terms:—" The island of Malta, with its dependencies, will appertain in full authority and sovereignty to his Britannic Majesty."

The incidents that have occurred worth narrating since the fortress of Malta fell under the sway of England have been but few. On the 3rd of April, 1807, a very serious mutiny broke out in the force then occupying Fort Ricasoli. During the progress of the war, the British Government had accepted the offer of a French noble called Count Froberg, to raise a regiment of Greeks for Mediterranean service. The Count collected together, from various quarters, a motley assemblage of Greeks, Albanians, and Sclavonians, who were enrolled under the title of Froberg's regiment, and stationed at Malta. In order to preserve any semblance of discipline amidst the discordant elements of this motley crew, it was found necessary by the officers, who were mostly Germans, to maintain great severity. A frequent use of corporal punishment was adopted, and as there was no bond of union between the officers and men, discontent soon ripened into revolt. The immediate cause of the mutiny was the fact of an officer striking a drummer on the face with a cane. Numbers of the men immediately rushed out of their barracks with arms in their hands; two officers were killed, and the remainder made prisoners; the gates were shut, the bridges raised, and Russian colours hoisted on the fort. A detachment of artillery, consisting of an officer and nineteen gunners, were in the place. One of these latter was killed whilst endeavouring to prevent the mutineers from obtaining access to the magazine. The remainder were compelled to load several guns and mortars, which were pointed towards Valetta. General Vilettes, the officer in command of the troops at Malta, determined to starve out the mutineers, it being known that they had but three days' provisions. The revolt took place at three o'clock on the afternoon of Saturday, the 4th April, and that same day a perfect cordon of troops was established behind the buildings and walls of the fields, beyond the foot of the glacis of the land front, and stretching from sea to sea. The mutineers threatened to put all their prisoners to death and to fire on Valetta, unless their terms were agreed to. These were that they should be sent back to their own country or Corfu in Greek or Russian vessels. They were informed, however, that nothing but unconditional surrender could be listened to.

On Wednesday morning about 400 of them, disgusted with their position and determined to surrender, rose against the ringleaders, killed the sentries who had been posted on the gates, and forced their way out, bringing with them all the officers, gunners, and women, and gave themselves up to the officer in command. Others continued to leave the fort in small detachments all that day and the next, until only eight of the most desperate of the ringleaders remained. On Thursday afternoon one of the mortars was fired. The shell fell in the centre of the Floriana parade ground without doing any damage, but so alarmed the inhabitants that many of them at once removed into the country.

To prevent further mischief it was determined to enter the fort by escalade, and this was effected before daybreak on Friday morning by a party of Maltese military artificers, under the command of an engineer officer. They selected the re-entering angle on the right of the gateway and reached the parapet before they were discovered. The mutineers finding their position forced, retreated to the magazine, and secured themselves in the lobby. The gates were at once opened, and the fort taken possession of by the troops.

Whilst this was being done two of the mutineers succeeded in firing three mortars against Valetta. One shell burst over the harbour, and the other two fell on the ramparts of the land front. The two men were not able to regain the lobby, but were made prisoners. The remaining six kept possession of the lobby, firing from the windows, and threatening to blow up the magazine if they were attacked.

No attempt was made to dislodge them, as it was known that they were without either food or water. On Sunday night three of them made their escape over the sea-line wall with ropes close to a small side door in the lobby, which could not be seen by the sentries. The remainder made arrangements for blowing up the magazine. This they effected by inserting one end of a piece of slow match into a barrel of powder and igniting the other end. They then crawled out of the door unperceived. Three sentries were killed, and the fort considerably damaged by the explosion. The three men were, however, at once secured.

Meanwhile a court-martial had been sitting to decide upon the fate of those who had surrendered or been captured. By the sentence of this court ten were hung and fourteen shot. These latter were executed on Floriana parade, and owing to mismanagement the duty was performed in a most barbarous manner. Pinioned, but not blindfolded, they were made to kneel upon their coffins, and after the first volley several still clinging to life rose up and ran about the parade pursued by the soldiers. One in particular made great efforts to escape; he succeeded in reaching the ramparts, from which he cast himself down headlong a height of nearly seventy feet. The soldiers in pursuit finding him still alive, put an end to his miserable existence.

The three men who had made their escape remained for

several days undiscovered: at length one evening a priest, passing by an unfrequented path in the vicinity of the fort, was assailed by a man dressed in the Froberg uniform, who pointed his musket at him over a wall. The priest, who was mounted on a mule, made his escape, and at once reported the circumstance to the police. Search was made, and the three men discovered in a state of actual starvation hidden amongst the rocks. They were secured without difficulty, and executed. The damage caused to the fort by the explosion of the magazine was very great, the whole of the left portion of the land front having been thrown down.

In the year 1813, a most violent outbreak of plague took place. The real cause of this attack is somewhat doubtful, and has been much disputed. Sir Thomas Maitland in his despatch of the 8th April, 1819, to Lord Bathurst, says— "As far as I have been able to ascertain, I think I am warranted in stating that the plague was brought to Malta by a ship from Egypt (the *San Nicola*), and conveyed out of that ship by a person smuggling some leather; this person and his family were the first sufferers from it."

The person alluded to was a shoemaker named Salvatore Borg, who with his wife, son, and daughter, all fell victims to the disease. The following list of deaths amongst the population from May to October, will show the intensity of the outbreak:—May, 118; June, 829; July, 1,602; August, 981; September, 664; October, 196; total, 4,390. After that date, no public statistics were given. The military suffered comparatively little, and the disorder was very much localized amongst the more crowded portions of the towns and casals.

The additions to the fortifications of Malta have not been numerous since the acquisition of the island by the British.

Chief amongst those that have been made must be ranked the intrenchments connecting the Cottonera with the Margarita lines, closed at the latter point by the Verdala barrack. The object of these works has been to form a keep at the highest point of the ground enclosed between the two lines, so that in case it is considered unadvisable to attempt to garrison the whole extent of the works, it shall still be rendered impossible for the enemy to maintain himself in any of the abandoned portions. A counterguard has also been constructed to cover the escarp of St. Peter's bastion on the Grand Harbour front of Valetta. This work, which is called the Lascaris counterguard, brings an additional fire to bear upon the Grand Harbour, and being casemated, is used as a barrack.

Under the rule of England the island still remains, and that Government, whilst prepared to maintain her claims against all comers, prefers to found her right upon the love and attachment of the Maltese. She does not need to mutilate the monumental records of the former governors of the island as the French have done. Secure in the love of her subjects, she can dare to recall to their memory the deeds of the heroes of old, and the Maltese who now enters the city of Valetta, passes beneath a gateway erected by the English, on which stand, as the legitimate guardians of the city, the statues of L'Isle Adam and La Valette.